Born in 1934, **Alasdair Gray** graduated in design and mural painting from the Glasgow School of Art. From 1981, when *Lanark* was published by Canongate, he authored, designed and illustrated seven novels, several books of short stories, a collection of his stage, radio and TV plays and a book of his visual art, *A Life in Pictures*. In November 2019, he received a Lifetime Achievement award from the Saltire Society. His books have been published internationally and translated into Italian, Russian and Japanese. His awards include the Whitbread Fiction Prize and *Guardian* Fiction Prize.

Also by Alasdair Gray

NOVELS

Lanark
1982, Janine
The Fall of Kelvin Walker
Something Leather
McGrotty and Ludmilla
Poor Things
A History Maker
Mavis Belfrage
Old Men In Love

SHORT STORY COLLECTIONS

Unlikely Stories, Mostly
Lean Tales (with James Kelman and Agnes Owens)
Ten Tales Tall & True
The Ends of Our Tethers: 13 Sorry Stories
Every Short Story by Alasdair Gray 1951–2012

POETRY

Old Negatives
Sixteen Occasional Poems
Collected Verse
Hell: Dante's Divine Trilogy Part One
Purgatory: Dante's Divine Trilogy Part Two
Paradise: Dante's Divine Trilogy Part Three

THEATRE

Dialogue – A Duet
The Loss of the Golden Silence
Homeward Bound: A Trio for Female Chauvinists
Sam Lang and Miss Watson:
A One Act Sexual Comedy In Four Scenes
McGrotty and Ludmilla
Working Legs: A Play for Those Without Them
Goodbye Jimmy
Fleck
A Gray Play Book

NON-FICTION

Why Scots Should Rule Scotland
The Book of Prefaces
How We Should Rule Ourselves
A Life In Pictures
Of Me and Others
Independence

This Canons edition published in 2022 by Canongate Books

HELL, PURGATORY and PARADISE first published
individually in Great Britain, the USA and Canada
in 2018, 2019, 2020 by Canongate Books Ltd,
14 High Street, Edinburgh EH1 1TE

Distributed in the USA by Publishers Group West
and in Canada by Publishers Group Canada

canongate.co.uk

1

The author gratefully acknowledges the support of Creative Scotland
towards writing this book

British Library Cataloguing-in-Publication Data
A catalogue record for this book is available on
request from the British Library

ISBN 978 1 78689 702 2

Typeset in Times New Roman by Palimpsest Book Production Ltd,
Falkirk, Stirlingshire / Biblichor Ltd, Edinburgh

Printed and bound in Great Britain by Clays Ltd, Elcograf S.p.A.

DANTE'S DIVINE TRILOGY

Englished
in very free verse by
Alasdair Gray
begun Thursday 8 August
2013

CANONGATE

HELL

LIST OF CANTOS

PURGATORY

LIST OF CANTOS

PARADISE

LIST OF CANTOS

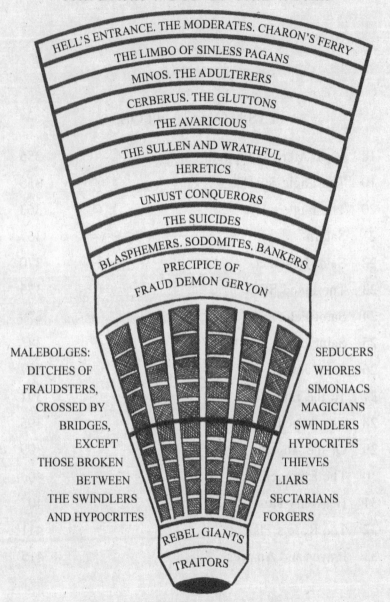

THE PLAN OF DANTE'S HELL

THE DARK WOOD OF THIS WORLD

HELL'S ENTRANCE. THE MODERATES. CHARON'S FERRY

THE LIMBO OF SINLESS PAGANS

MINOS. THE ADULTERERS

CERBERUS. THE GLUTTONS

THE AVARICIOUS

THE SULLEN AND WRATHFUL

HERETICS

UNJUST CONQUERORS

THE SUICIDES

BLASPHEMERS. SODOMITES. BANKERS

PRECIPICE OF

FRAUD DEMON GERYON

MALEBOLGES:
DITCHES OF
FRAUDSTERS,
CROSSED BY
BRIDGES,
EXCEPT
THOSE BROKEN
BETWEEN
THE SWINDLERS
AND HYPOCRITES

SEDUCERS
WHORES
SIMONIACS
MAGICIANS
SWINDLERS
HYPOCRITES
THIEVES
LIARS
SECTARIANS
FORGERS

REBEL GIANTS

TRAITORS

HELL

PART 1

FOREWORD TO HELL

There are more than a hundred English versions of Dante's epic and every two years another appears. Readers are always eager for them as, like the Bible, it answers important questions with fascinating stories. But unlike the Bible no governments have promoted one excellent translation. None exist. To compress dramatic action, thought and dialogue into a huge poem Dante invented a unique verse form: three line verses so cleverly unified by end-rhymes that most translators try to reproduce the same form. In Italian end-rhymes are easy because most words end in one of five vowels. In English end-rhymes are harder so most translators get them with language seldom used in daily speech. My version mainly keeps the Dantean form colloquial by using end-rhymes where they came easily, internal rhymes where they did not. My abrupt north British dialect has cut Dante's epic down to the range of my intelligence, which is less than Dante's. Critics who cannot read the original should compare it with any other English translation, which will be more accurate in the dictionary sense of the word.

Here are two examples of my abruptness. In Italy the heroine's name is pronounced with four syllables; *Be-a-trich-ay* is a poor phonetic approximation to that beautiful sound. In English the name is usually spoken with two syllables, almost rhyming with *mattress*. My rhyme scheme needs three syllables: *Be-a-tris*. Other Italian names should be pronounced with as many syllables as Italians use. Dante mentions two political parties, Ghibelline and Guelph, which I translate as Tory and Whig. The main difference (as in Britain's eighteenth and nineteenth centuries) was between old and new money, the older class being landowners, the new one merchants. Like all two-party systems the difference was constantly blurred by changing local alliances or intermarriage.

Other apologies for mishandling Dante's texts will be in the foreword to my *Purgatory* translation.

1: The Dark Wood. Virgil

1 In middle age I wholly lost my way,
   finding myself within an evil wood
   far from the right straight road we all should tread,

4 and what a wood! So densely tangled, dark,
   jaggily thorned, so hard to press on through,
   even the memory renews my dread.

7 My misery, my almost deadly fear
   led on to such discovery of good,
   I'll tell you of it, if you care to hear.

I cannot say how I had wandered there,   10
when dozy, dull and desperate for sleep
my feet strayed out of the true thoroughfare,

till deep among the trees an upward slope   13
gave to my fearful soul a thrill of hope
as rising ground at last became a hill,

and looking up I saw a summit bright   16
with dawn – the rising sun that shows us all
where we should travel by its heavenly light.

This quieted a little while the fright   19
that churned the blood within my heart's lagoon
through the long journey of that gloomy night.

Like shipwrecked swimmers in a stormy sea   22
who, tired and panting but at last ashore,
look back on swamping breakers thoughtfully,

I turned to view, though wishing still to leave,   25
the terrifying forest in the glen
no living soul but mine had struggled through.

My weary body rested then until,   28
rising, I climbed the sloping wilderness,
so that each footstep raised me higher still.

But see! The uphill climb had just begun   31
when suddenly a leopard, light, quick, gay
and brightly spotted, sprang before my feet,

dodging from side to side, blocking the way   34
so swiftly and with such determination
she sometimes nearly forced me to retreat.

37 The sun had reached a height dimming the stars
created with him on the second day,
after the birth of time and space and light,

40 and this recalled God's generosity,
letting me feel some good at least might be
within the leopard's carnival ferocity,

43 so dappled, bright and jolly was that beast,
but not so bright to stop me shuddering
at a fresh shock – a lion came in sight,

46 his mighty head held high, his savage glare
fixed upon me in such a hungry way
it seemed to terrify the very air.

49 A wolf beside him, rabid from starvation,
horribly hungry, far more dangerous,
has driven multitudes to desperation,

52 me too! For she established my disgrace,
(that worst of beasts) by killing my desire
to climb up higher to a better place.

55 A millionaire made glorious by gain
then hit by sudden loss of all he has,
cries out in vast astonishment and pain.

58 So did I, shoved down backwards, foot by foot,
by pressure of that grim relentless brute
till forced into the sunless wood again.

61 Appearing in its shade a human shape
both seemed and sounded centuries away,
murmuring words almost beyond my hearing,

therefore I yelled, "Pity and help me, please,   64
whether you be a living man or ghost!"
and pleaded, crouching down before his knees.

"Not man – though once I was, in Lombardy,   67
where both my parents dwelled in Mantua,
and I was born in Caesar's reign," said he,

"but educated in Augustan Rome   70
when the false gods were worshipped everywhere.
I sang the epic of Anchises' son,

pious Aeneas, who fled blazing Troy   73
and founded Rome. I was a poet there.
Why are you here? Why turn back from your climb

towards the bright height of eternal bliss   76
and come again to a bad place like this?"
"You must be Virgil!" Awestruck, I replied,

"Fountain of all our pure Italian speech!"   79
Rising, I bowed and told him, "All I know
of poetry derives from what you teach!

The style which makes me famed in Italy   82
I learned from you who are my dominie!
Help me again, for see at the hill foot

the brute whose threats have rendered me distraught! 85
Master, please save me – show me the right way.
That rabid wolf has driven me so mad

my pulse and every sense have gone agley."   88
I wept and, "Take another road," he said,
"and leave this wasteland, leave that wolfish whore

91 who lets none pass before she bites them dead.
Her starving greedy lust is never sated.
Her appetite increases as she feasts.

94 Mated with many beasts, she'll mate with more
till one great greyhound comes to hunt her down
whose fangs will end her life in deadly pain.

97 Wisdom, love, courage are his nourishment,
not gold nor land nor any earthly gain.
From birth among the lowly he will rise,

100 bringing new glory to the Italian plain
like the old Trojan colonists and kings
whose wars created Rome's establishment.

103 Out of each city state he will expel
the wolf before he fixes her at last
back in the place she came from, which is Hell.

106 That is not yet; so now you'll come with me
on a straight downward path into the jail
envy released her from, and see God's wrath

109 afflicting sinners who forever wail –
no second death will end their agony!
Then a high fiery mountain we'll ascend

112 past burning climbers, happy in their flame,
for they will one day join the heavenly choir.
The summit reached, since Heaven is your aim,

115 we two must part. A better guide than me
will lead you then. Living I did not know,
could not obey the last great law of He

who made the whole celestial universe.   118
His highest city, capital and throne
are places that I cannot hope to see.

Happy are those chosen to join Him there!"   121
I answered, "Poet, sent by the God whom you
(alas) can't know, let us be gone, I pray,

out of this danger, down that hard, hard road,   124
then to the heavenly gate Saint Peter guards,
seeing the poor damned souls upon our way."

We walked. I followed as he led me on.   127

2: Early Doubts Quelled

1 Day ended. Beasts and birds who love the sun
   homed to their dens and nests through dusky air.
   Mine seemed the only living body there

4 going to warfare, marching to battle where
   each step ahead would be a struggle of
   pity with dread in perpetuity.

7 O Muses! Highest altitudes of thought
   and memory, recording all I see
   by use of noble ingenuity!

10 Let me teach others, as I have been taught!
    "Poet!" I cried. "Tell me if I am fit
    to go the fearful way you're leading me.

13 You sang how great Aeneas followed it
    and living, saw the nation of the dead.
    God let Aeneas, for it was His plan

16 to found a pagan empire by that man –
    the Roman Empire Christ inherited,
    by crucifixion Christianising Rome.

19 He went through death and Hell to bring souls home
    to heavenly bliss Aeneas never knew.
    How can this living me follow these two?

Why me? Who has suggested that I go?   22
I'm not Aeneas, nor am I Saint Paul
summoned to follow Jesus by a call

direct from Christ. If feeble me submits   25
to enter Hell I'll maybe lose my wits!
Please! You know all! Why *should* I go with you?"

Blethering thus, unwilling what I'd willed,   28
I halted in an agony of doubt
from the brisk pace at which we'd started out.

Inside a darkened borderland I stood,   31
my courage to continue almost killed,
as if again within the evil wood.

"If I have grasped the sense of what you say,"   34
the ghost of splendid Virgil turned and said,
"cowardice, which leads most folk astray,

blocks (as its shadow on the road ahead   37
frightens a horse) the way that you should tread.
Listen to what should banish your remorse.

There came to me in Limbo where I dwell   40
(the only comfortable part of Hell)
a holy lady altogether lovely.

Her eyes like starlight and her quiet voice   43
angelically sweet, made me rejoice
to do the utmost thing she asked. Said she,

'Poet of Mantua, whose epic song   46
will last as long as stars and planets move,
someone I dearly love is going wrong –

49 If none will help he may be lost to me.
   On hearing this in Heaven I come to you.
   O courteous poet, listen to my plea:

52 I beg you, join him where he turns aside
   from the true track. He stands alone, astray,
   at foot of a grim hill. O pity him!

55 He needs your strength to guide him the right way.
   If you are not too late, say to him this:
   you have been sent by love and Beatrice,

58 for I am Beatrice, for whom you go
   to save both him I love and me from woe.
   The love that drew me from eternity

61 now draws me back. Soon I will see God's face
   within the glory of His sacred city
   and praise forever in that holy place

64 your goodness.' There she paused. At once I said,
   'Lady, by virtue of your heavenly love,
   the love that made God form the human race

67 with excellence that lifts it far above
   all other beasts within this world's small space,
   obeying you is what I most desire,

70 so much that done at once would be too slow.
   But there is something first I wish to know.
   Your blessed feet have carried you through Hell

73 yet you are not alarmed. How is that so?'
   'Because you wish to learn I will explain,'
   said she. 'God makes the innocent and wise

both blind and deaf to Hell's eternal pain,   73
but not to troubles of a living soul.
A gentle lady some call Heaven's queen

has mercy as her special ministry.   73
She often countermands God's stern decrees
to save a sinner's soul by purgatory –

a breach of justice to which God agrees.   82
She said to Lucy, "Saint of heavenly light,
your best disciple is about to quit

his upward climb to us, risking damnation.   85
Dante's in danger. Get him out of it."
Lucy sped to the height of contemplation

where I conversed (she knew) with sage Rachel,   88
noblest mother of the Jewish nation
and wife of flock-attending Israel.

"Beatrice!" she said, "in harmony with God!   91
Why, why, O why ignore a lover who
was taught to love divinity by you?

Can you not hear him miserably cry,   94
lonely and lost beside death's raving sea
and threatened by a foul rapacity?"

As soon as Lucy's words were understood,   97
nobody ever moved as fast as me.
I came to you whose wise and truthful speech

can heal my lover's hurt and do him good –   100
speech glorifying you and all who hear,'
she said, turning her face to hide a tear.

103 Its brightness urged me to this place. The wolf
still blocks the uphill path. We'll reach the top
going the long way round. With me your guide

106 and three celestial women on your side,
why hesitate? What have you got to fear?
Why all this cowardice? Have you no pride?"

109 As daisies folding petals up at night,
heavy with frozen dew, lean to the ground
until the rising sun's warm, gift of light

112 thaws and unbends and opens them, I found
at last my crippled courage stand upright.
Like one set free I cried, "Let us go on!

115 The great compassion of that heavenly she,
forbye the wonder of your courtesy
have cured my idiot timidity.

118 Your words have filled me with new confidence,
confidence,
making your will and mine a single will.
Guide, Lord and Master, come! Let us go hence."

121 The wild path that we followed led downhill.

3: Hell's Entry. Doom of Moderates. Charon's Ferry

ENTER THROUGH ME, CITY OF ENDLESS WOE, 1
ENTER THROUGH ME ETERNAL AGONY
ENTER TO JOIN THE WHOLLY LOST BELOW

CREATIVE LOVE, CREATIVE INTELLECT, 4
ESTABLISHED ME FOR ALL ETERNITY.
INFINITE JUSTICE IS MY ARCHITECT.

NOTHING EXISTED BEFORE I WAS MADE. 7
NOTHING EXISTING WILL ESCAPE MY SCOPE.
ALL YOU WHO ENTER HERE, ABANDON HOPE!

10 These fearful words carved deeply I could see
    above a great dark doorway, so I cried,
    "O Master, do these words apply to me?"

13 Like a good teacher giving calm advice,
    "Don't think that I mislead you," he replied.
    "By now you should have lost your cowardice.

16 I am assigned (recall) to help you view
    the final state of those dead sinners who
    chose to corrupt the goodness of their minds."

19 Smiling to cheer me on, he took my hand
    and led me in beside a dreadful band
    who hurt my ears with horrid lamentation.

22 Screams, wails, howls, groans and other ugly cries
    went blasting by us in a starless dark
    with skirls of rancorous denunciation,

25 wild curses yelled in tongues of every nation
    or hoarsely growled, or hissed in execration,
    mingled with bitter moaning, sobs and sighs

28 that had me weeping too in emulation.
    This madly squealing, roaring, snarling throng
    arms flailing, clutching hands and trampling feet,

31 went reeling, shambling, charging, tumbling by,
    like sands in whirlwinds, birling round and round
    until their foggy billows hid the sky.

34 This ghastly crowd and din so filled my head
    I gazed upon my guide and whispered, "Why?"
    "These timid sinners stand aside," he said,

"when strong oppressors tyrannise and slay.   37
They may feel sympathetic to the weak
but think it wise to keep out of the way.

When Satan, God's prime minister, first planned   40
to rule the universe, he raised a band
of rebels who split Heaven in two, it seemed,

till moderates united in a team   43
to stay aloof from holiness and sin
until they saw which side was bound to win.

They were the foremost damned when virtue won. 46
Outcasts of Hell and Heaven, here they run."
"But Master," I asked, "why do they yell so loud?"

He said, "This sorry crowd have the distress   49
of being altogether meaningless.
They envy now the fate of anyone

whose deeds and misdeeds will preserve their name 52
in memory, through good or evil fame.
Justice and mercy both reject them, so

we'll speak no more of them. Look, and let's go." 55
I looked and saw a whirling flag ahead,
chased by these multitudes. I never knew

such millions had been numbered with the dead, 58
but one I knew, that cowardly pope, who,
elected to reform the Church's sins,

fearing to foul his hands by that, withdrew,   61
true to himself, but to our God untrue.
Hornets that stung like daggers sped this race

64 of frantic nudity, so tears, sweat, blood
    splashing the ground from every limb and face
    were sucked by worms wriggling in trampled mud.

67 Beyond that rushing rabble I could see,
    though dimly lit, a mighty river's shore
    with quite a different crowd congesting it,

70 pressing and jostling. They seemed to me
    like people keen to reach the other side.
    I asked my guide, "What are they eager for?"

73 "Wait and you'll see," was all that he replied.
    We reached the river. From the other shore
    I saw a ferry-boat come shooting out,

76 rowed by a hoary ancient with white hair
    who, when he neared our side, began to shout,
    "Welcome to grief and welcome to despair,

79 you wicked ghosts! No glimpse of heavenly light
    for you again, condemned to endless night,
    with scorching heat or agonising frost.

82 Welcome to what forever hurts you most!
    But you – a living man – cannot cross here.
    My only business is to shift the dead,

85 so go another way, and fast!" he said
    I did not move. "Trespasser, go!" he roared,
    "I cannot carry you! Ghosts are my freight!

88 This boat can't bear a living body's weight."
    "Don't bluster, Charon. You'll convey this man,"
    my master said. "On high it has been willed

your boat *shall* take him, so of course it can."   91
The quiet reasoning of this reply
shut the grim captain's mouth, although his rage

glowed in a ring of flame around each eye   94
glaring upon the crowded landing stage
where his rude voice turned the bare bodies white

and made teeth chatter. Gibbering with fright   97
or wailing with it, those damned souls cursed God,
mankind, themselves, cursed worst their parents' bed,

the genitals and womb whence they were bred.   100
Beckoned by Charon, one by one they sped
downward. Like hawks they swooped into his boat

or spun down and round like drifts of leaves   103
abandoning a tree to coat the ground.
That demon with the eyes like flaming coals

packed tightly in his cargo of damned souls,   106
whacking the hindmost smartly with his oar.
I went out with them over the dark water

and as we left behind the nearest shore   109
I saw it was as crowded as before.
My kindly teacher said to me, "My son,

no nation is without a downward path   112
on which the dead are flocking here – each one
who dies within the shadow of God's wrath.

Their weight of guilt, by force of gravity,   115
drags them all quickly down for punishment
at the true depth of their iniquity,

118 a state they want, yet dread. No gleam of light
    (which they rejected) halts that downward flight.
    Charon precipitates their grim descent,

121 so hates conveying you who go elsewhere."
    We reached the further shore and disembarked
    onto a desolate and gloomy plain

124 shaking with earthquakes, and I saw it split
    by a great gust of wind that carried out
    black coiling clouds with crimson lightning lit.

127 So shocking was the sight that even yet,
    despite worse things I later saw in Hell,
    the recollection soaks my skin with sweat.

130 Exhausted then, I fell down in a fit.

4: Limbo of Sinless Pagans

A thunderclap jerked me at last awake   1
and upright, as if lifted by strong arms.
I found myself on a tremendous height

above so vast a slope of falling ground   4
it vanished under clouds beneath my sight.
I knew this pit must be the last abode

of every sinner cast away by God.   7
My guide, reading my thought, said, "It is so.
Here we must now descend, so let us go."

His face was deathly pale. I cried aloud,   10
"Master, I dare not! Surely you must see
I *cannot* follow where you fear to tread."

"Not fear but pity blanches me," he said,   13
"pity for those beneath. We've far to go,
so onward, come!" He led me straight ahead

onto the widest ledge circling the pit   16
where twilit air was tremulous with sighs –
no other sounds of suffering were there.

My sadly smiling guide asked, "Do you know   19
who dwell within this painless part of Hell?
This is my place, with those who did not sin,

22 born before Jesus, therefore not baptised.
Limbo is where all sinless pagans dwell
outside the radiance of gospel's grace.

25 Lacking baptism, you see, we did no wrong,
but cannot truly love the Trinity
and give to it the praise that is its due.

25 This is the only cause of our distress."
That noble souls are thus condemned to pain
forever, and condemned to it in vain

31 depressed me for a while, and so I said,
"Now tell me, sir, please tell me, Master dear . . ."
(for now I needed utter certainty

34 about our faith which strikes all error dead)
". . . has no one any time escaped from here
by their own virtue, or by virtue lent?"

37 My guide exactly knew just what I meant.
"Soon after I entered this zone of Hell,"
he said, "a Hero crowned with victory

40 passed through and down to pull out of the pit
Adam and Eve and all His ancestry –
Abel their first born son of righteous mind –

43 Noah the just whose ark preserved mankind –
Abraham patriarch of everyone –
Rachel whom Heaven put such cares upon

46 and wife of Jacob renamed Israel –
lawgiver Moses, psalmist David too –
and many more than I could tell or see

He raised to Heaven where I will never be."   49
We passed as he was speaking through a crowd –
men, women, infants who forlornly stood

like rustling trees within a twilit wood,   52
but gradually between them there appeared
a light that grew much brighter as we neared,

until I saw it was a dome of light   55
with such fine folk inside I asked my guide,
"Why are these brightly lit and set apart?"

Said he, "Heaven ratifies the glory   58
given by art and story." A great shout
rang out: "The prince of poetry is home,

returned to us from distant wandering!"   61
Four solemn figures came towards us then
with neither joy nor sorrow in their looks.

My guide explained, "Their leader with the sword   64
first sang of warfare – also was the first
to have his verse immortalised in books.

His name is Homer. Horace close behind   67
brought wit and satire into poetry;
next, Ovid, singer of love's mysteries

and those transformed by angry deities;   70
and lastly Lucan, singer of civil strife
who knew that One in Heaven is lord of life.

These four are reigning kings of poetry   73
yet think (for it is true) I am the best.
I must confer with them, which is their due."

76 The band of poets gathered round my guide.
He spoke with them and then at his request
made me the sixth in that small company

79 of eagle-winged strong souls whose poetry
outsoars the rest. My master smiled at this.
We walked together, these wise men and me,

82 slowly upon our way to better light,
talking of things profound and good to say,
six kindred souls within that gracious place

85 until a splendid city came in sight,
a stream of pure clear water flowing round.
We walked on it as though it were dry ground

88 then faced a gateway in a lofty wall
with seven towers. Passing between two,
I found a lovely space of smooth green lawn

91 where noble people, moving gracefully,
spoke to each other very quietly.
I asked my guide, "Master of every art,

94 what *privileges* these majestic folk,
apart from obvious nobility?"
He said, "Their names still famously resound

97 on earth, and heavenly powers respect them too,
believing privileges are their due."
We two then walked a little way apart

100 up a small hill. Good light allowed a view
of these great ghosts. Nothing so thrills my heart
as thinking of these spirits I have seen:

Electra, and the heroes she conceived;   103
Hector; Aeneas ancestor of Rome;
Caesar in armour with his hawk-like eye;

huntress Camilla; Amazon warrior   106
Penthesilea; first Latin king Latinus,
with daughter Lavinia; Brutus who

expelled Rome's last king Tarquin; Julia –   109
Lucretia – Cornelia – Marcia –
standing apart, the mighty Saladin.

Raising my eyes I saw the kings of mind: 112
Aristotle master of those who know;
Socrates close behind; Plato also;

Democritus who said atoms and chance   115
made everything; cynic Diogenes;
Anaxagoras; the herbal healer

Dioscorides; Thales; Orpheus;   118
Tully; Livy; moralist Seneca;
geometer Euclid; geographical

astronomer Ptolemy; the doctors   121
Galen and Hippocrates; and the best
of Aristotle's great expositors:

Avicenna and Averroes. O!   124
I cannot tell you all I saw because
too many times my words demean my thought.

My company was growing very small.   127
Our group of six had dwindled into two.
My bold wise guide and I at last withdrew

into a place where nothing shines all.   130

5: Minos. Doom of Adulterers

1 Descending to the second ledge of Hell,
a smaller circle of intenser pain,
I heard again the sound of sorrowing.

4 Here demon Minos with his dragon tail
grins as he passes judgement on the dead
then sends them down to their due punishment.

7 Each ghost before him gibbers out its crimes.
The times he winds his tail around himself
show to which depths the wicked ghost must go.

10 Hell has ten rings. The demon's tail is long.
The throng of souls, ceaselessly pouring in,
are never slow in blurting out their sin,

13 then hurl themselves down through appalling space
onto the right ledge of the hellish pit
that is forever now their dwelling place.

16 "YOU have no place here!" Minos bawled at me,
seeing we did not pause but walked straight through,
not stopping to be judged, "Take care! Beware!

19 Hell's open door is not kept wide for you!"
"Minos," my guide replied, "forces too high
for you to know insist this man may go

unhurt through every door there is in Hell.   22
Our business is not yours, and so farewell."
New sounds of lamentation reached my ear,

a rushing tumult mixed with howling yell.   25
We entered darkness – darkness bellowing
like ocean tempests combating together.

A hurricane of ghosts went wailing past   28
under the lofty cliff that was their coast.
I saw lost souls tossed, spinning in the blast

and buffeted again, again, again,   31
against the granite wall that penned them in.
I knew this endless storm of sorry souls

must be the just and proper doom of all   34
who sin because their overwhelming lust
quelled reason's light. A rockslide in the cliff

had formed the gap we came through. Seeing us   37
the storm of fleeing, yelling ghosts blasphemed
much louder, wheeled like starlings in their flight,

screaming onwards like cranes hopeless of rest   40
or lesser pains. "Master," cried I, "name some
so mercilessly whipped by this dark air."

He said, "There's one whose history you know –   43
wife of a king who made her empress queen
of all the lands now ruled by the Sultan.

Her sexual appetites were so obscene   46
she legalised all kinds of viciousness.
Her name is Semiramis. Dido there

49 swore she would only wed one man. Him dead,
she took instead another mate and then
committed suicide when he escaped –

52 Helen of Troy, so opportunely raped –
Cleopatra whose expertise in love
was legend – see too the many men –

55 Paris – Achilles – Tristan – Lancelot—"
He pointed out so many souls condemned
for fleshly lust, it filled me with dismay

58 to see such noble people led astray
by love that ought to be our greatest joy.
"Poet," I said, "let me talk with that pair

61 who seem more gently carried by the air."
Said he, "If they come near enough to hear
Invite them by the love they clearly share."

64 The wind now tossed them close. "O harried souls,"
I cried, "if none forbid, please talk to me!"
Like homing doves they glided to my side.

67 One said, "Dear good and kindly living soul
who frees us briefly from our storm-tossed state,
if we could pray we'd pray that you find rest –

70 that blessed rest that cannot be our fate.
The only way to show our gratitude
for these few moments out of whirling Hell

73 is telling you all that you wish to know.
My birthplace was a town where River Po
enters the sea. I married lovelessly

a hard old man. His brother at my side   76
whom I love still, had youth and gentleness.
As he enjoyed my body we were found

and slain. Our killer's place in Hell will be   79
among the murderers who followed Cain."
Sighing, I bowed my head. My guide enquired,

"What thought distresses you?" "Sorrow for youth   82
and what befalls youth's sweetness," I replied,
"Francesca, please believe I pity you,

but tell me what occurred that led you to   85
the deed you knew was sin." "Worst grief," said she,
"is happiness recalled in misery.

Your master knows this well and if you need   88
to understand, I'll tell as you command.
To pass an idle hour one afternoon

we chanced to read of how Sir Lancelot   91
was overcome by love of Guinevere.
This youth who never shall depart from me

trembling all over, dared to kiss my mouth.   94
That book seduced us. There's no more to say
except, of course, we read no more that day."

She wept. The other spirit wept – me too.   97
The three of us shed tears without restraint.
Because I could not give them any help

I clutched my head and fell down in a faint.   100

6: Cerberus. Doom of Gluttons

1   Returning to my senses once again
from sorrow that confused them utterly,
I saw a different multitude in pain,

4   not reeling, writhing, spirits spinning round,
but corpulences stuck in muddy ground
under a freezing hard unending rain

7   of filthy water, hailstones, blasts of snow
descending through a murkiness of fog
to make the earth below a stinking bog

10 from which the sunken souls halfway protrude.
Across this mire prowls a rude vicious beast
three-headed, each head howling like a dog.

13 His name is Cerberus, his eyes blood-red,
black hair and beards befouled by greasy phlegm,
his belly gross, each paw with knife-like claws

16 that stab and rip sinners they prance upon,
who also howl like dogs. They cannot stop
squirming to turn their downside up again

19 to shield their upside from the dreadful rain.
Cerberus, glaring on us, snarled and showed
three pairs of open jaws with dragon fangs,

his body twitching, bristled to attack.   22
My guide stooped swiftly, scooped up blood-rich mud,
then accurately flung a handful down

each throat. Howling and snarling stopped at once.   25
Like hungry hound gorging on juicy bone
he left the damned alone as we moved on

across the swamp where footsteps often sank   28
down through a groaning ghost to mud below.
Then one, twisting half up beside our way

cried out, "O Dante, surely you know me?   31
We met in Florence years before I died."
"To me you seem a stranger," I replied,

"but hellish woe has maybe altered you.   34
Please tell me who you were, the thing you did
that brings such suffering. Worse punishments

no doubt exist, but few so sickening."   37
Said he, "Within our sunlit native town
the citizens once knew me as the Hog.

I thought rich food the best thing life could give, 40
so rot in rain here like a sodden log,
but not alone, the others that you see

are also damned for selfish gluttony."   43
I said to him, "Poor Hog, I pity you!
But ghosts can know much more than living men

of what time has in store. Please tell   46
if Florence which engendered us will come
in course of time to rule her people well.

49 *Must* party politics divide our state?
No just men lead us to co-operate?"
He told me, "Old disputes will never end.

52 Divided still by envy, pride and greed
our government will come to civil wars,
bloodshed and banishment. Our councillors

55 will fight for who pays most, changing their side
to any that pay more. A few will fight for
civil rights, justice for those in need

58 and be ignored by envy, pride and greed."
I wept at that, begging, "Tell me about
good men I knew who wanted to do well –

61 Arrigo, Mosca and Tegghiaio,
Jack Rusticucci and Farinata –
where are they now?" "Go deeper into Hell,"

64 said he. "You'll find them there. All I ask now
is this: when you return to Italy
remind the folk that I, the Hog, am here.

67 I'll say no more." His eyes went squint. He fell
down flat and blind and speechless as before.
My leader said, "He'll hear no other word

70 till the last trumpet summons bodies up
to reunite with souls. Then will resound
the Judge's final word of doom, that word

73 that locks the damned forever in their tomb."
We waded slowly onwards through the scum
of muddy shadows, stinking fog and rain,

talking a little of the life to come.   76
I asked him, "Master, will these feel their pain
harder or lesser or without much change

after that judgement's passed upon the dead?"   79
"Think scientifically," my guide said,
"when things are more complete the more they show

and feel, if sensitive, delight or pain.   82
No hint of ease can be within this pit.
Body plus soul must feel the opposite."

We spoke of other things I don't recall   85
upon that path which gradually bent
round in a circle to the next descent.

Here we found Plutus, enemy of all.   88

7: Plutus. Avaricious. Styx

1   "Daddy Mephisto! Daddy Bugaboo!"
    gargled the demon. Like a bulging sack
    his bloated body almost filled the gap

4   torn in the cliff our track descended through.
    "Never fear *him*," murmured my gentle guide.
    Pointing at Plutus' swollen face, he said,

7   "Shut up, you wolfish clown! Chew your own gut!
    Our journey into Hell is willed on high
    where archangelic swords cut rebels down!"

10 As billowing sails of scudding ship
    crumple in tangles if the mast collapse,
    so crumpled Plutus. We descended past,

13 arriving at the fourth shore round the bin
    all evil sinks to, where I stared amazed
    by the insanity that raged therein.

16 Justice of God! I cannot understand
    why men condemn themselves to endless pain
    by madly chasing earthly loss and gain.

19 Think of a mighty river wild with spate
    plunging in torrents till abruptly blocked
    by counter-torrents of an equal weight.

Think of the smashing splash as these two crash   22
together and the turmoil and recoil.
Imagine now each wave of this stramash

a man shoving a boulder with his chest,   25
each limb and muscle with the utmost strain
holding the weight or pushing it away,

the difference impossible to say,   28
though when their boulders clashed one party yelled,
"Hold tight!" the other shouted out, "Let go!"

Disgusted by the sight, "Master," I cried,   31
"who are they? Those with tonsures on the right,
are they all clergymen?" "Both right and left,"

said he, "in their first life neither could keep   34
nor spend with decency. To hoard or waste
is what divided them, and yes, the bald

were greedy priests and cardinals and popes   37
who loved gold more than souls." "Point out the worst!"
I cried, "When I am back in Italy

my book will make their vices more accursed."   40
"It's stupid to commemorate," said he,
"people whose names deserve to be forgot.

How short a comedy it is, my son,   43
this play of wealth that only luck has blessed,
since all the gold that glows beneath the moon

can't buy a single soul one moment's rest."   46
Said I, "Please tell me more about this luck
who seems to hold the world's wealth in her fist."

49 Said he to me, "O creatures of the dark!
    You human brood, unlit by reason's spark!
    Allow my sentences to do you good.

52 The mind who formed the universe took care
    that every one could have an equal share
    of sunlight, moonlight, starlight and sweet air.

55 On earth such widespread goodness cannot be.
    Most goods become a private property
    even inside a small community.

58 Within a city or a nation state
    great force or cunning can accumulate
    properties, making some cliques dominate

61 until the angel with so many names –
    luck, chance, fate, fortune, mutability –
    makes new cliques prosper, other cliques decay,

64 whether by vice or virtue, who can say?
    But those who trust, not virtue, but to luck
    have gone astray, aye, very far astray.

67 A day and night have passed since we set out.
    We must not linger longer on our way
    but go to look at deeper misery."

70 We dodged right through that boulder-shoving mob
    and on the far side found a bubbling spring
    of water, black as night, from which a stream

73 led us around to a cliff-edge crevasse
    where, tumbling in, it spilled to lower ground.
    A steep dark stair by that weird waterfall

brought us to where black liquid filled a ditch   76
under the overhanging precipice –
a wide, dank, moatlike ditch known as the Styx

giving off chilling mist. Its outward bank   79
sloped down towards a marsh in which I saw
great multitudes of figures in a fight,

naked and mud-stained, grappling upright   82
or wrestling prone, legs kicking, punching fists,
fingers that gouged or tore and teeth that bit.

Walking between the Styx and that foul sight   85
my master said, "Outrageous violence
condemns these souls to mindless, endless spite.

Now turn your eyes and look the other way   88
to the black slime bubbling like boiling broth
caused by the sighs of damned souls underneath.

I'll tell you what they'd like to say but can't.   91
*On earth we were so full of our own woe
we saw no good in any gift of God.*

Not space, time, air, sunlight or love itself   94
could woo us from our miserable state.
Eternal sullenness is now our fate.

Aye, could they speak such words would be their chant. 97
Bubbles are all that will be seen of them."
Conversing, we eventually came

to the foot of a great tower that had no name.   100

8: The Wrathful. Gate of Dis

1 Before we reached that lofty tower I saw
two horns of flame spring from the very top
and on the far side of the marshy pond

4 I saw through vapours distant flames respond.
I asked the fund of knowledge at my side,
"What do these signals indicate, and why?"

7 He answered, "Wait and see. The marsh mists hide
the ferry we desire, but not for long."
Then, speeding rapidly towards our shore

10 like arrow twanged from bow, there came a skiff
rowed by an oarsman roaring out at me,
"Hooray, you wicked beast! Got you at last!"

13 My guide called back, "Phlegyas, Phlegyas,
you're wrong about this man. He will not stew
inside this filthy ditch where you are boss

16 or any ditch in Hell he passes through.
What you must do is carry us across."
As if defrauded of his rightful wage

19 the demon strove to bottle up his rage.
My leader stepped aboard the ancient craft
then beckoned me. Unused to heavy freight

it settled lower with my weight, was rowed   22
much, much more slowly to the other shore.
then, from the stagnant fen beside the boat

a muddy figure rose and said to me,   25
"Who are you, coming here before your time?"
"I am not here to stay, but who are you?"

said I, "One who must weep," was his reply.   28
I said, "Good. Stay weeping in misery
Filippo Argenti, for I know you

despite your filthy dress." He stretched his hands   31
to grasp the boat. My master shoved him off crying,
"Stay here with other dirty dogs!"

Clasping my neck, kissing my cheek, he said,   34
"Blessed be the womb that bore you and also
your righteous indignation. Argenti

was horrible. His spiteful arrogance   34
encouraged spite in others. It is right
he weeps enraged for all eternity."

I said, "I want to see him suffer more."   40
"Before we reach the shore," my master said,
"that good wish will be gratified," and then

(I thank Power on high for this) a shout   43
burst out. "Filippo Argenti!" it cried
so loud it seemed yelled by the whole damned marsh.

Beneath the ooze I saw them tearing him   46
while with his teeth that proud Florentine soul
tore at himself. Enough of this. Anon

49 I heard new sounds of grief in front and stared
   eagerly forward. "Son," explained my guide,
   "we now approach Hell's greatest garrison,

52 the citadel of Dis." Said I, "Ahead
   I see beyond the battlements what look
   like tops of red-hot mosques." Said he, "They are.

55 The heat of nether Hell creates that glow."
   We reached the dismal city's iron wall,
   were rowed around it till the boatman bawled,

58 "Get out. This is the only entrance gate."
   Beside the gate a thousand angels stood,
   those ugly ones expelled from Heaven's light.

61 Said they, "Nobody living gets through here!"
   My master signed he'd talk to them apart.
   They said (though only slightly mollified),

64 "Yes, you can come, but not that other one
   who'll have to find his own insane way back
   without you as a guide!" Reader, my heart

67 sank at these words. "Dear leader," then I begged,
   "you who have helped me through so many
   threats,do not abandon me. Take me instead

70 back where we came from." "Do not be afraid,"
   my guide said. "None can stop our pilgrimage
   since One has ordered it. You rest a bit

73 and cultivate good hope. I will return
   and not desert you in this lower pit."
   My gentle padre left me to remain

76 with *yes* and *no* contending in my brain.

9: Citadel of Dis. Furies

On seeing him return from that shut gate,　　　1
so absolutely did my courage fail
I knew my face was turning deadly pale.

My guide restrained *his* pallor at the sight,　　　4
and as no eye could see through the grey mists,
he stood a while intently listening

and thus I overheard him murmuring,　　　7
"We'll win through somehow, I've no doubt unless . . .
But help *is* being sent . . . I wonder when . . ."

These words were meant to save me from distress　10
but only made me worry even more.
To change the subject, this is what I said:

"Master and guide, has anyone before　　　13
left Limbo to explore as deep as this?"
"I did," said he, "when civil war split Rome

well over thirteen centuries ago.　　　16
The witch, Erichtho, keen to know who'd win,
forced me by spells too sinful to repeat

straight down to Satan's lowest seat in Hell –　19
we used to call him Demogorgon then –
he said Caesar would gain the victory.

22 This downward path is therefore known to me
    though barred to you by Hell's hostility.
    We need that gate. On every other side

25 the wall stands sheer above the muddy tide of
    wrathful souls, so we must wait for aid.
    Some new thing frightens you?" I pointed where

28 upon the iron battlements of Dis
    three bloodstained female figures had appeared,
    bat-winged and belted with green snakes, their hair

31 writhing with smaller snakes. All glared at me
    so fiercely that I clung hard to my guide
    who said, "These are the Furies – torturers

34 of the most guilty souls. She on the left
    is Megaera; wailing on the far right
    Alecto, with Tisiphone between."

37 Tearing their breasts with talons eagle-like,
    they yelled, "Medusa, come! Change him to stone!"
    "Turn round!" my guide cried. "Don't look, shut eyes tight,

40 cover your face! Gorgon Medusa's glare
    can petrify you here so use both hands."
    Ensuring these commands he swung me round,

43 pressed my hands to my eyes with both his hands.
    Some intellects should find a lesson there.
    But then a mighty thunderclap rang out,

46 a crash advancing through the muggy fen
    like a tornado smashing down great trees,
    and driving on dust, beasts and fleeing men.

My guide then freed my eyes and said, "Look hard   49
at who is coming where the fog's most thick."
As snake spreads panic through a pond of frogs

who dive deep into mud, the wrathful souls   52
sank from the path of one who, dry shod, strode
across the foggy marsh of their abode,

fanning the fumes away before his face –   55
an almost absent-minded exercise
because his thoughts seemed in another place.

This was my helper. Unsure what to do,   58
I watched my guide who bowed, so I did too.
The helper from on high seemed not to see.

He passed us, touched the gate which opened wide.   61
To demon janitors cowering inside
he, standing on the threshold, cried aloud

in a great ecstasy of indignation,   64
"You stupid, wretched, miserable crew,
still rebels to He who created you!

Know again that insubordination   67
can alter nothing that is willed on high
and only multiplies your woe. Goodbye!"

Then he went back across the filthy bog   70
without a word to me who, fearless now,
followed my leader through the gate of Dis.

None stopped us as we passed the stronghold's towers 73
and walked into a land of different pain.
By Rhône at Arles, Pola in Italy,

76 are graveyards where the ancient, plundered tombs
gape at the sky, with slabs once shutting them
lying close by. So was the plain of Dis

79 except for this: each tomb was spouting flame,
being a furnace hotter than a forge,
and from which, also, dreadful outcries came.

82 My guide said, "See the doom of heretics
and of their followers, for every tomb
has room for many more than you can see,

85 each heated to a different degree
according to the error's magnitude."
So there we stood between high battlements

88 and all the flaming graveyard's punishments.

10: Doom of Heretics

Round between iron wall and flaming graves,   1
my leader led me by a hidden track
until I said, "Master, each ring of Hell

is known to you. Tell me, would it be hard   4
for me to speak with people in these tombs?
Their lids are off. No one is standing guard."

"On judgement's final day," responded he,   7
"bodies join souls, the lids are clamped down tight.
These heretics thought Epicurus right

who taught souls die with bodies. What you say   10
is said for reasons you withhold from me,
but knowing them I'll let you have your way."

"Master, you understand my inmost thought   13
so why waste words?" said I. "O Florentine—"
these words came from a fiery tomb nearby,

"O you who walk alive between Hell fires,   16
please pause and talk with me. Your dialect
proves you too are native of my city,

to which I sometime showed hostility."   19
In terror I moved closer to my guide
who said, "What's wrong? Did you not ask for this?

22 See Farinata standing in his flame,
    well known to you by name, so speak with him."
    I gazed on one waist-deep within his grave

25 whose face appeared contemptuous of Hell.
    As I approached he gazed as hard at me
    then, with disdain, asked who my people were.

28 I told him willingly. His eyebrows rose.
    "My enemies!" he said, "They led those Whigs
    I twice expelled." "The Whigs came back," said I.

31 "Your folk did not." There popped up at his side
    the face of someone risen to his knees
    who stared about for one he could not see

34 then weeping cried, "Where is my son? Surely,
    if poetry lets living souls through here
    my Guido should be standing beside you."

37 I said, "A greater poet is my guide."
    "Then tell me, does he live and breathe sweet air?"
    Because I hesitated to reply

40 he sank from sight with cries of great despair
    while great-souled Farinata stayed erect,
    with dauntless face continuing our talk.

43 "My family in exile still?" said he.
    "That is a more tormenting agony
    than are the pains of burning in this bed.

46 Not fifty months will pass before you know
    the pains of exile too. Tell me the cause
    that Florence and its laws are merciless

to members of a noble family?"   49
I said, "The blood you shed – that victory
staining a river red – is still recalled

and will not be forgot." He shook his head,   52
sighing, and said, "My side had also cause,
but when the Tuscan aristocracy

would have demolished Florence utterly   55
my opposition stopped that happening."
"May your descendants find a resting place,"

I said, "but what I cannot understand   58
is how you can tell what future years will bring
and not what happens now." "Defective sight,"

said he. "Heaven allows us light to see   61
what lies ahead, but nothing earlier.
News of today depends on visitors,

so after judgement day we dead in Hell   64
will have no memories of anything –
knowledge of nothing but our suffering."

That horrid thought recalled me to a fault.   67
"Please tell the father who fell back," said I,
"his son still breathes the air and is my friend.

Absence of mind alone made me unkind."   70
I heard my master call. In haste I begged
to know who else was there. "A thousand plus,"

said Farinata, naming emperors   73
and cardinals. Refusing to say more
he sank from sight and I, pondering hard,

76 followed my guide again. "Why lost in thought?"
   he asked. Said I, "A prophecy of pain –
   exile from home." "Remember that," said he

79 and raised a finger, "this too! When you stand
   in the sweet sight of she who cares for you,
   your life may look more perfect than you think."

82 Leaving the wall, we went across the plain
   between the flaming graves that covered it
   and down a slope towards the nether pit

85 from which arose a most disgusting stink.

11: A Lecture on Hell

Huge boulders fenced the clifftop round the ledge 1
but did not block the stench from lower Hell.
Retreating from that edge we went behind

a monument inscribed, *I hold the Pope* 4
Anastasius, who was led astray
by Photinus. My guide said, "Let us stay

here till accustomed to the evil smell." 7
"Agreed, but please use the delay," I said,
"to tell me what lies deeper down in Hell."

Said he, "I mean to. Know this cliff, my son, 10
surrounds three circles, each diminishing,
as do the upper circles we've passed through,

each built to satisfy eternally 13
God's justice. I will say who occupy
these rings of punishment, and tell you why.

Evil is justice wronged by force or fraud. 16
In the next circle down you'll meet the souls
who forcefully crushed justice openly –

homicides, tyrants, plunderers who took 19
their neighbours' lives and properties and lands –
suicides too, destroyed by their own hands –

22 those who blasphemed the Highest One of All –
and last, perverters of His greatest gifts:
bad buggers and bad bankers rich through loans.

25 Each sort receives a different punishment
that splits their circle into treble zones.
Fraudsters are in the second circle down.

28 Fraud is the sin the Highest hates the most,
since fraud kills love, that bond between the just
which could unite us all. Untied by fraud,

31 this bond is changed to hatred by mistrust
that worst of sins against the Holy Ghost.
Hence in the circle further down you'll see

34 seducers, pimps, prostitutes, rotten popes,
sorcerers, bribed officials, hypocrites,
thieves, scandal-mongers, lying experts who

37 twist people, money, words, assisting liars
who dominate each unjust government.
Last, lowest, smallest circle of the pit

40 is centre of our world and universe
where our descent concludes. There you will see
a lake of solid ice where traitors freeze,

43 traitors to kin and homeland, guests and these
to whom they owe profoundest gratitude,
frozen around the hugest fraud of all."

46 "My thanks, dear guide," said I, "for making clear
the ranks of sinners down in the abyss,
but think of those outside the walls of Dis –

racing through fog, tempest-tossed, clawed by dog   49
in rain, battering together boulders,
gurgling in slime and fighting all the time –

surely they suffer less than those below,   52
and if so, why?" "Stop talking like a fool,"
was his reply. "Aristotle's *Ethics*

defines three kinds of sin: incontinence   55
caused by an excessive natural lust,
is first and commonest and not the worst.

Violent malice vexes Heaven more,   58
and fraud's mad beastliness is most accursed.
You know this well, yet sit there asking why

all sinners don't go to Hell's deepest pit?"   61
"Master," I told him, "hearing you untie
that knot of doubt is truly a delight.

Untie my last. The loan of wealth for gain –   64
capitalism which priests call usury –
why is it judged as foul as sodomy

and so deserving of as great a pain?"   67
"True wisdom and philosophy," said he,
"give reasons you will find in Genesis

and Aristotle's *Physics*. These explain   70
natural things are Heaven's handiwork
and humankind should live by daily toil

through honest use of its materials   73
as all good farmers, tradesmen, housewives do
and poets too who show realities.

76 Despite the endless labour One commanded
on sending Adam out of Paradise,
money itself is not against His law

79 when it helps people share the goods we need.
But those who make money their merchandise
breed money out of money in their greed

82 until their banks of it leave others poor,
impeding flow of goods and common sense.
Foul unearned incomes are the consequence.

85 They worship Mammon, Midas, Mercury –
false golden gods. And now let us go hence.
Somewhere above, day is about to dawn

88 and so we must descend a precipice."

12: The Minotaur, Centaurs and Unjust Conquerors

Where a vast canyon cleft the clifftop edge   1
I saw, as from an Alpine mountain's height,
a rock fall sloping down between dark walls

so steep and far I shuddered at the sight.   4
Think of that avalanche of ruined stones
near Trent, that people call the Slides of Mark,

which spills from lofty summit to the plain.   7
Such was our stairway down through the ravine,
while sprawling across the top I saw

that monstrous and bull-headed shame of Crete,   10
the bastard of depraved Queen Pasiphaë
whom only a bull's prick could satisfy,

and crouching in a hollow wooden cow   13
got what she craved. On seeing us, her child
bellowed and bit his dewlaps, wild with rage,

at which my master cried, "No, this is not   16
Duke Theseus who slew you long ago.
This man must see the violently wrong

you guard below, so, beast, out of our way!"   19
As bull stabbed fatally by butcher's knife
before death strikes, has breath to plunge and kick,

22 so did the Minotaur. My guide said, "Quick!
    Let us slip past while fury blinds the brute."
    We did, both stepping down the scree of stones

25 that shifted under my more weighty foot.
    I pondered this until he said, "Perhaps
    you contemplate these rock falls which permit

28 your easier descent into the pit.
    They were not here when last I came this way
    before that Hero from the world above

31 rescued so many souls from sin and shame.
    In Limbo then I heard a joyful shout
    as if our universe was cleft by love,

34 and certainly an earthquake split these cliffs
    when He came here to fetch His people out.
    Now look below. You will begin to see

37 a flood of boiling blood devised to pain
    those who by force hurt other folk for gain."
    Between the cliff foot and a wide red moat

40 that curved around that level's inner ring,
    I saw a troop of centaurs galloping,
    all armed like bowmen out to hunt for deer.

43 They stopped as we came down. Three left the troop,
    put arrows in their bowstrings and drew near.
    One called, "Halt, you from above! Stand there! Declare

46 what torture you deserve – speak or I'll shoot!"
    My guide called back, "What I am here to say
    is for the ears of Chiron – not for you,"

and leading me towards that well-drilled band   49
murmured, "that speaker tried to steal the bride
of Hercules, who shot him dead for it.

Chiron, the centaur chief, once kept a school   52
for heroes where Achilles, Hercules
and others trained. His troops patrol the shore

of this hot moat, ensuring souls don't rise   55
more than they should above the scalding flood."
We stood before this chief, our heads below

the line at which the horse and man combine.   58
From his great height Chiron regarded us,
then took a dart and with the feathered end

parted his beard, exposing his wide mouth,   61
and said to the companions at his side,
"Look at the one behind – the follower

whose feet imprint the soil. *He* is not dead."   64
"Not in the least!" swiftly declared my guide.
"He has been sent by one on high to view

the depths controlled by you, the wisest beast.   67
I pray you, by the Power that led us here,
let one you trust escort us to the ford

and carry this man over on his back –   70
he is no spirit who can fly through air."
Chiron addressed the centaur on his right:

"Nessus, do what he asks. Take care of them.   73
Make sure no other troops cause them delay."
We and our new guide paced along the bank

76 amid dank steam that rose from the canal
of bubbling blood, with many a piercing scream.
Those sunk to eyebrows in the hellish stew

79 could make no outcry, though they suffered most.
"And should!" our centaur cried. "These plunderers
gloried in slaughter, spilling blood like water,

82 seizing by force nations not rightly theirs.
That bald dome was the boss of Sicily,
Dionysius, poisoned at last,

85 who pestered Carthage, Greece and Italy.
That scalp is Alexander's, called *the great*
for grabbing states from Greece to India,

88 dying when thirty-three. He over-ate.
Those black hairs in the soup reveal the place
of tyrant Azzolino who brought woe

91 to Padua, Verona, Brescia.
The fairer hair nearby belongs to grim
Obizzo of Ferrara, rich with loot –

94 vile gains for which his own son murdered him."
Wondering how my master liked this guide,
I looked at him and, smiling, he replied,

97 "Let me be dumb a while and learn with you."
As we advanced, above the simmering gore
wild shrieking heads emerged, and we saw more

100 such people as the moat grew shallower.
One waist-deep soul a little way apart,
our centaur said, was Simon Montford's son

who had avenged in church his father's death   104
by stabbing England's crown prince to the heart.
Screaming among those grand aristocrats

were pirates, highway robbers, human dregs,   107
though now the moat boiled only lower legs.
Where feet alone were stewed I recognised

faces I knew. Not wanting tête-à-têtes,   110
I looked aside and so we did not speak.
"Now we can cross," the centaur Nessus said.

"Beyond the bed sinks to the other side   113
where Attila and such as he abide
so deep that none will see them any more."

So on his back I reached the further shore.   116

13: Doom of Suicides

1 Nessus had not regained the former shore
   before my guide and I were in a wood
   more grim than that where I encountered him.

4 No bough was smooth, but torn and warped askew.
   No leaf was green, but withered black and brown.
   No fruit was seen, but many a poisoned thorn,

7 and only harpies nested in the trees –
   foul things with women's heads between their wings,
   big feathered bellies and gigantic claws

10 wounding the branches that they perched upon.
   My master said, "This ring of Hell is like
   a hedge between the boiling moat we left

13 and scorching sands to come. Look well here, please.
   Before you do I cannot tell of it
   and be believed." I stood and looked around,

16 hearing a kind of moaning wail like wind
   except for something human in the sound.
   I think he thought I thought it came from folk

19 hiding among the trees. I stared at him.
   He said, "Break off a twig." Puzzled, I did
   from a large thorn tree that I stood beside

and then, "Why are you breaking me?" it cried.   22
As a green branch with one end in a fire
hisses while sap trickles from out the other,

both words and blood came from the break I'd made.   25
I dropped the twig, looked to my guide for aid
as the voice said, "You would not be unkind

to smaller animals. Why pitiless   28
to soul turned into tree?" "Poor wounded tree!"
my master said. "Your hurt was caused by me.

I knew no other way to show this man   31
the fate of sinners in your hellish wood.
But tell him now the name you bore on earth –

returning there he may renew your fame."   34
"God bless your courtesy," the tree exclaimed.
"Good reputation was my life-long aim

which my bad end undid. If people know   37
I was not all to blame, one soul in Hell
will feel some consolation. Listen, please.

For twenty years I served great Frederick,   40
Emperor of Europe, sometimes called
the *stupor mundi*, wonder of the world.

I was his chancellor, using two keys,   43
reward and punishment, with quiet art
till none but me knew his most secret heart.

My faithfulness robbed me of sleep and strength,   46
but jealousy, whore of all royal courts,
made me so hated that my Emperor

49 also distrusted. Suddenly disgraced,
blinded, in chains, I who had been so just
to others, to myself became unjust.

52 I, Pier de Vigny, battered out my brains,
but promise by the roots that feed me now
I never once betrayed my Emperor.

55 If you return to earth tell others so,
for envy is still dirtying my name."
Silence ensued, then Virgil said to me,

58 "Don't miss this chance. He's wise. Ask what you like."
I said, "For pity's sake, I can't. You ask,"
so ask he did. "How did it come to pass

61 that souls like yours are tied in wooden knots?
Will nothing make you free?" The tree
again squeezed out more air turned into words:

63 "Minos flings all such souls down here like seeds,
and where we fall we root and start to sprout.
The harpies, feeding on our leaves, cause pain

66 and open cuts through which we can cry out.
We too will join our bodies when time ends,
but not be clothed in our old corpse again.

69 Suspended from the tree we have become,
we'll feel its weight forever, and be dumb."
Intent upon these words we were surprised

72 to hear a sudden noise, a crashing roar
swiftly approaching us, sounding as if
fierce hunters were pursuing a wild boar.

Upon our left two naked men raced past,   75
the first one screaming, "O come quickly, death!"
The second panted, "You were not so fast,

Lano, in battle, where folk killed you last."   78
Breath failing him, he fell into a bush.
Bounding behind, immense black bitches came

as ravenous as hounds loosed from a chain,   81
and biting fallen man and leafy spray,
tore him to bits and carried them away.

My guide now led me over to that bush   84
which wailed through all the fractures I could see,
"Jackie San Andrea, why fall in *me*?

Why should I suffer for your guilty life?"   87
"And who," my master asked, "are you, who through
so many gashes pours complaints and blood?"

"One who was born beside the Arno's flood,"   90
it said, "where Florence and its civil strife
made me detest my miserable life.

I made my house the gibbet where I hung.   93
Forget my name! Please put my broken shoots
nearer this trunk where they will feed my roots."

Our birthplace made me honour his request.   96

14: Blasphemers. Phlegethon and Giant History

1 And then we reached a boundary between
the second and the third ring round the edge,
where agony to come was clearly seen.

4 Vengeance of God! O say with what dismay
all should read here just what they might endure.
As the moat ringed a wood, so the wood lay

7 like wreath around a hot and sandy plain
where nothing grew but hordes of naked men
lamenting wretchedly their kinds of pain.

10 Fire-flakes were always slowly falling down
like Alpine snowflakes, big on windless days,
on some who lay flat out, or crouched down squat,

13 but most raced round in crowds. The huge sparks clung
till battered off. Pain-crazed, they punched themselves,
left, right, above, below, all hands were sent,

16 making new room for pains none could prevent.
Where flakes touched sand they blazed up like a torch
doubling the pain. The flat-out folk screamed most.

19 "Poet," said I, "Master of all in Hell
except the sullen gatekeepers of Dis,
please tell me who that stubborn big man is

who shows disdain of fire that falls on him."   22
The man, seeing I noticed him, cried out,
"What I was living, I will always be –

hater of Zeus who claims sole deity!   25
Zeus never can achieve his vain desire –
his stupid aim that all adore his name!

However long he keeps me under fire –   28
however many folk think Zeus supreme,
my will at least can disallow that claim!"

In contact with a citizen of Hell   31
my guide had never been so cross before.
He cried, "You do not know whom you blaspheme!

A true faith thirteen centuries ago   34
abolished Zeus! Best punishment for you
is suffering the rage in which you stew."

Then with a kinder look he said to me,   37
"Capaneus, once a Greek warrior boss,
went out to conquer Thebes. The fool denied

that any God could ever conquer *him*.   40
Defiance now for him is endless loss.
Come, we will not set foot on burning sand

but keep within the coolness of this wood   43
until we reach the way that leads across."
In silence we went on to where a stream

gushed from the wood to the blasphemer's plain.   46
I shuddered, for it looked like boiling blood.
Its heat had baked both banks to solid stone,

49 also a path that lay along each side.
   This long straight aqueduct, this narrow flood
   must have been very deep. Its steam repelled

52 fire-flakes above the stream and walkways too.
   My guide said, "Of all I've shown to you,
   this stream by far is most remarkable."

55 "Please tell me why," I begged, "What is the source?"
   What follows are the words of his discourse:
   "Crete is an island in earth's Middle Sea,

58 that mighty lake whose shore is shaped by coasts
   where Africa, Asia, Europe meet.
   Crete, ugly now, was once so fair a place

61 some thought it near the Earthly Paradise
   God gave to parents of the human race.
   Here for a thousand years all enjoyed peace

64 and fruitfulness. Their king was wise and just.
   This Golden Age lacked rage and theft and war.
   Mount Ida is the highest mountain there,

67 now bare, but then enriched by splendid trees,
   blossom and bird-call, waterfall and caves.
   The inmost cave is ceilinged by a dome.

70 Erect beneath a great old giant stands,
   his back to Asia, his face to Rome,
   reflecting on it. He is History

73 with pure gold head, bright silver chest and arms,
   bronze belly, the rest iron *not* all way.
   The right foreleg is terracotta clay

'on which (alas) he mainly leans today.   76
Under the golden chin, a straight-down wound
splits torso through the baser metal skin,

a fissure bleeding juices from the heart   79
of History since mankind turned to sin.
This mix of tears and blood, always renewed,

this woe of History pours to the cavern floor,   82
slips down through rocks then floods three moats of Hell,
moats on the way down here you've seen before.

At Charon's ferry it is Acheron,   85
the Styx where it surrounds the walls of Dis.
Upon this ledge we call it Phlegethon

before it falls and turns to frozen ice   88
as Cocytus. There nothing is more low."
I said, "The floods you name are separate!

So how can they appear as one stream here?"   91
Said he, "You know this pit is circular.
Descending we've been walking to the left

and have not made a single circuit yet.   94
Apart from passing near one waterfall
you've seen no others that connect this place.

The next will bring great wonder to your face."   97
"I know that Acheron, Styx, Phlegethon,"
I said, "are rivers here, but will I view

Lethe? That is a sacred river too."   100
He said, "You will see Lethe, not in Hell,
but where forgiven sinners are made well.

Now we must leave this wood, so follow me."   103

15: An Old Sodomite Friend

1 In misty steam that quenched the falling flames,
   we sped on the firm track beside the stream
   along a dyke like those shielding Dutch fields

4 from North Sea tide, or saving Padua
   from Brenta's springtime flood. Not wide or tall
   as those, it raised our feet man-high above

7 the scorching plain on which impious hordes
   suffered their fiery rain. On looking back
   I could not see the wood, but saw a pack

10 of nearby racers peering up at us
   like tailors squinting through their needle's eye.
   One gripped my coat hem, crying, "Marvellous!"

13 I, staring down upon that baked-black face,
   knew him, cried out, "Brunetto! Are *you* here?"
   Said he, "O my son, let your old teacher

16 jog by your side a little further on."
   "I want that too," said I, "and a good chat,
   if my guide lets me sit a while with you."

19 "O son," cried he, "if one of us should pause
   he must lie flat out for a hundred years
   under this fire. Let us go side by side

until I meet colleagues of mine again."   22
I dared not join him on the plain, but bent
respectfully to him as on we went.

He said, "What chance or fate brings you down here   25
alive? Who is your guide?" "In middle age,"
I said, "I went astray, but yesterday

this poet came to lead me the right way."   28
"Then follow him to Heaven's height!" said he,
"I died too soon to strengthen your great work.

Inside our city two main cliques contend –   31
the worst descended from Attila's Huns,
the other one from Rome's nobility.

Both, envying your work, will hate your name.   34
Let the fools nourish weeds and kill with hoes
anything great that sprouts on their dunghill.

When Italy's great writing grows again   37
and other states are honouring your fame
they'll try to claim, too late, a part in you.

Such goats won't cultivate our golden grain."   40
"You would not suffer as you do," I said,
"had my prayers any force, for I recall

how well you taught me, many hours each day,   43
how good work fits us for eternity.
What I say now I will write down elsewhere

so that my gratitude is widely known,   46
and by a lovely lady close to God.
Despite what folk say, how Chance turns her wheel,

49 I will obey my own uncommon sense –
your teaching – Virgil's – my experience,
joined by good hope into one conscience."

52 At this my guiding spirit turned and said,
"Words worth remembering," but even so
I asked Brunetto if his company

55 were men worth knowing. "Some were good priests,"
said he, "and scholars, both sorts damned like me
by one bad sin. Some, of course, are scum.

58 I see a cloud arising from the sand,
showing folk come with whom I must not be.
My worth lives in *The Treasure*, my best book.

61 Please, back on earth, make sure it still is read.
That's all I ask!" and away he sped
like one who begins racing for a prize,

64 not like a loser, but like one who'll win.

16: Sodomite Patriots

A hum like distant beehives filled the air   1
from where the stream fell to Hell's lower pit,
then three souls left a crowd and ran to us

yelling, "Tell us the news from Florence, you   4
whose clothing tells that you belong there too."
Alas, the ugly scabs burnt into them,

old, fresh, big, small, I hated to behold,   7
grieve to recall. My guide said, "Be polite.
Another chat won't hurt you." As we paused

they moved by the dyke like wrestlers about   10
to grapple in a ring, but wheeling round
sideways while moving feet, bodies and heads

to keep their faces to me, then one said,   13
"Our blistered baldness on this ledge of Hell
may cause contempt, but let our fame incline

to some respect in you. He, naked, flayed,   16
and in whose steps I tread, served Florence well
with counsel and with sword – Guido Guerra

was his name. He behind me was the lord   19
Tegghiaio Aldobrandi, whose word,
if heeded, would have saved us hopeless strife.

22 I am Jack Rusticucci, driven here
through vices fostered by my prudish wife."
I wanted to leap down, embrace each one,

25 which my good master surely had allowed,
but dread of roasting held me back. Instead
I bowed and said, "Not contempt but dismay

28 is mine on seeing you in such a state –
heroes of our old city's government
which once kept Florence gloriously great.

31 I will return there in due course, but first
must pass among the lowest of the cursed."
He cried, "Long life and fame to you, but say

34 how Florence is today. Do courtesy
and courage still survive? Are they quite gone?
Some recently who joined our company

37 brought most displeasing news." Raising my face,
I cried, "New men enriched by trade parade
in Florence – using ill-got gains to rule

40 in ways to make you weep." My hearers stared
at each other, sharing that dismal truth,
praised me for talking straight of what I knew,

43 begged when beneath Italian skies again
I'd speak of them, then broke their wheel and ran
with legs as quick as wings over the plain,

46 vanishing before I could say, "Amen".
We too moved on until the waterfall
blattered so loud it almost drowned our speech.

Just as at Forli in the Apennines   49
the river Acquacheta from an edge
leaps down a height a thousand falls might use,

the thunder of the waters stunned my mind.   52
I wore a cord around my waist, the kind
Franciscans wear to tell them to stay chaste.

At his request I gave it to my guide,   55
who cast it far out into the abyss.
"Surely," I thought, "now something very strange

will come of this," and so indeed it did.   58
To state a fact that people won't believe
is most unwise – they'll think that you deceive,

but if I do not tell truth here, my tale –   61
this Comedy – is surely bound to fail.
As I gazed deep down through the murky air,

I saw come swimming slowly up a shape   64
that would amaze the bravest of the brave.
Like a huge thing long drowned below the tide

but freed to rise, it rose with arms spread wide.   67

17: Fraud Demon Geryon. Bankers

1   "Behold the monster with the stinging tail
    who bores through mountains, ruins mighty walls,
    equally crumbles arms and armaments,"

4   my leader said, beckoning me to where
    the causeway stopped and overhung thin air,
    and there I saw the foul big form of Fraud

7   resting his chest upon the causeway end,
    his lower parts writhing in space behind.
    The face was like a kind wise man's, the rest

10 was scorpion, with two great clawing paws
    hairy to armpits, but no Persian rug
    had such gay patterns as his back, sides, breast,

13 in shifting colours like chameleon skin.
    As boats lie half ashore and half afloat,
    the foremost part stayed put, the stinging part

16 stayed airborne, quivering. "We need this brute,"
    my guide said, "for we can't descend by foot."
    At the plain's rim we passed a squatting group.

19 "Stay here," he said, "while I negotiate,"
    and on he sped while I glumly remained
    near the extreme edge of the seventh ledge.

Here bankers' frantic hands were beating out   22
flakes of fire endlessly from skin, air, sands
like dogs in heat stung mad by fleas, wasps, flies,

yet still they stared with bloodshot, pain-crazed eyes 25
into a sack slung around each one's neck.
I knew none there, but saw upon their sacks

old coats-of-arms: lion on yellow ground,   28
white goose on red, also a pregnant sow
azure on white. "Get lost!" one of them said.

"The living have no place in this damned pit.   31
I, a Paduan among Florentines,
spit in your face!" He tried to, pursing lips,

protruding tongue. I hurried from that place   34
and found my guide seated astride that brute.
"Come on," said he, "be brave. We need this lift.

Climb up and sit in front and you will find   37
I shield you from the stinging tail behind."
This struck me into a vile trembling fit,

teeth chittering as with cold. Shame alone,   40
such as good teachers can make pupils feel,
set me astride those shoulders none should trust.

I tried to say, "Please hold me tight." My fright   43
was so extreme no words came out, and yet
he clasped me hard and said to Geryon,

"Go now, but make your flight both wide and slow   46
to suit the greater weight you bear." As ships
back slowly from a quay, so Geryon

49 drew back, and when quite clear, turned tail to where
his chest had been – stretched tail out like an eel,
then pulled air to him with his paws and swam

52 out into space. Fear gripped me as it gripped
Apollo's child who, letting go the reins,
sent chariot sun scorching across the sky,

55 or Icarus when feathers fell away,
hearing his father yell, "You've flown too high!"
No worse fear could be mine than when I saw

58 only the air and thing to which I clung.
We wheeled, descending slow, but all I knew
was air blew in my face from far below.

61 Once, noticing the falling waters roar,
I raised my head, looked down, saw fire, heard
moans,
then cowered back, recalling what I'd known –

64 worse pains were coming up on every side.
Our aircraft glided to a rocky floor
below the cliff. We climbed down. Geryon

67 zoomed swiftly off like arrow from a bow.

18: Love Frauds

The circles here are called the malebolge,   1
of iron-coloured stone as is the cliff
enclosing them. Bang in the centre gapes

a deeper pit. The ledge around is split   4
into ten round ravines with dykes between,
like ten successive moats around a fort.

Just as such forts have bridges to their gates,   7
so from the base of the enclosing cliff
arched bridges span ravines from dyke to dyke

towards that pit of which I won't speak yet,   10
but each ravine and dyke and bridge slopes down
quite gradually lowering to it.

We stood upon the outer dyke when dropped   13
from Geryon's back. My poet led me left,
so on our right I saw new sufferers

and torturers, because within that moat   16
two naked streams of sinners trudged around,
nearest towards us, others trudged away.

Horned demons with great whips were lashing them – 19
O how they raised their heels at every stroke!
None waited for a second or a third.

22 Then suddenly I saw someone I knew.
    When my guide granted leave to speak, the ghost
    tried hard to hide his face till I cried out,

25 "Venedico Caccianemico!
    Why do you stare so hard upon the ground?
    What got you in this mess?" He sighed and said,

28 "I don't like answering, but still, your speech
    recalls old times and so I must reply.
    I sold my sister Ghisolabella

31 to Marquis Este. I'm not the only one
    this ditch holds from Bologna. If you need
    proof of this, recall our greed for gold."

34 At this a scourging demon lashed him well
    shouting, "Gee up, pimp! No girls here to sell!"
    I joined my leader. We walked on until

37 a bridge was reached and crossed. Halfway we paused
    to watch those coming from the other side.
    "Heartless seducers all," explained my guide.

40 "That kingly pair, Jason and Theseus,
    despising pain, display no sign of grief.
    Jason was thief who stole the Golden Fleece,

43 helped by Medea who he then betrayed,
    and earlier had left Hypsipyle
    with child among more women he'd beguiled.

46 Ariadne helped Theseus to slay
    the Minotaur. He sailed from her next day.
    Aye, all who so deceive deserve this fate.

Let's go to the next ditch." Crossing the ground   49
between two bridges, I could hear a sound
of gurgled groans, snuffling and smacking hands.

The bank ahead was filthy with a slime   52
dropped from thick fumes which rose above the ditch,
hurtful to eyes, appalling to the nose.

I could see nothing underneath these fumes   55
until I reached the bridge's greatest height
and glimpsed below some heads in so much filth

it seemed earth's privies filled that ditch with shite.   58
So badly smeared with ordure were these heads
that tonsures and long hair looked much the same,

and yet I heard one shout, "Why stare at *me*?"   61
I said, "Unless I'm seeing wrong, you were
Alessio of Lucca whom I knew

when his head was dry. If you're he, why here?"   64
He sobbed and punched his head and cried aloud,
"By sordid flatteries, to further my career

I damned my soul." My master called,   67
"Come, look upon this slut straining to lift
her head above the shit while scratching it.

She's Thaïs, the famous whore. When clients   70
wanted more and asked how she'd liked it last,
always, *Stupendously!* Thais replied.

With that bad end let us be satisfied."   73

19: Simoniac Popes

1 O Simon Magus, first of phoney priests
   to sniff for money in the wounds of Christ,
   and you simoniacs who coin it there,

4 wearing Christ's garments, stripping bare the poor
   who gladly serve Christ well without rich feasts,
   now is the time to see your doom in Hell.

7 At the third malebolge we climbed the bridge
   and saw strict justice underneath, supreme
   in Heaven, earth and also in that ditch.

10 Bottom and sides were pierced by same-sized holes,
   round like the font in Saint John's baptistry
   I broke to save a boy who would have drowned

13 had I not done so, a fact which some folk doubt.
   From each stuck out a sinner's feet and legs
   up to the knees – the rest was underground –

16 and every foot-sole was on vivid fire,
   the legs writhing so madly that I thought
   the joints were bound to snap like broken strings.

19 Like flames on surfaces of oily things
   so moved these flames about on toes and heels.
   "Who is that kicking harder than the rest,

in redder flames?" I asked. My master said,   22
"Ask him yourself." On the fourth dyke he turned,
lifted me down the bank and at the base

deposited me in a narrow space   25
by he complaining wildly with his feet.
"Though you are planted downwards on your head,

unhappy soul, tell me your name," I said.   28
A muffled voice cried, "Is that Boniface?
They lied who said many more years would pass

before you came. Are you dead so soon from   31
gluttonising on the Church you raped?"
Speechless I gaped until my guide murmured,

"Tell him you are not whom he thinks." I did.   34
The ghost, twisting his feet together, groaned,
said, "Since you ask, I was Pope Nicholas,

who cared less for my flock than for my kin.   34
I pursed gold for them. Pursing is the sin
that pens me in this fissure. Under me

are former popes guilty of simony.   40
I must be driven further in when he
I took you for arrives. Longer than I

he'll lie within this trench with roasting feet,   43
before the papacy, sold to the French,
is torn in two by greedier deceit."

In rage I cried, "What was Saint Peter's fee   46
when Christ said *follow me*? Briefly the Jews
worshipped one golden calf with just one head.

49 Your thousand golden gods have each a head,
    tail too. Are coins the Christ that popes should preach?
    When Constantine made Christianity

52 the Roman Empire's one official creed
    he acted well, but pensioning the popes –
    his great donation – stimulated greed.

55 Forgiveness for their sins can now be bought
    by the kings of every wealthy nation.
    This fornication between Church and State

58 brings endless warfare and profanity
    foretold to us in Saint John's Revelation."
    I chanted all this to the holy cheat

61 as, moved by anger or by conscience,
    he kicked hard with both feet. This pleased my guide.
    Carrying me back up the ditch's side,

64 he did not stop until he put me down
    upon the highest point of the next bridge
    from which the dreadful fate was clearly seen

67 of those who walked around the next ravine.

20: Magicians

This, the twentieth chapter of my book,   1
first section of my triple enterprise,
must put new matter here before your eyes.

Along that circling valley I could see   4
a wailing crowd of folk approaching me
at pace of priests chanting the litany.

I saw their nakedness from feet to necks   7
but higher they were faceless – there appeared
the backs of heads. No epileptic fit

could twist a human head so wholly round.   10
I turned, saw grieving faces move away
with tears flooding each spine to buttock cleft,

and these distortions of our human shape   13
made me weep too until my guide said, "Stop!
Pity for those in Hell is impious

so lift your head. See Amphiaraus.   16
An earthquake swallowed him because he hid
from death he had foretold. His chest is now

his shoulder-blades. He goes backwards with the rest   19
who used black arts to see too far ahead
so can't see forwards now. See Tiresias.

22 His belly is in front of Aruns' bum,
   prophet who read the stars from his high home,
   the cave of marble in Carrara's cliff.

25 See her with breasts concealed by flowing hair,
   Manto, the daughter of Tiresias
   and virgin witch who founded Mantua,

28 my birthplace, of which I will tell you more.
   Forced out of Thebes, Manto first roamed afar
   in search of a new home. In Italy

31 among the mountain ramparts of the north
   she saw Lake Garda fed by Alpine snow.
   The overflow led her to Mincio,

34 a sluggish stream spreading in marshes round
   a plot of firm ground, uninhabited.
   On this she lived secure until she died.

37 Over her bones the scattered folk nearby
   built, fortified the town of Mantua.
   Tell all you know the truth of my account

40 which some misguided fools deny." "O yes!"
   cried I, "but, please, first tell me more about
   the sinners trudging in this dreary ditch.

41 Which is that brown old man with the white beard?"
   "Eurypylus," my guide explained, "the priest
   who chose when Greeks should sail to Trojan war.

46 I've written of him in my *Aeneid*.
   On his lean shanks see stalking Michael Scott,
   the Caledonian astrologer –

Guido Bonatti, another sly cheat   49
who told the Montefeltro when to fight –
Asdente, Parma's toothless shoemaker

sorry he'd not stuck to his former trade –   52
with many wretched women who betrayed
their sex and sold to neighbours magic drinks,

curses, revengeful hocuses and worse.   55
But let us leave this place, for high above
moon sets and day dawns. It is Saturday,

a golden morning before Easter Day.   58

21: Swindling Councillors

1   We went from height of bridge to bridge's height
     of the fourth malebolge, the blackest moat
     by far to greet my sight, brimful of tar

4   from side to side, boiling like the vats in
     Venice's great arsenal where the state
     builds its new ships, makes old ships water-tight.

7   No furnace lit by hand but wrath divine
     made bubbles in the pitch welter, expand,
     burst, rise again within that scalding ditch

10 at which I stared down till my leader cried,
     "Take care!" pulled me aside. Fearful, amazed,
     I gazed at a black demon speeding by,

13 bat-wings spread, claws clutching a sinner's feet,
     with thigh over each shoulder, roaring out,
     "Come, comrades! See a new town councillor

16 from Lucca – I am flying back for more.
     No lack of politicians there to swear
     that yea is nae for cash, then for more pay

19 to vote the other way." He flung his freight
     face down into the pitch. The victim shrieked,
     arched back, tried to rise. From below the bridge

leapt demons wielding hooks and pitchforks who   22
forced him down like cooks plunging boiling meat,
yelling, "You cannot swindle us, so sink,

you bastard, sink! Go under! Drink our tar   25
or feel us rip and scar!" My master said,
"These boys are rough. You go behind that rock

while I talk sense to them." Gladly I hid   28
and saw the horrid crew rush out at him
as dogs attack a beggar. Unafraid,

he told them, "Before you risk prodding me,   31
a word first with your captain. Which is he?"
"Old Stinkytail!" they cried and moved aside

from one who grunted, "Talk will not save your hide."   34
My guide replied, "See I have reached this place
clean and unhurt, proving that heavenly grace

is leading me. This force you must obey,   37
to help me and a friend upon our way
down to Hell's deepest pit. This you must do

or boil in your own stew." I never saw   40
a villain so downcast as Stinkytail.
He gulped then panted, "Bring your pal out here –

I'll see what I can do." Trembling with fear,   43
I joined his crew like Pisans I have seen
pass between ranks of Tuscans, whom they must

trust not to kill but cannot wholly trust,   46
I clung close to my leader's side among
these glaring demons wielding blades and prongs.

49 "One wee jag in the arse will do no harm?"
"Why wee? Why not a few?" two whispered, but,
"Scratcher and Gasher, shut your stupid gobs,

52 or feel me fork *your* bums!" roared Stinkytail,
then to my leader said, "The bridge ahead
fell in a quake twelve hundred, sixty-six

55 years ago yesterday at noon. You need
a bridge much further round this dyke. I'll pick –
that's if you like – good men to take you there."

58 I whispered, "Master, *please* let us go alone."
He murmured, "Please control your cowardice.
These demons hate us, yes, but fear me more,

61 so stop those scowls which show how foul they are
so must exasperate." He said aloud,
"Thanks. We accept." Stinkytail grinned and cried,

64 "Clartyclaw, take command of these: Snotbeard!
Dogspew! Ratsnout! Toadspit! Tusker! Pigshit!
Snatcher! Scratcher! Gasher! And Cuntycrab!

67 Aye, these good men will do, so now, you lot,
give both my guests the care that is their due
to the next bridge's arch, but let no part

70 of swindler's arse show above tar you pass.
Now, forward march!" He gave a bugle call
out of his anus, very loud and clear.

73 As counter-sign each fiend stuck out his tongue
and farted just as loudly in the rear.
Dreading each one, I started marching too

76 along beside my guide, sweating with fear.

22: Swindling Devils

I have heard cavalry and infantry 1
march off to bang of rocket and of gun,
drum ratatat, trumpet tantantara,

bell clang, bagpipe yell and hornpipe hoot. None 4
disconcerted me like that rude salute
which sent us on our march along the dyke

with ten fiends guarding us. From what? And why? 7
Not able to imagine a reply,
I stared hard at the moat where sometimes gleamed

the backs of souls, daring to ease their pain 10
like dolphins, before sinking down again.
Folk say, in Rome behave as Romans do.

Walking among this crew so eased my fear, 13
I learned their names and almost felt at home,
among their ghastly camaraderie.

Most souls I saw clung froglike to the shore, 16
nose above tar, but dipped as we came near.
One clung so long that Snatcher leapt ahead,

speared hair with pitchfork, yanked him into air, 19
hurled him upon the ground and briskly said,
"Right, pussies – here's your mouse. Who wants first bite?"

22 I shuddered, shouted, "Please, first ask his name!"
"Tarface," snarled Dogspew, "spit your old name out."
The wretch moaned, "Ciampollo of Navarre,

25 King Tybalt's chancellor, then barrator,
distorting laws for all who paid me well,
damning my soul to everlasting Hell."

28 "Hooray!" howled Scratcher, ripping a wide strip
of skin away, but Clartyclaw cried, "Halt,
a guest has more to say." My master asked,

31 "Are there Italians underneath that tar?"
"Many," whimpered the native of Navarre.
"I've just been dragged from one who is my pal,

34 a very famous magistrate indeed –
no bigger swindler sat upon a bench—"
"You talk too much!" yelled Gasher. With a hook

37 he wrenched a muscle from the speaker's arm.
Clartyclaw told my guide, "Talk fast before
they mangle him some more." My master asked,

40 "Who was your friend?" Staring upon his wound,
the Navarese groaned, "Great Fra Gomita,
deputy governor and magistrate,

43 so kind to gangsters in Sardinia,
they all spoke well of him, also his mate
Zanche of Logodoro, chief swindler

46 of the lot. O how the fiends gnash teeth and
roll their eyes at me! If you want to see
Tuscans and Lombards let me whistle, then

at least seven will appear. By that sign   49
we tell each other that the coast is clear.
I'll do that for you, though of course at first

you must stay out of sight." Ratsnout snorted,   52
"I smell a trick." The swindler said, "You do.
I am so much a trickster that from spite

I'll fool my pals because I can't fool you."   55
Then Pigshit cried, "If managed well this lad
will be our tool, our bait. He sits on dyke,

we wait behind. He whistles like a lark.   58
When enough are lured ashore, we charge out
slashing, goring, buggering how we like!"

"While he escapes?" sneered Ratsnout. "Daft idea.   61
One bird in hand is worth flocks in the air."
"My arms are long," said Snatcher, "crouched behind,

I'll keep him in my reach, and if he leaps,   64
I have wings, will swoop. Before he hits the tar
I'll grab his balls. We'll take off balls, tongue, skin,

teeth, nails and hair. Trickster, will you like that?"   67
"Escape? I would not dare," the swindler swore.
Now even Ratsnout thought the plan was good.

The demons placed the bait where they thought best   70
and crouched down low behind, we with the rest,
till Snotbeard whispered, "Whistle!" and the bait

drew a deep breath, paused, jumped. Snatcher, too late,   73
grabbed for him, yelling, "Got you!" but terror
outleapt wings. Snatcher's downward swoop did not

76 carry him up because Ratsnout, enraged,
    had also taken flight. Mad for a fight,
    he tackled Snatcher in mid-air. Both plunged

79 in scalding tar where the Navarese sank.
    Pain disentangled them, but pitch-clogged wings
    stuck them screaming, struggling in the ditch till

82 Clartyclaw sent four fiends to the far bank.
    By hooks from each side Snatcher and Ratsnout
    were dragged up, pulled out raving and laid down,

85 each one well cooked inside his crusted hide.
    This uproar, pandemonium, stramash
    was not our business so we did not wait,

88 but left both fiends and swindlers in that state.

23: Hypocrites

Silent and unaccompanied we went   1
along the dyke-top path, me after my guide,
pondering on the turmoil left behind.

It called to mind Aesop's tale of the frog   4
and mouse both killed by their own deceit.
What would our fiendish guards do, joined by two

recovered from the tar-bath's scalding heat?   7
Demons are only bound to keep one law –
sinners must suffer in their ring of Hell.

They knew we saw they had not kept it well,   10
been swindled into clownish capering.
Whom would they blame for their incompetence?

Malicious folly will not blame itself   13
for lack of sense. And now I seemed to hear
a distant yell draw near. "Master!" I cried.

He turned and said, "You're right in what you fear.   16
See, soaring they approach with bat-wings spread,
baying like bloodhounds after blameless hares."

As mother wakened by a fire alarm   19
lifts baby at her side and runs, he grabbed,
raised, held me to his chest, and leapt into

22 the other ditch, slid down the side on his back
    like water down a sluice. My lucky ride
    baffled our foes who, snarling, stood above,

25 powerless to leave the ring they must patrol.
    In the sixth malebolge we also stood,
    watching another kind of suffering.

28 At first sight what I saw was glorious –
    a line of richly patterned golden gowns
    enamelled with such peacock colourings

31 kings might have proudly worn them, though grand hoods
    hid every face, and from these tears streamed down.
    The fancy dress was causing this distress.

34 Its agonising weight made them all move
    so slow I thought at first that they did not.
    A weary dress to wear eternally!

37 My poet led me left, the way they went,
    not fast, but each step passed a sobbing wretch
    until I begged, "Have none here names I know?"

40 "You with the Tuscan tongue, don't rush away!"
    a voice behind us cried. "Stay in that place.
    When closer to you I will give you names."

43 My master said, "Yes, let us wait for them,
    then if you wish, go forwards at their pace."
    I saw behind two trying to come near.

46 "Their coats are light," one said. His friend replied,
    "He whose throat moves when talking is not dead."
    When opposite the last looked sideways, spoke:

"Tuscan, though you may fear hypocrisy,   49
know that to you I will talk honestly.
Before I do, tell me first, who are you?"

I said, "My body, born by Arno's flood,   52
grew up within that city set on it.
I keep that body yet, but tell me why

your eyes distill such tears. How did you get   55
the punishment you wear?" He groaned and said,
"These gilded robes are lined with thickest lead,

so those who bear such weight are bound to creak.   58
Once we were priests sworn to protect the weak
and work to end the bitterness of feuds

which dominate every Italian state.   61
When Florence found no able magistrates
to keep God's peace inside the city gates

it gave two jovial friars the job –   64
me, Catalan, and Loderingo here,
both Bolognese." Horrified, I yelled,

"Peacekeepers? Bah! You raised the mob who smashed   67
the Guardingo, home of the Uberti!"
He sobbed and muttered, "We did wrong, that's true.

Eager to please, we pleased the great too well.   70
Pope Clement wished to hurt the Uberti.
He is now in Hell." I began to say,

"Friars, your iniquities . . ." but was struck   73
silent by a new piece of divine wrath:
an old man crucified across our path

76   was trodden underfoot by all who passed.
He writhed most under me for my foot pressed
heaviest, since I lived. Catalan said,

79   "That was Caiaphas, priest who thought it best
one blameless Jew should benefit the rest
by crucifixion. Staked around this ring

82   are other rabbis who supported him,
forever now condemned to feel the weight
of dreadful falsehood in each sinner's heel."

85   Virgil had died before our Saviour's birth.
He marvelled at the sight, then told the friar,
"We need a way to climb out of this ring

88   upon the right. Please, is there such a thing?
If not I must command a black angel
to fly us up astride his ugly wing."

91   Catalan said, "There is a way at hand.
Bridges across this malebolge all fell
in the great earthquake when Christ harrowed Hell.

94   It left big slopes of rubble down each dyke,
mainly the lower side upon the right.
We're nearing one – climb up it if you like."

97   My master halted for a while then cried,
"That demon, Captain Stinkytail, lied to me!"
The friar said, "In Bologna I learned

100 devils are beasts with several vices.
It seems that telling lies is not the least."
With angry face my leader strode ahead.

103 Of course I hurried after where he led.

24: Doom of Thieves

Just as a shepherd, baffled by late spring,   1
frowns upon fields where grass is white with frost,
then smiles when sunlight thaws it for his flocks,

my master frowned upon the broken rocks   4
that must become our stair. Gazing aloft,
he chose the best line of ascent with care,

then turning, smiled and beckoned. Up we went,   7
he leading till high boulders blocked our way.
Stooping, he lifted me. I gripped the top,

then dragged my body up over the edge   10
and pulled him after – he was very light.
And so by lifts and pulls, from ledge to ledge,

we climbed above that static avalanche.   13
Breathless, and tired on what I thought the top
I lay flat out, thinking the summit reached,

but no! The dyke in front sloped higher yet.   16
I groaned at that. My master said, "Get up!
Sloth is no way to win enduring fame.

Great works demand effort to stop your name   19
fading like smoke in air, foam into sea.
Come, we have harder climbs than this ahead."

22 Pretending to a strength I did not feel,
rising I said, "Lead on. I'm not afraid."
We toiled up that sore steepness to the ridge

25 where the next bridge began. We mounted it.
Halfway across, a cry from underneath,
angry, prolonged and wordless, made me stare

28 down into dimness. I saw nothing there
and asked, "Who is below?" Said he, "You'll see,"
and led me off the bridge. At last appeared

31 the seventh malebolge and what it held.
I shudder when that vision comes to mind.
It was not deep and squirming at our feet

34 were many kinds of reptile – limbless,
many-legged, blind, goggle-eyed – snakes, lizards,
crocodiles, wriggling in piles or chasing

37 naked men who raced around, their hands bound
tight behind by serpents whose heads and tails,
thrust between thighs, entwined their genitals.

40 One of them paused beneath us by the dyke.
A tiny lizard leapt and bit his back
where neck and shoulders meet. His head flamed up.

43 Like wooden statue blazing from the top,
he stood there burning downwards into ash
spreading like thin white carpet on the ground.

46 Smoke from the burning hung in a pale cloud
that did not fade but stayed, thickened, sinking
to the ash that rose, meeting the haze

in lump, hump, pillar. Ash and smoke condensed, 49
became that shape the burning had unmade.
He stood where he had been, blinking, aghast

like epileptic waking from a fit, 52
bewildered still by recent agony.
My master asked his name. "Vanni Fucci

of Tuscany," said he, "called too the Brute 55
of Pistoia, which was my town and den
where I was absolute, me and my men."

"Master," I told my guide, "don't let him go 58
before he says why he is here. I know
he was brutal, bloody, caused much grief

like other party bosses – never knew 61
the Brute of Pistoia was also thief."
The sinner glared at me, blushing with shame.

Said he, "You finding me so low in Hell 64
hurts worse than dying did. Since I must tell,
know it was I who, from Saint Zeno's Church,

stole all the holy vessels. For this crime 67
an honest man was jailed. Now listen more!
Learn to regret you ever met the Brute.

Your party has some strength in Florence still – 70
not for much longer. Those who wish you ill
are growing stronger. Allied with Pistoia,

the party hating yours will force a war, 73
a stormy battle on Picene's plain.
Your people will be thunderstruck and mine

76 will win, and give the beaten side no choice
   but death or exile, therefore I rejoice!
   You'll never see the town you love again.

79 I'm glad that fact will bring you endless pain."

25: Doom of More Thieves

Having said that, the Brute flung up his fists,   1
each with two fingers parted in wide Vs,
and screamed, "Up your arse, God! Fuck you and yours!"

A friendly snake, coiling round throat and head,   4
choked cursing short, while one between his thighs
tied hands to genitals. He could not move

a finger without pain so, speechless, fled.   7
Pistoia, Pistoia, burn yourself down
rather than breed such brutes from Fucci seed!

In all Hell's halls I have met none who so   10
shamelessly, arrogantly hated God,
not even he struck dead on Theban walls.

A centaur charging past cried, "Where is he?   13
Where is that filthy beast?" Maremma's swamp
along the Tuscan coast had not more snakes

than writhed upon his back. Behind the head   16
a dragon rode his shoulders, bat-wings spread
and snorting flame. "That's Cacus," my guide said.

"He was that cattle-thief Hercules slew,   19
so is not good enough to share the job
of keeping tyrants in the moat of blood."

22 I heard voices below cry, "Who are you?"
and down there saw three Florentines too rude
to give their names. Not knowing them I laid

25 finger from nose to chin, suggesting that
we watch them silently. I heard one say,
"Where is Cianfa?" in a worried way.

28 Maybe you won't believe what happened next.
It seemed incredible to me. A reptile,
six-legged, sprang and clung to the speaker's front.

31 Mid limbs clasped belly, top claws clamped his arms,
jaws like a vice gripped cheeks. The lowest part
grasped thighs, squeezed tail between and up behind.

34 Never did ivy bind an oak so tight,
then both forms started merging like hot wax,
colours and shapes becoming interfused.

37 "Agnello, you are neither one nor two!"
the others cried. Two faces shared one head.
Torso and legs grew twice as thick. Two arms

40 stretched twice as long. Sickened, I gladly saw
that jumbled monster stumbling away.
His friends stayed put in spite of their dismay.

43 If they felt safer near us, silly they!
As in hot summers, over sunlit roads
the lizards flash from hedge to hedge, through air

46 a wee red goggle-eyed beast flung itself
like dart at belly, hit one where it stung
the part through which the unborn child is fed,

then fell down, crouched, gaped up at the bitten one 49
who, hypnotised, gaped back and even yawned.
Smoke from his navel, smoke from the beast's snout

came squirting out and mingled in a cloud. 52
Lucan's *Pharsalia* tells how bite of snake
turned Sabellus into a pool of pus, and how

Nasidius swelled spherical and burst. 55
Ovid's *Metamorphoses* tells of how
Daphne, Arachne, Arethusa changed

into tree, spider, fountain. I am first 58
to tell how substances were interchanged
between two kinds, so Lucan, Ovid,

listen to me. Under that smoky veil 61
the lizard's tail split while the bitten man
pressed feet, knees, thighs against each other till

difference vanished. The forked tail took shapes 64
legs lost. Meanwhile arms drew into armpits
while the beast's forelegs grew. Its hind claws clenched,

changing into those parts good men conceal – 67
the wretch's private parts became wee feet.
As one sank down the other rose erect.

One head went bald, the other head grew hair. 70
Colours exchanged, yet through the misty air
they still stared eye to eye from changing heads.

The upright one grew brows, cheeks sprouted ears, 73
nose formed above and chin below his mouth
in which the cleft tongue rounded, fit for speech.

76 The croucher's face had sharpened to a snout,
   ears pulled inside as snail retracts its horns.
   The tongue thinned, forked and flickered. The smoke stopped.

79 The soul, now lizard, squirmed and hissed and fled.
   The soul, now human, spat and turning said
   to he who stayed, "So now let Buoso

82 run on all fours a while as I have done."
   I thus knew how none in this robbers' den
   could call their souls their own for very long.

85 The man, reconstituted, limped away.
   I recognised him: crippled Puccio.
   Francesco followed, lizard, thug and thief

88 who brought the folk of Gaville such grief.

26: Liars and Ulysses

Florence rejoice, famous on land and sea,   1
where florins are the common currency.
That crowds of thieves swarm from you into Hell

cannot delight, does not astonish me.   4
Cardinal Prato tried and failed to quell
the bitter feuding that corrupts your state

so prayed it suffered total overthrow   7
to end your boastful posturing. I too
pray that this happens soon. The more I wait,

the horrider must be my city's fate.   10
We left that dyke, set foot on the next bridge,
surmounting rocks so jagged and abrupt

we could not move without the help of hands,   13
and as we struggled up I grimly thought
of how so often mighty powers betray,

mislead so many. Being Florentine,   16
I swell with hope and pride when I survey
the scope of what I plan to say in rhyme.

What if my talent leads me far astray?   19
I too must pray for more humility.
At last we rested on the bridge's height.

22 As peasants, with the coming of the night,
   pause on a hillside before going down
   into a valley where the fireflies glow,

25 we stared into the malebolge below
   and saw a flow of sparks. "Each is a flame,"
   my master said. "Clothing a counsellor

28 whose lying words fooled people into war."
   I shuddered, wondered could such words be mine?
   Could things I write become excuse for sin?

31 I clutched the crag to stop me falling in
   as we climbed downwards for a nearer view.
   Some spires of moving fire within that ditch

34 were taller than the rest and cleft in two.
   My master said, "Each of these double flames
   contains a pair united by their crime.

37 Here comes inventor of the wooden horse,
   Ulysses, with beside him Diomed
   who made the Trojans think it was a gift

40 proving the war was past, the Greeks had left.
   Both mourn within that fire their stratagem
   which burned down Troy, city of Aeneas,

43 who fled and founded Rome, as I have sung.
   They bemoan also other crafty tricks
   whose outcomes they did not see." I cried out,

46 "Master, if they can speak within their flame,
   I pray you please, please let them speak to me!"
   He said, "I like that prayer, so I agree.

Leave talk to me. Greeks will despise your speech." 49
When the flame came to where my guide thought best
I heard him cry, "Please pause, hear our request.

We are two poets who would be your friends, 52
and wish to know what we have never read
in Homer's epic – how you met your ends."

One flaming horn, the biggest of the pair, 55
first roared and wavered, as if struck by wind,
then the point flickered, speaking like a tongue.

"Bound back from Troy I lost my way, my men, 58
my ships through storms, monsters and women's wiles,
till winning home at last I found myself

unfit for quiet life with wife and son. 61
Choosing a crew of some I knew from Troy
we put to sea, sailed west and reached that strait

twixt Africa and Spain, leading into 64
the boundless ocean circling the globe.
Hercules put a pillar on each shore

inscribed *do not sail through*, and so none had. 67
'Shipmates!' said I. 'Did we dare, share, survive
a thousand dangers in a quest for rest?

No! Greeks seek knowledge, virtue. Strife for these 70
is the best of life. Let us sail ahead,
discover a new world, and if we fail

73 what grander way to end can old men find?'
    They cheered and plied their oars, would not have ceased
    to drive us onwards had I changed my mind.

76 We sailed for five moons south. Equator crossed,
    strange constellations shone above at night.
    Then to the east one day as dawn light spread

79 we saw, by distance dimmed, a splendid sight –
    a land wider than Italy, rising
    higher than any mountain into the sky.

82 Our joy soon changed to grief. From that land came
    a storm that struck and whirled us three times round,
    heaved our stern high, plunged the prow under waves

85 that closed above us. As God willed, we drowned."

27: Another Liar's Fate

The flame now burned erect and silently   1
till my sweet poet said that it might go
and so it did, but then another came

that clearly also wished to speak with him.   4
The noise it made was first a roaring din
like uttered by that red-hot roaring bull

when its inventor baked to death therein.   7
Breaths in each flame were cries of agony
till they articulated at the tip.

1We heard it say, "I aim my words at you   10
who in my dialect, dismissed that Greek.
Though scorching in this ditch I crave the speech

of lovely Italy, and my ears know   13
that you, like me, come from high lands between
Urbino and the Tiber's upper flow.

Romagna is where I committed crimes   16
for which I burn. If newly come from there,
please tell me if the states are still at war."

My guide, nudging my side, said, "You reply."   19
Having leaned down to hear, I quickly said,
"You, hidden in flame below, should know

22 our Romagna is never free of war
from scheming hearts of many tyrants there.
There was no open fighting when I left.

25 Ravenna stands as it has done for years.
Speaking heraldically, I will say
the Eagle of Polenta's pinions still

28 guard it and Cervia. Forli, once saved
by Guido Montefeltro from the French,
is under the Green Lion's claws. The jaws

31 of dogs – mastiff and whelp – chew Rimini.
Blue Lion, switching politics each year,
holds onto Faenza and Imola.

34 Cesena, between mountains and the plain,
is torn between freedom and tyranny.
Having replied, I beg to know your name,

37 and make it spoken in the world again."
The flame roared louder, waved its point about
more wildly, longer, before words came out.

40 "If you could make my name spoken again
by living men I would be dumb, but since
only the dead come here I need not fear

43 to say how damnable I've been. I, Guido
Montefeltro, am he who beat the French,
as you have said – a thorough man of war,

46 who, in the flesh my mother bore, was more
a fox than lion, skilful to mislead
my many enemies in word and deed.

Thus I earned fame and praise, yet knew of One   49
on high who forbids bloodshed, lying too.
Time came when evil ways no longer pleased.

I hauled in sails and punted to the shore.   52
Confession and repentance made me friar
wearing the slender cord Saint Francis wore.

Alas, that did not save my soul from Hell.   55
The highest priest of all, Pope Boniface,
that princely Pharisee, asked me to help

destroy – not Saracens or Jews – his foes   58
were Christians, a family of those
with whom he'd signed a pact to keep the peace.

Emperor Constantine sent for a pope   61
to cure his leprosy. Pride tortured
Boniface. Only I, he said, could cure

his raging fever for a fight. To me   64
he sounded drunk. I was afraid to speak.
Forgetting supreme office, holy vows,

me and the cord I wore to keep me meek,   67
he said, 'Trust me, my son! I hold the keys
the last pope never used, the keys that open

Hell and Heaven where all my will is done,   70
as it is *not* on earth without a fight.
Do as I ask and dying you'll do well.

I now absolve you of what some think sin   73
if you help me win the Penestrina,
stronghold of the Colonna.' Silence fell.

76 When more of it would give offence I said,
    'Father, if you have saved my soul from sin,
    absolve yourself from breaking holy vows

79 to keep the peace.' He did, and when I died
    Francis arrived, a coal black cherub too
    who roared, 'No cheating! Penitence alone

82 lets wicked souls dodge Hell. None can repent
    while willing sin – a contradiction.
    Amazed, are you, to find fiends logical?'

85 My wretched soul was dragged to Minos, who,
    enraged, wrapped his tail eight times round me, then
    bit it, howling, 'Go to where penitence

88 is learned by frauds wearing the scorching gown,'
    and O indeed it does! It does! It does!"
    The flame, waving and twisting, moved away,

91 roaring aloud in wordless agony.
    We left that ridge by climbing the next bridge
    over the ninth malebolge, a pit full

94 of those vile souls who split humanity.

28: Doom of Sectarians

If unrhymed prose could easier describe   1
the blood and wounds appearing in that ditch,
I'd certainly resort to it, Hell knows.

All speech falls short, there are no words to tell   4
of all the carnage we enact on earth
and re-enact repeatedly in Hell.

Below the bridge there seemed an endless flow   7
of all those mutilated in the wars
of Troy, Greece, Italy and Africa.

Gashed bloody bodies with sliced heads, stumped
limbs,   10
staggered along or hopped or crawled or reeled,
their inner parts obscenely unconcealed.

From chin to fart-hole one was so far split   13
that all his entrails hung between his thighs
with under those the bags of piss and shit.

Seeing me stare, he raised hands to his chest,   16
declaring, "See me divide myself," then
pulled the gap wider still, shouting aloud,

"thus is Mohammed maimed! Ali ahead   19
is cleft from hair to chin. Everyone here
created what the cowards call *discord*.

22 Behind us stands a demon with a sword
who chops us up like this. Trailing again,
again, again around, we slowly heal

25 until we feel *again* his slicing steel.
But who are you, standing upon that dyke?
Is viewing punishment a thing you like

28 before you have to suffer with us too?"
My master said, "He is not damned like you.
I, who am dead, conduct this living man

31 to see all the conditions of the dead."
At this over a hundred in that ditch
halted, forgot their wounds. Each raised his head

34 to gape at me. Mohammed said, "When back
in Italy, see Brother Dolcino,
leader of those who would restore the faith

37 of Christians to old simplicity.
Crusaders menace them and Muslims too.
Tell them to get in food before the snows

40 give victory to their Navarese foes."
Mohammed lurched away and then came one
with half a face – ear, nose and mouth sheared off.

43 Out of his severed windpipe red with blood
with sides that moved like lips, these words wheezed up:
"O you alive and innocent! Unless

46 appearances deceive, we've met before
on that sweet plain sloping from Vercelli
down to the mouth of Po. If you return,

speak of Pier da Medicina. I   49
was a scandal-monger there. Tell my friends
who govern Fano of their dreadful ends

prepared by one who means to grab their town.   52
He will invite them for a peaceful talk
and send a ship. Unless my words from Hell

prevent, at sea they'll be flung in to drown   55
by Malestino, whelp of Rimini."
A yell then silenced him till he explained,

"The name of Rimini is agony   58
to one damned here for something he said there
forty-nine years before the birth of Christ."

I said, "Yes, I will speak of you on earth,   61
but first say why that name causes such woe."
In answer Pier, gripping the yeller's jaw,

wrenched the mouth open wide so that I saw   64
the tongue slashed to a wordless stump inside.
I cried, "But why? For what?" Pier replied,

"A stream near Rimini called Rubicon   67
was Roman frontier. Caesar halted here.
For the Republic he had conquered Gaul.

If now he marched his mighty force across   70
many in Rome would hail him Emperor
and so provoke a bloody civil war.

No wonder Caesar hesitated till   73
Curio spoke: "Delay is dangerous –
march on before too late." So Caesar did.

76 Curio shares the fate of those whose tongue
   has overflowed with bad persuasive speech.
   A handless wretch came waving stumps sprouting

79 blood across his face. He shouted, "I, Mosca,
   Florentine, began *our* civil war by
   crying, *Kill the Buondelmonte clan*!"

82 I said, "That war killed your clan too." Grief-struck,
   he staggered off, then I saw a sight
   almost beyond belief. A headless man

85 ran to the bridge. One hand held by the hair
   his head. He stopped and raised it lantern-like
   to see me nearer, help me hear it speak.

88 After a moan of deep despair it said,
   "O breathing soul, look at this mournful thing!
   Does greater misery than mine exist?

91 I am paid thus for splitting a young prince
   off from his father Henry, England's King,
   as Achitophel goaded Absalom,

94 against dad David, King of Israel.
   So is my head divided from the rest.
   Such retribution is indeed my due,

97 but carry news of me to earth again:
   Bertran di Born, of Périgord's High Fort,
   a fighting statesman, a Cistercian monk

100 and troubadour whose songs are known to you."

29: Doom of Forgers

The sight of all these mutilated souls   1
made my eyes drunk with grief. I stood and wept,
pondering long upon the crowd below,

till Virgil said, "Come – we have far to go,   4
much more to see. The sun is overhead,
the moon under our feet. Why linger here?

No malebolge before has held you long."   7
"I hope my Uncle Geri will appear,"
said I. "He must be in this dismal throng

for starting one of feuds that dislocate   10
every Italian state." "True," said he.
"While you were talking with de Born

he pointed a stern forefinger at you   13
who did not see him, so he went away."
"He was stabbed," said I, "so thinks I betray

our family by not avenging him.   16
I sympathise but have to disagree."
Talking, we left the dyke, climbed the next bridge

and heard such piercing cries that from pity   19
I pressed hands hard on ears, almost thinking
we now approached a plague-struck city street.

22 The truth was much more horrible. Suppose
each hospital there is in Italy,
Sardinia and Sicily and Crete

25 flung all the patients with their putrid sores
into a mighty trench. I saw that sight.
The stench of it also attacked my nose.

28 Too weak to sit up, half the souls lay flat.
The rest sprawled over them or feebly crawled.
The quickest movements were their frenzied hands.

31 They would have welcomed flame or scalding pitch
to stop the endless itch they had to scratch.
A pair propped back to back at the ditch side

34 were thickly blotched with scabs from head to toe.
No stable boy or one wakened by lice
ever employed so fast a curry-comb

37 as fingernails with which each scratched his hide,
stripping off scabs as cooks scrape skins from bream
or fish with bigger scales. To one of these

40 my master said, "You who distress your skin
with fingers used like pincers, do you know
Italians here?" Weeping, he replied,

43 "We are, although disfigured. Who are you?"
Virgil announced, "I am an escort sent
by One on high to lead this living man

46 down through the rings of Hell and up again,
so that he can report upon your pain."
The sinners, trembling, broke apart to look.

My master murmured, "Tell them what you like." 49
I faced them and declared, "If it's your wish
to be in history for years to come,

don't let your foul damnation keep you dumb, 52
but tell your tale to me." At this, one said,
"I, Griffolino of Arezzo was

burned by a bishop as a sorcerer, 55
though that was not my sin. Purely for fun
I told his idiotic bastard son

I'd teach him how to fly like Daedalus. 58
I could not so I died for nothing done.
Albert of Siena was the fool's dad.

My burning was that bishop's mad decree. 61
Minos, a better judge, sent me down here
for I had truly practised alchemy."

I said, "The Sienese are silly folk – 64
even the French are not so light of mind."
The other leper cried, "Unfair! Unkind!

You have forgot their great academy – 67
the Spendthrifts Club where the wise Sienese
teach poorer citizens to pawn their goods

to buy rich clothes, exotic whores and foods 70
and booze and horses shod with silver shoes.
But Dante, I am one you used to know.

When students, I was called Capocchio. 73
Physics for you led to philosophy.
For me, knowledge of metal under heat

76 fed my fantastic dreams of alchemy,
and turning lead to gold and sour to sweet,
making bodies live eternally,

79 though what I made was always counterfeit."

30: Doom of More Falsifiers

The pagan gods were moved by earthy lust.   1
Spite against women whom her husband raped
made Juno far, far crueller than most.

Juno annoyed the Theban Semele   4
by bringing madness to her family.
One, thinking wife and children were wild beasts,

slaughtered his son and drove the rest to drown.   7
Enslaved after her city was destroyed,
Hecuba, wife of Priam, king of Troy,

was also maddened by the same false gods.   10
Seeing her daughter slain upon the tomb
of Achilles, her son's corpse on a beach,

she did not weep but barked like rabid dog.   13
No madness out of Thebes or Troy was worse
than two I saw now – bare white hungry ghosts

who quickly crawled on hands and knees around,   16
goring the helpless invalids like hogs.
One from behind bit Capocchio's neck

and dragged him, thus gripped, painfully away,   19
face down and belly ripped by the rough ground.
Griffolino, shuddering with dismay,

22 said, "Know that ghoul was Gianni Schicchi,
mimic and forger of a dead man's will,
thus mutilating his identity

25 so he is damned to mangle dead souls still."
"As you are not tormented by the other,"
said I, "please tell me who that other was."

28 "Myrrha, a Greek who broke two moral laws,"
said he, "for in disguise she fucked her father.
In stolen shapes that pair indulged their greed.

31 Now they must gnaw at us like starving apes
though that was not how they preferred to feed."
As the two furies vanished from my sight

34 a sinner close at hand said, "Look at me –
pity poor Adam's miserable plight."
So dropsically swollen up was he,

37 at first a belly like a giant lute
was all that I could see, then saw attached
his shrunken head with raw cracked lips that said,

40 "Once I owned all a man could want, but now
water, just one wee sip, is what I need.
The land I love, the place of my misdeed,

43 has cool wells, small refreshing streams that slip
between green hills down Casentino's vale
into the Arno. Stern justice decrees

46 these memories hurt more than my disease.
A master goldsmith in Romena, I
forged the bright florins for Romena's counts

thus helping them pay off outstanding debts.   49
To know my fakes required uncommon sense –
twenty-two parts were gold and three pretence –

but forgery was proved. I burned for that,   52
being a workman and an employee.
Aristocratic folk employing me

suffered no loss of life or liberty.   55
O, how I long to see the wretches here –
Guido, Allesandro and their brother.

I've heard that one is here. My spite is such,   58
I'd gladly go (did weight not tie me down)
a hundred miles to gloat upon the sight

though I could only crawl an inch each year."   61
I said, "A couple on your right-hand side
are reeking like roast meat. Have you their name?"

He said, "They were here long before I came.   64
Potiphar's wife is one who falsely blamed
Joseph for her adulterous desire;

next to her is Sinon, the Greek liar   67
whose falsehoods led to setting Troy on fire."
Annoyed by this reply, with sudden fist

the Greek punched the massive paunch. Like a drum   70
it boomed. The goldsmith smote the other's face.
"Feel how my arm has strength my body lacks!"

The answer came: "You loved flames while your arms   73
had many coins to fake, but liked them less
with arms chained to the stake." The coiner cried,

76 "Since that fake horse disgorged your countrymen,
Sinon is now a name for treachery."
The Greek cried out, "Enjoy forever now

79 the thirst that cracks your tongue, that rotten bung
that can't let out the foulness in your paunch,
swelling it to a hedge that hides your face."

82 The coiner sneered. "Again your tongue has wagged
in vain. You crave cool water more than me.
The scorching fever makes your thirst the worst."

85 Then suddenly my master said to me,
"Listen much longer to this sorry stuff
and we will start to have a quarrel too."

88 He spoke so angrily I blushed with shame,
knowing I was to blame. Seeking excuse,
I longed for words and found that no words came.

91 The fun I'd found in their vile argument
seemed a bad dream from which I could not wake.
I stood there dumb with my head bowed until

94 he smiled and said, "Cheer up. Do not regret
faults you will not forget, so won't repeat.
Less shame would clean you of a fouler sin,

97 but joy in spiteful talk is always mean."

31: Ancient Giant Rebels

After his stinging tongue reddened my face   1
it laid that soothing ointment on the place,
just as a lance which Achilles possessed

healed by a second touch the wound it made.   4
We turned our backs upon that wretched ditch,
finding the dyke-top now a wider space

but dimly lit. Advancing with my guide,   7
I found the view ahead obscured by mist.
From this a mighty trumpet blast rang out

which would have made a thunderclap seem faint. 10
Not even the great horn that Roland blew,
bursting his heart to summon Charlemagne,

sounded so full of dreariness and woe,   13
and then I saw what seemed a row of towers
similar to the battlements of Dis,

and asked the poet, "What city is this?"   16
Said he, "The distance has confused your sight –
when nearer you will see." Changing his mind,

he halted, took my hand and kindly said,   19
"Remember, no danger threatens you at all,
but still, prepare for what may be a fright.

22 These shapes are giants in Hell's lowest pit
     standing upon its floor and looking out.
     Their waists are at the level where we stand."

25 As we drew near the brink of Hell's last sink
     I saw more clearly, and my terror grew
     at how these monsters towered above the land

28 though half their bulk was underground. I knew
     nature right to stop making men so big
     when they inclined to wickedness, unlike

31 such gentle beasts as elephant and whale.
     The nearest baleful head loomed over us,
     as far above as Peter's dome in Rome,

34 and from the neck I saw a huge horn hung.
     The fierce mouth opened wide and, gibbering,
     cried, "Agargal grabgeeky glubdrib yak!"

37 "Idiot, blow your horn!" my guide yelled back.
     "It toots more sense than does your senseless tongue."
     To me he said, "Nimrod, this immense fool,

40 founded the first of cities, Babylon,
     then mad with pride, employed humanity
     to build a stair so high that all could reach

43 Heaven without having to die. Heaven
     stopped that, depriving us of single speech.
     Now none can understand what Nimrod says,

46 and all they say is meaningless to him.
     Let us be gone." We did, still going left.
     A bowshot further on, there came in sight

a bigger, fiercer beast, and by what hand   49
he had been pinioned there I could not think.
A chain wound five times round above his waist,

the links so tight both arms were firmly bound.   52
"That is Ephialtes," my leader said,
"one of those Titans who attacked the might

of pagan gods, giving them all a fright   55
until he was put down by One Supreme."
"If you'll permit, I'd rather see," I said,

"Briareus, the biggest." He replied,   58
"You'll next see Antaeus, who's just ahead.
He is unchained, knows speech, will lift us down

to Hell's last floor. The one you ask to see   61
is further on and much like this one here,
though far more strong." Maybe Ephialtes

grasped what these words meant. With sudden roar he,   64
earthquake-like, flung his belly's weight against
the cliff he faced. The ground under our feet

shuddered so much that I, despite that chain   67
sweating with terror fearing it might break,
gladly hurried away beside my guide.

We came to Antaeus, who looked on us,   70
his face ten yards above. Virgil spoke thus:
"In Africa there is a famous place

where Scipio made Hannibal retreat,   73
and you once slaughtered lions for your meat.
Some say, had you too fought the heathen gods

76 your giant brothers had not known defeat.
I ask you to perform a simple chore –
set us please down upon Hell's frozen floor.

79 Don't sneer! The poet at my side can give
what many here desire, a well-known name.
He will return to life and write a book

82 to renovate the fame of all he's met."
In the two hands that Hercules had gripped
Antaeus prepared to take Virgil up,

85 who called, "Come to me, Dante," clasped me tight,
and like a single parcel we were raised.
Stooping to lower us the Titan seemed

88 much like Bologna's lofty leaning tower,
the Carisenda, seen from underneath
when clouds pass overhead. I'd have preferred

91 descending by another way, but he
put both of us down carefully at last
where Lucifer and Judas dwell, before

94 springing upright again, straight as a mast.

32: Doom of Traitors

I lack the grinding, jagging words to tell   1
about this dismal hole, this evil pit,
this Hell to which the world's vast weight slopes
down.

The language other people use in fun,   4
or soothe a baby with, or call their mum
is unfit to describe the bitter fear

and chilling numbness of that dreadful state.   7
I pray to all the mistresses of art –
Muses who helped the poet Amphion

make music that raised high the Theban wall –   10
please guide me still! Do not depart until
I have described the steep path into light.

But can good rhyme describe those ugly souls   13
whose strongest doings were propelled by spite?
Better for them had they been goats or sheep.

Arriving at the bottom of this well,   16
I edged down backwards from the giant's feet,
then Virgil said, "Mind your own feet because

you're very liable to kick a head."   19
I turned and saw a lake of ice so clear,
so solid that we seemed to walk on glass.

22 Neither the Danube river nor the Don
in Austria and distant Russia
on coldest winter nights freeze down as thick

25 as did that lake. A granite mountain flung
upon the edge would not have made it creak.
Like frogs in ponds with their heads out, I saw

28 agonised souls ice-bound up to their necks,
teeth chattering as loudly in their jaws
as does the clattering of a stork's beak,

31 and all these heads were bent towards the ice.
A pair so face-to-face their hair was mixed
were at my feet. "What brought you here?" I said.

34 They lifted up their heads to see my face,
opening eyes from which tears spilled and froze,
instantly blinding them. Enraged, like goats,

37 each banged the other with his brow until
a nearby head, earless from frostbite, cried,
"What right have you to pester us like this?

40 If you must know, these twins were sons and heirs
of Alberti, Lord of Bisenzio, who left
half of that pleasant valley to each one.

43 Each tried to gain the whole by fratricide.
All of us in this zone have sinned like Cain,
killing our kin. For this we are iced in.

46 Focaccia upon my right once slew
his cousin. See in front, blocking my view,
Mascheroni, his nephew's murderer

(known to you, being a Florentine) and   49
lastly, to end your queries, know that I,
Camicion de' Pazzi, have betrayed

to death a cousin, so I now await   52
Carlino, another cursed Pazzi who
will make me seem more sweet by being worse."

As Virgil led me on I had to see   55
a thousand heads with teeth in snarling grins.
Puddles with ice since then, however wee,

horrify me. Through that eternal chill   58
I was led shivering towards one point –
that universal centre where is not

a lower thing, nor can there ever be   61
Upon the way, by chance or fate's decree,
I kicked a face. Weeping, it loudly said,

"Why hurt me more? Is this revenge because   64
on Montaperti's battlefield, through me,
the side you hated won the victory?"

"Master," I begged, "please wait. This man must clear   67
a doubt I have, then we'll walk very fast."
My leader paused. To he who still complained

I said, "Give me your name." He answered, "No.   70
Why give my name to one who kicks like you?"
"I am alive," said I, "so to win fame

tell me your name." Said he, "I want the opposite –   73
I crave oblivion. Please go away."
Gripping his scalp, I said, "Your name! Or else

76 your head will lose its hair." "Aye, strip me bald,"
said he, "but I won't tell." I ripped off tufts;
he howled till I heard someone cry, "Bocca,

79 what in Hell's wrong? Do your head's clicking teeth
so madden that, dog-like, you howl instead?"
Releasing him, I said, "Bocca, shut up!

82 Now I can tell Italy the final fate
of one who is a traitor to the state
that nourished him." He snarled, "Say what you like,

85 but also tell the name of he who gave
you mine – he is Buoso, paid by France
when France invaded us. If any ask

88 who else is cooling here, Beccheria –
he betrayed Florence too – and further on,
see Gianni de Soldanieri,

91 a Whig like me who joined the Tory crew;
and Ganelon, traitor to Charlemagne;
and Tribaldello – when Faenza slept,

94 he crept to let in Whigs who massacred
the Tory refugees." So we left him,
garrulously, furiously raving

97 against his kind. Later we came on two,
frozen neck-deep in the same icy hole
with he behind capping his neighbour's head

100 and chewing it where the brain joins the neck
as starving men bite bread. I said, "You hate
the man you eat. Tell me your name, and his,

and cause of this. If it be sufficient,   103
when I return to life on earth again,
trust me to justify the pain it gives

while the grand poem of my journey lives."   106

33: Doom of More Traitors

1   Ceasing to eat, the sinner wiped bloody mouth
on hair that still grew on his victim's head
and said, "You ask me to renew a grief

4   so desperate that speaking of the cause
will wring my heart. Let it! If words can blast
this traitor's name, then listen while I weep.

7   Names first. I was the Count Ugolino,
he Archbishop Roger, friend and ally,
so I thought. Listen well and be taught why

10   I gnaw his head in Hell. That he had me
trapped, fooled and killed is well known, but few know
how cruelly death came, although they call

13   the prison where I died the Hunger Tower.
Through a thin loophole in the dungeon wall
I saw several moons wax full then wane

16   before a bad dream prophesied our pain.
On hills dividing Pisa and Lucca
Roger on horseback, wearing hunting gear,

19   whipped on a pack of dogs. Beside him rode
all the chief Tories with their lean, fierce hounds,
hunting a wolf and cubs. After a short run

I saw father and sons fall, saw sharp fangs   22
tear them apart. I woke before dawn,
heard sons and grandsons weeping in their sleep,

begging for bread, then I knew our jailor   25
had been told to lose his key. You must be
heartless not to shed tears for my children,

innocent in spite of guilty me. All   28
were now awake. It became the hour when
food used to be brought but instead we heard

the door of the tower being nailed shut.   31
I stared at their faces and I could not weep,
feeling like stone inside. I heard them weep.

My little Anselm said, 'Daddy, what's wrong?'   34
Even then I shed no tear throughout that day
or the next night. A new day dawned. One ray

of light shone in on us. By it I saw   37
their faces were like mine and bit my hands
for grief. They thought it was for food. One said,

"Father, you gave us flesh – eat ours instead."   40
I became calm to save them from more pain.
On the fourth day Gaddo fell at my feet,

cried, "Father, can you do nothing?" and died.   43
During days five and six the other three
fell one by one and I, now blind, groped round,

stroking their faces, calling them by name   46
till famine finished me as grief could not."
Having said this his eyes went blank. He bit

49 that wretched skull again as dog bites bone.
O, you disgrace to Italy –
famous as Thebes for all atrocity!

52 Perhaps strongholds were lost by treachery
of Ugolino – it was still a crime
to kill Uguccione, Brigata

55 and the two others mentioned in my rhyme.
We walked on to a place where rugged ice
fixed heads of sinners in a way that made

58 all faces stare straight upwards so that tears
could not be wept away. They filled the space
under the brows with a hard layer of ice

61 whose icicles pierced eyes. The freezing air
drove feeling from my face although I sensed
a wind and asked, "Master, what moves this air?

64 No heat makes motion here." "What makes that wind,
you'll see," said he. From near our feet a cry
went up: "O please remove this icy mask

67 that I may weep a while before my tears
freeze up again." "Say who you are," said I,
"then if I don't do what you ask, let me

70 be under thicker ice than you." He said,
"I am Fra Alberigo, Jovial Friar,
who gave feast of reconciliation

73 to show my brother who'd insulted me
that I forgave him, though my pudding course
for he and son was assassination.

In ice I get my just dessert." I cried,   76
"But you are still alive!" He said, "Not me.
I will explain why, as you offer to

unglaze my eyes. Some sinners yield to fiends   79
before death is due, so at once fall down
into this pit's worst part. The fiend takes on

their body, move it as it used to move.   82
Branca d'Oria, shivering nearby,
is just like me and has been here for years."

"Impossible!" I cried. "Branca still lives,   85
eats, drinks and sleeps and puts clothes on and off."
Alberigo said, "So I hear. The fiend

replacing him enjoys the life he led.   88
Now, as you promised, please let free my tears."
Treason to such is highest courtesy

so I did not. He was a Genoese   91
whose town deserves the fate of Pisa too.
O Genoa, curse of the earth you grieve

with your foul cluster of corrupting dens!   94
Many you bred have been hurled into Hell
and fiends are now your richest citizens.

My guide reminded me, "Now we must leave."   97

34: The First Traitor. Hell's Exit

1   "The banners of Hell's potentate appear!
    Do you see them, Dante?" asked my guide.
    I stared into the mist ahead and saw

4   a vast dim distant something, windmill-like,
    with moving sails perhaps, or were they wings?
    A wind came from it like the worst of gales.

7   Only the shelter of my strong guide's back
    enabled me to walk. Now we were where
    (with fear I write this) every soul appeared

10 wholly below the ice like straws in glass,
    some lying flat, some standing up erect
    or upside down, or bent with face to toes.

13 My leader halted, stood aside and said,
    "See Dis himself, the origin of wrong –
    once brightest of archangels in the height,

16 and here the lowest beast in Hell's foul pit."
    Wind from in front had grown to such a blast
    I had to crouch not to be overthrown,

19 but saw the vast thing clear, ice to its chest,
    yet mountain-high above the icy plain.
    My height is closer to a giant than

a giant is to what I saw of Dis.   22
Since this was part, how huge must be his whole?
If, before frowning on the highest good,

his beauty equalled present ugliness   25
no wonder out of him all woe ensued!
I bent head back to view the awful face

and saw that he had three joined at the brow,   28
the middle red, pale yellow looking left,
the right face black as Abyssinian.

Below each face there sprang up pairs of wings 31
fitting a bird like that – I never saw
a ship with sails so big – and like a bat

featherless. Their flapping could not raise him   34
as he frantically wished. They drove three
arctically chilling winds away, made

Cocytus a lake of ice. Tears flowed down   37
from his six eyes, mingling with bloody foam
from mouths in each of which a soul was chewed,

shredded by shark-like jaws of teeth within,   40
while outside claws were tearing at the skin.
My guide said, "He who suffers most up there

is Judas, head-first in the scarlet face,   43
legs prancing out, and from the black muzzle
see the head of Brutus, from the yellow,

Cassius. You know both murdered Caesar,   46
trying to kill Imperial Rome that spread
worldwide the gospel I have never read.

49 Their murder elevates them here, but you
     have now seen everything that Hell can show.
     To reach a higher place we'll go below."

52 He made me clasp his shoulders from behind,
     and raised me piggy-back; waited until
     the wings were high and wide then ran beneath,

55 grasped the beast's shaggy hide and, tuft by tuft,
     climbed down a gap between ice and the side
     of Dis. At the hip by straining very hard,

58 he turned us till heads were where feet had been,
     and then (I thought) climbed right back into Hell,
     although I heard him gasp, "Hold tight. This stair

61 takes us from wickedness." Panting as if
     his strength had almost gone, he put me down.
     Squatting, I raised my eyes to see the head

64 of Dis, but saw instead his vast legs pointing up.
     I was not sitting on an icy lake
     but on the rough floor of an ill-lit cave.

67 "Arise!" my leader said. "We've far to go
     and it is almost day." Rising, I said,
     "Dear Master, first clear my perplexity

70 before we leave. Why is he upside down?
     Where is the ice? Why, in so short a time,
     has the sun shifted round from night to day?"

73 He said, "While on the pelt of this foul worm
     we passed the central point of gravity –
     the whole world's core to which all weight inclines.

Here Satan stuck when he could fall no more.   76
Our solid earth recoiled before his face
leaving that void, that cone-shaped terraced space

called Hell inside the Northern Hemisphere   79
under the lands where living men draw breath –
Europe and Africa and Asia,

where the One Sinless Man was done to death.   82
We are now standing on a little ground
whose other side is underneath the ice.

Far, far below our feet in the north sky   85
the sun sets as it dawns above our heads.
It's time for us to go now you know why."

He first, with me behind, climbed back to light   88
in blackest shade without the use of sight,
but led ahead by sound. A trickling stream

had made a tunnel through the rock that wound   91
in easy slopes down to the tomb of Dis.
We ascended this by a long day's march

nor stopped to rest till, having travelled far,   94
under an arch appeared a sky of moon
with things as heavenly, and so at last

we stood outside, and saw the evening star.   97

PURGATORY

PART 2

REDEMPTION

THE EARLY
PARADISE

LUST

GLUTTONY

AVARICE

WRATH

SLOTH

ENVY

PRIDE

DOOR TO THE PURGING LEVELS

ANTEPURGATORY
FOR SOULS DELAYED BY
SUDDEN DEATH
LATE REPENTANCE
EXCOMMUNICATION

SHORE FOR SOULS NEWLY ARRIVED

PLAN OF MOUNT PURGATORY

FOREWORD TO PURGATORY

Hell is underground, Heaven high above. Where on Earth is Purgatory? No heretics believed in it. Thomas Aquinas called it a fact human reason could not locate so should leave to God. Dante never feared imagining more than orthodox Catholics, and by combining their theology with Pagan science he placed Purgatory firmly where we place Australia.

Greeks and Romans had no evidence of land outside Europe, Asia and Africa, so thought a vast ocean covered the rest of the globe. Their geographers deduced that the polar regions furthest from the sun were too cold to support life, and the equator nearest the sun was too hot. Some wondered if the south temperate zone supported life but were sure this could never be known, as the equator would roast or boil explorers trying to cross. This meant Atlantic voyages could discover nothing good, so across the Strait of Gibraltar they imagined a sign: *THUS FAR AND NO FURTHER.* Dante decided this was a divine prohibition, because shortly before his time Italian merchants sought a faster way than overland to import Indian spices and Chinese silk. They sailed out past Gibraltar meaning to circumnavigate Africa and never returned.

This enforced Dante's Catholic cosmography. When God expelled the rebel angels (said theologians) they fell into an underground pit He had prepared for them. Dante described Hell as a conical space, the point at the centre of the world where Satan was stuck like a worm in a bad apple. Matter that formerly filled Hell's cavity had been expelled as an island-mountain in the south's ocean, exactly opposite Jerusalem in the north land mass. This was Purgatory, ringed by terraces with steep cliffs between, the lowest cliff surrounded by a coastal plain for new arrivals. Round the low cliff trudged sinful souls saved from Hell by last-minute repentances, but delayed from climbing to Heaven by excommunication. From a cave in that cliff Virgil led Dante after they ascended from Hell.

1: Cato, Warden of the Shore

1   The little ship of my intelligence
    furls sails, drops anchor, leaves the cruel sea.
    I stand upon the second kingdom's beach

4   and now can sing of where each sinful soul
    is purified, made good by reaching up
    to paradise. O teach me, poetry!

7   Be with me Calliope, holy muse
    of epic song who treats voices that sing
    of lesser things as if unpardonable

10 magpie chattering! In Heaven's clear height
    I saw sweet blueness deepening down to
    the horizon where that lover's planet

13 Venus gladdened my eyes, shining above
    the constellation of the fishes, now
    rising from the sea. To the right I saw

16 a galaxy unknown to living folk
    except the first, before they came to sin –
    four great stars, points of a brilliant cross.

19 Poor northern sky, to be without that sight!
    Dropping my eyes I saw beside me one
    lit by that starlight, bearded and white-haired,

his face so full of venerable might 22
I wanted to adore him as his son.
"What are you," he demanded, "you that flee

eternal punishment? What guide, what lamp 25
lit your path out? Has Heaven changed its decree,
letting the damned souls free? Say by what right

you stand below my cliffs!" By word and hand 28
my guide made me bow knee and head then said,
"We have not come by our own will. Hear why.

When this man stood in peril of his soul 31
Heaven sent a lady, saying I should
lead him through Hell up to the highest good.

Now he has seen the deeps. May I show now 34
those sinners purified upon the steeps
where you preside? Be kind to him. He seeks

the liberty that you in Utica 37
perished to keep, shedding your coat of clay
to proudly wear it on the Judgement Day.

Our journey breaks no law. This man still lives. 40
Minos never judged him or me. I dwell
in the virtuous ring of Hell, close to

chaste Marcia, the wife who worships you. 43
For her sake let us climb the blessèd stairs
that lead to Heaven's grace. When I return

to Limbo she will hear how kind you are." 46
I saw this warden of the purging hill
was Cato, Caesar's foe, who stabbed himself

49 rather than see the Roman Empire kill
the glorious Republic that he loved.
Shaking his head he said, "Aye, Marcia

52 deserves all kindness, but since she has gone
beyond death's river, Acheron, and I
stay here, why mention her? Since you obey

55 Heaven's commands you need not use her name
for I obey them too. Lead him you guide
down to this island's shore. Above the beach

58 in soft mud grow the reeds that never die.
Pluck one of these and tie it round his waist.
Wash his face first. Angels hate the sight

61 of grime from Hell. After, don't come back here.
The rising sun will show a better place
to start your climb. Goodbye." He disappeared.

64 I stood up when my leader said, "Dear child,
this plain slopes seaward. Let's do as he told."
A morning breeze fleeing before the dawn

67 came from the distant glitter of the sea.
We crossed that lonely plain like wanderers
seeking a path who fear they seek in vain.

70 The low sun's level rays began to warm
the turf we trod, when my guide paused beside
a boulder's shadow on a patch of grass

73 still misted with pearls of dew. I halted,
knowing what he would do. He stooped, wet hands,
washed my face clean of crusts left by fearful,

pitiful tears, restoring how I looked   76
before invading Hell. We reached the shore
no living foot had ever touched before.

Here, as instructed, Virgil plucked a reed,   79
and as he bound it round my waist I saw
a miracle, for where that rush once stood

sprang up another, just as tall and good.   82

2: Newcomers

1   By now the sun had left the northern sky
     where at high noon it lights Jerusalem,
     leaving the Ganges in the deepest night.

4   Seen from our shore the sky above the sea
     took on a rosy glow, into which slid
     that golden sphere of light. We stood and gazed

7   like wanderers who tarry on a road
     before their journey starts. Then I beheld
     beneath the sun, across the ocean floor

10   a sight I hope to see again – brightness
     speeding so swiftly to us that no flight
     of bird could equal it. When I gazed back

13   from questioning my master with a look,
     it had grown brighter. On each side I saw
     a whiteness I could not make out, above

16   something becoming clearer as it neared.
     My master did not say a word until
     the whitenesses appeared as wings, and then

19   seeing who moved that ship he cried, "Bend knees,
     clasp hands, bow down before a cherubim
     of God, for you will soon meet more of these.

See how without a sail or oar the ship   22
is driven by his Heaven-pointing wings –
by pure eternal plumes that never moult."

The brightness of this dazzling bird of God   25
made me half close my eyes. He stood astern
of ship so light that the prow cleft no wave.

More than a hundred souls within it sat   28
singing King David's psalm, *When Israel
escaped from Egypt's land*, chanting *Amen*

on feeling that their vessel touched the strand.   31
The angel signed the cross over these souls
who sprang ashore. His ferry sped away

fast as it came. Passengers on the beach   34
stood looking round like strangers anywhere.
The sun had chased stars from the sky when one

approached and said, "Sirs, there is a mountain   37
we must climb. We do not know where to start,
can you show the way?" My guide said, "We two

are pilgrims just as ignorant as you,   40
come by a road so rough that further climb
to us will be child's play." A whisper grew

among these spirits that I lived and breathed.   43
They stared as if I were good news. One face
I knew, so ran to embrace that man. Alas,

my hands passed through his shade and hit my chest.   46
He smiled, withdrew. I cried, "Stay Casella –
I love you – tunes you gave my poems

49 make them popular! Why die before me?
And months ago! Why so long getting here?"
The sweet voice I knew said, "And I love you,

52 though gladly Heavenward bound. Remember
exactly thirteen centuries ago
Christ died for us. Our Pope proclaims this year

55 a Jubilee. All who hear mass in Rome
will have their sins forgiven. Hope of that
draws hoards of ancient dying pilgrims there.

58 The port for all not damned to Hell is where
Tiber joins the sea. Queues for that ferry
are very long these days, hence some delay

61 not troublesome to me. Heaven's decree
is best, but say why you stand *breathing* here!"
I said, "I live, so must return this way

64 when dead, like you, by the same ferry. Please,
if death has not deprived you of your art
sing verses I once wrote to cheer my heart."

67 He sang, *Love that converses with my mind*,
so sweetly that it sounds within me still.
My master and the others listened too,

70 as if it wholly occupied their will
till, like a thunderclap, Cato appeared
shouting, "You lazy louts, why linger here?

73 Run to the mountain! There strip off the sins
hiding your souls from God!" As pigeon flock
pecking the ground for seed, at sudden shock,

explodes into the air, these travellers   76
in panic fled that terrible old man
and spread across the plain, at the same time

racing blindly uphill, wholly unsure   79
what he or she was bound to find ahead.
Having no clue what better we could do

I and my leader were not far behind.   82

3: The Foothills

1   Our pace became more dignified upon
the foothills of that mount where climbing joins
goodness and reason. Since he had let me halt

4   to hear a song, Virgil had said no word.
His noble mind, believing no fault small,
suffered the sting of being in the wrong.

7   The rising sun shone rosy on our backs.
I gladly viewed the upward slope ahead
then felt it incomplete, for only one

10   shadow lay on the ground before my feet.
Afraid that suddenly I climbed alone
I gasped with dread. My comforter enquired,

13   "Why, even now, do you distrust my aid?
In Naples, underneath a monument
my shadow is entombed among my dust.

16   That I am shadowless is not more strange
than all the starry spheres of Heaven are.
Admiring wonder is the right response

19   to everything beyond your wisdom's range.
Thought alone *cannot* know the infinite
eternal Three-in-One creating all.

If human science could bring men to God   22
Mary need never have borne Jesus Christ,
or we in Limbo live unsatisfied

in outer Hell, far from the greatest good   25
where Homer, Plato, Aristotle dwell
with many more." He fell silent again,

staring with troubled face on ground we trod   28
until we reached Mount Purgatory's base.
The wildest mountainside in Italy

would look an easy staircase seen beside   31
this cliff too sheer, this granite precipice
too high and smooth for any mountaineer.

My master sighed and murmured, "Lacking wings,   34
we need to find a slope that legs can use.
It must exist. Do we turn left or right?"

He pondered where the ground met the rock wall.   37
I, looking round, saw, a sling-shot away,
a group of souls approaching from our left,

walking so slowly that at first I thought   40
they did not move at all. I shouted out,
"See Master! These may know where we should go."

He looked, then spoke with confidence renewed.   43
"Indeed they may, my son. Let us enquire
and never cease to hope." A thousand steps

brought us to where the flock of souls, like sheep,   46
walked timidly, heads bowed, behind a few
dignified leaders pacing slowly too.

49 "Hail, holy ones!" cried Virgil. "You have died
    as Christians, so are sure of Heaven's grace.
    Unlike you we must ascend at once. Please

52 where is the right place? Do you know of one?"
    The leaders halted, stared and then drew back.
    Their flock was scared and huddled to the rock.

55 My shadow on their track caused this dismay.
    Virgil declared, "You need not feel surprise.
    I will explain. My friend is still alive,

58 his body therefore splits the light of day.
    Heaven demands we climb without delay.
    Where can we do so?" "Turn and go with us,"

61 a leader of these good souls said. We did,
    walked at a slow pace. "Perhaps," said one,
    "you know my face?" I looked. He was fair-haired,

64 handsome, debonair, an eyebrow broken
    by a scar. I admitted I did not,
    whereupon, smiling, "Look at this," he said,

67 opening his vest to show in his chest
    a much worse wound, adding "I am Manfred,
    ruler of Sicily, Tory warlord

70 who defied the Pope, so died by the sword.
    As my blood flowed I gave my soul with tears
    to Him who saves all sinners who repent,

73 even of crimes as horrible as mine.
    The victors built a cairn over my bones.
    He that comes to me I will not cast out,

Christ said that but Pope Clement disagreed,   76
had the cairn broken, bones scattered around,
on unholy ground battered by wind and rain.

We in this troop though excommunicate,   79
will be redeemed at last, though for each year
unconfessed souls normally wait to climb

the purifying stair to Heaven's gate,   82
we under papal ban wait thirty more.
That time can be reduced by living souls.

I beg you please when back on Earth again,   85
tell my daughter Constance, Aragon's queen,
mother of kings, to pray well for my soul.

Despite Pope Clement I am not in Hell."   88

4: The First Ascent

1   Pleasure or pain can fill us up so full
    they dominate all ways we think and act,
    a fact disproving Plato's rule that souls

4   are triple – vegetable, animal
    and logical. Words can so occupy
    our soul, we do not notice passing time.

7   Manfred so pleased me that I did not see
    the sun rise to its fiftieth degree.
    Mid-morning passed before our company

10   aroused me, crying, "Here's the place you need!"
    I saw in the cliff face a gap as wide
    as in a vineyard hedge that peasants block

13   with a forkful of thorn, yet wide enough
    to admit a man into a deep crack
    sloping steeply up. My guide, stepping in,

16   started climbing on all fours, rock beneath,
    beside and above his back. I followed,
    bidding the slowly moving flock goodbye.

19   You may rush down Noli, up San Leo,
    mount Bismantova's summit on your feet.
    Urgent desire drove fast my hands and knees.

I scrambled after Virgil, did not stop   22
until we reached the precipice's top
and stood upon the edge of a broad ledge

of that bare mountainside. "Master," said I,   25
"where now?" "Upward," said he, "and do not halt
before you meet a wiser guide than me."

He turned to lead me up a steeper slope   28
than we had tackled in the creviced rock.
Exhausted I cried, "Pause kind father, please!

You're leaving me behind – I need to rest!"   31
"My son," said he, pointing not far ahead,
"drag yourself first up there." I forced my feet

to follow him up to a level ground,   34
a terrace curving round the mighty hill,
and sat facing the way we came (often

the finest view) due east. First I gazed down,   37
feasting eyes on the sea below, then raised
them to the skies, amazed to see the sun

shining upon my left. "How can this be?"   40
I said. "This island mountain," he replied,
"is central to the southern hemisphere,

just as the land where Christ was crucified   43
is central to the north. Halfway between
lies the equator. When the setting sun

crossed that, it left the north in night and brought 46
light here, to the western point, which is not
upon your right, but on the other hand.

49 Do you understand?" I did, then asked him,
"Have we much more to climb? The height ahead
is out of sight." He said, "The hardest part

52 of leaving sin is always at the start.
The climb is easier as you go up.
Near the top you will feel climbing is like

55 floating downstream in a boat." A voice said,
"You'll sit down pretty often before that."
We turned and saw a rock within whose shade

58 folk squatted, looking totally fatigued.
The speaker hugged his knees, head sunk between.
I told my guide, "That is Belacqua, sir –

61 a Florentine well-known for being slow."
Belacqua raised an eye above his thigh
and grunted, "Busybody, up you go

64 now you know why the sun shines on your left."
Smiling a bit at that I said to him,
"You need not grumble friend. You're safe from Hell

67 but why sit here? What are you waiting for?
Have you not shaken off your laziness?"
"Brother," he groaned, "I cannot go up yet,

70 I died too soon to properly confess
my life of sinful sloth before my death.
The angel-warden of the higher gate

73 cannot admit me up to cleansing pain
until I've squatted here for sixty years –
the years before I gave my soul to God.

No living souls will pray to lessen these   76
and my despair. O how I envy you!"
Virgil, climbing ahead, called back to me,

"Time to go on!" I left Belacqua there.   79

5: The Unconfessed

1   I left these ghosts to follow him uphill,
    and then heard other voices shouting, "Look!
    Sunlight won't pierce him, so he is not dead!"

4   Turning my head I saw an eager crowd
    staring upon my shadow and at me.
    "Words should not turn you – face the uphill track,"

7   my leader cried. "Good heads should imitate
    strong towers undisturbed by windy blast.
    Ignore what people say. Distracted minds

10 go easily astray because each thought
    cancels the last." "Coming!" I called (for what
    else could I say?) and blushing with shame,

13 climbed up to him. From round the hill above
    penitents came, chanting King David's psalm,
    The Miserere, grieving for past sin.

16 At sight of me their chant became an "Oo!"
    and two ran down to us, crying, "Please say,
    what kind of man are you?" My guide replied,

19 "Tell your folk that he (as his shadow proves)
    is flesh and blood, able to do them good
    if they respect him as they should." No cloud

soared swifter through the sky than they returned   22
to that crowd who, hearing their news, then wheeled
round like a troop of cavalry and then

came charging down. My guide said, "Know that these   25
will beg you to take word of them to Earth,
but don't stop climbing. Listen as you go."

"O lucky soul, ascending to delight,"   28
one cried. "On legs your mother made, please
look at us hard. Do you see any here

whose names you could take back to those we love?   31
They do not know the manner of our deaths,
deaths so obscure that we could not confess

but are not damned to Hell. A final pang of grief   34
for our past sins admitted Heaven's Grace,
which brought us here where prayers from pure hearts

can make us fit to see God's face, and these   37
are now our agonising need." I said,
"I see none here I know. Tell me your names,

if that will ease your pains and speed your climb   40
if it does not halt mine. I must obey
one who forbids delay while leading me

from world to world, but truly I declare,   43
by peace we all desire, to do my best."
"No need to swear – we trust your kindly words,"

their spokesman said. "I will first give my name: 46
Jacopo Cassero, Fano my town
between Naples ruled by Charles of Anjou

49 and states claimed by the Pope. Please visit there.
Ask people to say orisons that will
help shed the sorry burden of my guilt.

52 The Marquis of Ferrara spilt my blood
in secret, just to gratify his wrath.
At Oriaco near to Padua

55 (that traitor's town) his men ambushed my path.
Stabbed and confused I fled quite the wrong way
into the marsh, stumbled through mud and reeds,

58 fell bleeding, and saw my heart's blood at last
stain a pool red." Another spoke to me,
"May you meet what you seek upon this hill,

61 then back on Earth find some who'll pray for me.
I am from Montefeltro, once its count,
foxy old Guido's son, but few there now

64 care for me. My widow Joan does not,
and so you find me here with troubled brow."
Surprised, I cried, "But you and I once fought

67 at Campoldino! Afterwards I heard
your corpse was missing. None knew where it went.
Was that through malice or by accident?"

70 He said, "A demon drowned my solid part
after my soul was saved. I will explain.
I left that fight unhorsed and with slashed throat,

73 my blood dabbling the plain until I reached
a stream called Archiano that flows down
into the Arno from the Apennines.

Falling upon its bank I lost my sight 76
praying to God, and died with Mary's name
on my wicked lips. Let the living know

what happened then. God's angel took my soul. 79
The fiend from Satan yelled, "I have been robbed!
You carry off this man's eternal part

all for one tiny tear! See what I do 82
to his remains!" With wind and mist he swelled
clouds over the plain from Protomagno

to the mountain range, then burst them into 85
more torrential rain than earth could contain,
flooding to overflow gully and stream.

Bursting Archiano's banks, they swept my corpse 88
into the Arno, breaking it apart.
The bits were sunk in mud." A third shade said,

"When back on Earth and rested from your climb 91
tell people of La Pia. My birthplace
was Sienna. Maremma saw my death

as he knows well, the man who wedded me." 94

6: Of Italian States

1   Gamblers breaking the bank are thronged upon
    by some who hope good luck rubs off on them,
    and others wanting shares in what they gain.

4   Souls pressed on me like that, so very thick
    I waved my hands in air to drive them back,
    promising all these violently slain

7   to do the best I could. First, the good judge
    stabbed in court by that man of blood, Tacco;
    Guccio who, fleeing Campoldino,

10 was swallowed too by Arno's stormy flood;
    the Pisan who forgave the enemies
    who slew his son; Frederick Novello;

13 Count Orso; Peter Brosse wrongly hanged
    by the Queen of Brabant. (Let her beware
    of joining ugly company in Hell.)

16 When free of these and others begging me
    to tell their kindred they needed prayers
    I begged my guide, "Master, enlighten me.

19 Your *Aeneid* says that divine decree
    cannot be altered by the human will.
    Surely that means these beg my help in vain?"

"I wrote plain truth," said he, "but wrote before   22
God came in mercy to humanity,
was born as a divinely honest man

who suffered and defeated wretched death.   25
Since then, when justice is embraced by love
in a last moment of pure penitence,

justice and mercy form one healing flame.   28
Be patient if you do not understand.
Enlightenment awaits you high above,

smiling in bliss. Her name is Beatrice."   31
I shouted, "Master, let us hurry up!
I am not tired now, and before sun sets

will climb up very fast to reach the top."   34
"Before that Heavenly event," said he,
"the sun will set twice more, but just ahead

sits one who may know an easier ascent."   37
Him we approached was Lombard. With calm pride
he gazed on us as resting lions do

out of moving eyes. When Virgil asked   40
where lay the way up he did not say,
but asked from where we came. My leader said,

"Mantua," at which the soul, leaping up,   43
embraced him, cried, "My city! Know that I,
Sordello, am poet of Mantua,

only excelled by one born long ago."   46
Then Virgil happily embraced him too.
O Italy, you hostelry of slaves!

49 You vessel, captainless in stormy sea!
Why cannot souls who love their cities well
co-operate to keep their country whole?

52 Even within a single city wall
new money fights with old, each wrestling for
a strangle-hold, making alliances

55 with foreigners through bribery, bad pacts
which are not kept, preventing unity.
There is no peace within Italian shores.

58 Unlike beehives who recognise a queen
you are a brothel, ruled by squabbling whores.
The Emperor Justinian once made

61 a legal code to pacify his land
which other lands employ – not Italy,
which won't submit to legal spurs and bit.

64 None is allowed to take the reins in hand.
Devout priests should obey our Lord's command
and let a Caesar ride our Latin steed.

67 O German Albert, Holy Roman King,
all Europe should be yours, but you don't heed
its central garden which has run to seed.

70 Come, govern us! Our wretched noblemen,
Montagues, Capulets, Filippeschi,
Monaldi dread each other! Unite us

73 under one head we all should recognise!
Rome, a poor widow, weeps for your great work
of restoration. Pity and help Rome

become the Queen of Christendom again   76
or pity your reputation. And may
almighty Jove, once crucified for us,

not turn away from our chaotic state.   79
Tyrants dominate Italian towns
where mob-rule is not led by rascal clowns.

My Florence, this digression won't touch you   82
where citizens take public good to heart
and to their tongue. You are too smart for rule

by mob or tyrant. Athens and Sparta   85
did not legislate constantly like you.
Elsewhere folk dodge the burdens of the state –

your people grab for office before asked,   88
and so are peaceful, rich – except when not!
You change your constitution in a week,

laws, government and coinage restlessly,   91
improving nothing like a sick woman
tossing and turning in her bed and sure

each new position may achieve a cure.   94

7: The Climb Halts

1   Those Mantuans, Sordello and my guide,
    embraced each other happily until
    the first drew back enquiring, "Who are you?"

4   "A soul from Hell," the greater poet said.
    "Augustus, the first Emperor of Rome,
    buried my bones before the Christian faith

7   let saved souls make a staircase of this hill,
    so I, Virgil, will not reach paradise."
    Like one who thinks, "This is . . . it cannot be!

10 It must . . . but surely not?" Sordello stood
    wondering, as if his eyes perceived
    a marvel far too great to be believed,

13 then bowed as low as anybody could.
    "You are the glory of the Latin race!"
    he cried, "Through you our language is as strong,

16 will live as long, as Gospel scriptures do.
    Tell me the miracle that brings you here,
    and if you think me fit to know, from which

19 cloister of Hell." Said Virgil, "I have come
    through all the rings of Hell, but dwell with souls
    who do not suffer pain. Ours is the state

of babies who die before christening   22
cleans off their sinful stain. We do not weep
but sigh for what we, living, could not know

so cannot now enjoy eternally –   25
true faith, hope, charity. But even so
Heaven has ordered me to lead this man

up to the mountain's height. Since sunset casts   28
its shadow on us we will climb by night,
having not reached real Purgatory yet.

Sordello, can you tell us the right way?"   31
"Yes, I will be your guide a while," said he,
"but not uphill at once. Now you must halt

and be escorted to a resting place   34
where you will find folk you'll be glad to see."
"Why? Who bans our divinely ordered climb?"

my master cried, "Do you?" Sordello stooped,   37
drew a line with his finger on the ground,
and said, "When light departs you won't cross this.

None forbids night climbing here, but darkness   40
abolishes all wish to climb, though letting
any drift backward down the way they came."

My master brooded, then said, "Lead us please   43
to where you say a rest will do us good."
He led us in the gloaming a short way

toward a corrie hollowing the slope,   46
then said, "Here we will wait for a new day
deep in the mountain's lap." A winding path

49 that rose and fell brought us to that deep dell.
We stood upon the edge where, gazing down
there still was light enough to see below

52 a glowing lawn as green as emerald
with blossoms golden, crimson, pearly white,
silver and azure and pure indigo.

55 All colours of the rainbow were surpassed
by blooms feasting our eyes. Their fragrances
blent in one sweetness, lovely but unknown

58 to living men before I breathed that air,
and there sat souls unseen by lower folk
singing the Holy Hymn to Heaven's Queen.

61 "Before the sun now setting leaves the sky,"
Sordello said, "we need descend no more.
Why? Those below are clearly seen from here.

64 He who sits highest of that kingly crew,
too glum to move his lips in sacred song
was Rudolph, Emperor, who failed to heal

67 wounds that have mangled Italy so long.
Trying to comfort him is Ottocar,
King of Bohemia, in his nappies

70 better than bearded Wenceslaus, his son
who lazily now occupies his throne.
That snub-nosed chap beating his breast in grief

73 regrets how he disgraced the Crown of France.
That vicious thief, his son, has gone to Hell
but see *his* daughter's husband, formerly

the Prince of Anjou, also torn by grief.   76
You see two monarchs sing in harmony –
stout Tory King of Aragon beside

the manly-nosed Whig King of Sicily.   79
Their sons have none of their nobility.
How seldom vigour in a parent tree

enters its branches! Only God knows why.   82
See England's Henry sit apart, alone,
a simple king whose Edward, Prince of Wales,

is now a hammer of the French and Scots.   85
Lowest and looking up, unluckiest
prince of this age, William of Montferrat

who, tricked by foes, died in an iron cage."   88

8: The Vestibule

1   When church bells toll the knell of parting day
    the traveller, whether on land or sea
    remembers home and loved ones far away.

4   While pondering Sordello's final word
    I saw a kingly soul below arise,
    showing by gestures that he would be heard.

7   Joining his palms he lifted them in prayer,
    and gazing to the east, began to sing
    sweetly the evening hymn to Heavenly light.

10 The rest melodiously joined the hymn
    while also gazing on the bright clear stars
    which were, I noticed, starting to appear.

13 Reader, sharpen your mind's eye to the truth
    I try to show you through my poem's veil
    which should be thinnest, most transparent here.

16 The noble company fell silent, all
    looking up humbly and expectantly,
    to where I saw descending through the air

19 a pair of angels holding shining swords
    shortened because their points were broken off.
    Their wings and robes were green as fresh spring leaves.

One stopped above our heads, the other stood   22
upon the mountainside just opposite.
Though I could clearly see their flaxen hair,

the brightness of their eyes quite dazzled me.   25
Sordello said, "Mary, Mother of God,
sends them to guard the valley at this time

from the foul snake, our spiteful enemy."   28
Unsure of where that snake would come, I pressed
against the trusty shoulder of my guide.

"We will descend and greet some noble shades,"   31
Sordello said, "for speech with you will please
that company." By three steps I went down

to where I saw (though air was darkening)   34
a man whose face I knew, as he knew mine –
noble judge Nino. That he was not damned

delighted me. "When did you land upon   37
this island's shore?" he asked. "At dawn today,"
I said, "although I did not cross the sea.

I am not dead, but came on foot through Hell."   40
He started back, then said to someone near,
"Conrad, arise! See what God's grace has willed."

Then said to me, "By that great gratitude   43
you owe to Him whose deepest purposes
cannot be known, when back in Italy,

beg my child Joan to pray God for my soul.   46
He will respond to prayers of innocence.
My wife, who wed again, loves me no more,

49 showing how soon the flame of women's love
    dies lacking sight and touch to kindle it.
    She cannot long enjoy her present mate.

52 Her husband flaunts a viper on his shield.
    Carved on her tomb it will not look as fair
    as would the chanticleer she had from me."

55 The indignation showing in his face
    came from the heart, but I was staring up
    to that high centre where stars move most slow.

58 My leader asked, "What are you seeing there?"
    "Three starry torches new to me," said I,
    "with which the southern sky is all aglow."

61 Said he, "The four great stars you saw at dawn
    have sunk from view and are replaced by these."
    And it was then Sordello cried aloud,

64 "See! There's the enemy!" pointing to where
    the valley's side dipped low, for there a snake
    was sliding in, maybe that subtle one

67 who first had given bitter food to Eve.
    Through grass and flowers it undulated on,
    an evil streak, twisting at times its neck

70 to lick its back with flickering forked tongue.
    So swiftly did Heaven's hawks swoop down at him
    I only heard their green wings cleave the air

73 before that serpent fled and they returned.
    He whom the judge had called to look at me
    had not since looked away. Approaching now

he said, "May your will to ascend this hill   76
not fail before you reach the greatest height.
If you have word of Val di Magra or

places near by, then tell it to me please   79
for there I once was great, known by the name
my father had, Conrad Malaspina.

My too much loving of my family   82
here must be purified." "I was never
in your land," I replied, "but in Europe

where are you not renowned? Guilty tongues fail 85
to slander your name, for it still resounds
for generosity of purse and sword –

a family famous for going straight."   88
He said, "Years hence I happily foresee
experience will prove your friendly view

of my folk's generosity still true."   91

9: The Entrance

1   Upon the little valley's verdant floor
    I, Virgil, Sordello, Nino the judge
    and Conrad Malespina spoke no more

4   and I, imperfect man, slept deep until
    that early hour when swallows, sensing dawn,
    mournfully cheep and sleepers, not disturbed

7   by dreams of bodily and mental stress
    sometimes see visions of pure blessèdness.
    A golden-feathered eagle seemed to be

10   hovering overhead with wings outspread.
    I thought, "That bird seized Ganymede to be
    butler in Paradise, so fair was he.

13   He won't want me!" Then like a thunderbolt
    it swooped and, snatching, soared with me up, up,
    up to the height of Empyrean fire

16   where the imagined heat fused us in one
    before at last (of course) awaking me.
    The mother of Achilles carried him

19   asleep from Crete to a Greek island where
    his opening eyes knew nothing he could see.
    Two hours after day dawned I woke like that,

cold, weak, and staring at the ocean's shore   21
far, far below. My comforter and guide
seated at my side said, "Do not be afraid.

Your state is excellent. Before day broke,   25
as you were fast asleep upon the flowers
that clothe the lower dell, a lady came.

She said, *I, Lucy, come to lift this man*   28
and take him, sleeping, further on his way.
Sordello stayed with other noble souls

as when this clear day dawned she took you up,   31
I following until she laid you here
and pointed to that gate before she left."

Made confident once more I rose to face   34
the rampart of the mountainside, my guide
leading me up to a much higher place

than we had been before. Reader, please know   37
I must rise to a higher theme, sustained
by greater art. We reached what at first seemed

a cleft in that rock wall, but was a gate   40
above three coloured steps, each different.
On the threshold a silent warder sat,

his face so bright I could not bear the sight,   43
and in his hand he held a naked sword
I also could not look on steadily,

for it reflected light so dazzlingly.   46
"Where are you from? What do you seek?" he said.
"If no Heavenly escort brings you here,

49   beware! This upward climb may do you harm."
     "A messenger from Heaven," said my guide,
     "recently pointed us toward this gate.

52   Her name was Lucy." "Enter then, and climb,"
     the courteous warder said, so I set foot
     on a white marble slab so polished smooth

55   it mirrored me exactly as I am.
     The second step was purple, rough and cracked
     throughout its length and breadth. The topmost step

58   resembled porphyry, as red as blood
     spurted from vein. The angel's feet reposed
     on this. The threshold where he sat above

61   was clearly of the hardest adamant.
     On these three steps my leader led me up,
     saying, "Now ask him to fling wide the gate."

64   I threw myself down at his holy feet,
     and after beating on my breast three times
     begged him to mercifully let me through.

67   With his sword point he etched upon my brow
     seven Ps, then said, "As you climb within
     these will be healed away." Out of his robe

70   of ashen colour he removed two keys,
     one gold, one silver. Turning in the lock
     the white first, then the yellow, he explained,

73   "When both keys do not turn the gate stays shut.
     One is more precious but the other needs
     more skill, more wisdom, to make it unlock.

Peter who gave them told me if I erred   76
to err on mercy's side, so in you come
but don't look back or you will be expelled."

When Caesar burst in through a temple door   79
to rob Tarpeian gold, they thundered loud.
The hinges here roared louder grinding round,

but entering I heard sweet voices sound   82
blending with organ chords, and ringing clear
in the *Te Deum*, mighty mirthful hymn,

which most of all on Earth I love to hear.   85

10: The First Terrace

1   And so the angel warder let us through
    that gate locked fast to those of evil will.
    We climbed a narrow track in the cleft hill,

4   nor did I dare look round when at my back
    the gate shut with a clang that shook the ground.
    Our steep path zig-zagged sharply left and right.

7   Said Virgil, "This will test your climbing skill,
    so concentrate." I did. It was near noon
    when I emerged from that tight needle's eye.

10   Footsore and tired I stood beside my guide,
    like him, unsure of where to go again:
    sheer drop behind, on each side empty plain,

13   ahead a sheer cliff three men's height away.
    We had not moved a step before I knew
    the cliff we faced was marble, pure and white,

16   splendidly carved with shapes so well devised
    they could not be the work of human hands
    and recognised just One could make them so.

19   We saw the angel Gabriel announce
    the birth of Jesus Christ, the Prince of Peace
    for whom mankind has wept through centuries.

He seemed to say, *Hail Mary, full of grace!*   22
and the humility of her reply,
Here am I, God's servant, glowed in her face

so I believed I heard her with my ears.   25
"Look over here," my guide said, pointing to
images of a more crowded scene:

oxen pulling a cart holding the ark   28
brought by King David to Jerusalem.
Seven jubilant choirs surrounded it.

My eyes declared, "They sing!" my ears, "They don't!"   31
and where, in marble, clouds of incense rose,
eyes disagreed with nose. Before the ark,

the psalmist monarch with his robe tucked up   34
danced like a happy clown. His wife looked down
from a high window, smiling scornfully

at his humiliating lack of pride.   37
Beside this was another crowded scene:
Emperor Trajan riding forth to war

with knights and retinue. Eagles above   40
flapped golden wings. A poor widow clung
to his bridle, cried, "Sir, my murdered son

should be avenged!" "He will be, when I return."   43
"But if you don't?" "My heir will do what's right."
"If you don't do what's needed now," cried she,

"then why should he?" "True!" Trajan said, halting,   46
"none should delay just acts." Justice was done.
Our best Pope since Saint Peter, Gregory,

49 esteemed this just humility as proof
   of Trajan's noble Christianity,
   so he is now redeemed in Paradise.

52 These splendid visions of true humbleness
   pleased me by showing truth and beauty one
   'till I heard Virgil murmur, "Here come they

55 who should point out the stair to the next heights."
   I looked to see some kind of cavalcade,
   then said, "There are no people in my sight!

58 Here's a slow avalanche of heavy stones
   advancing on the ground. Sir, please explain."
   Said he, "Stoop down and look. Under those weights

61 see once proud sinners crawling on their knees."
   I cried out, "O you poor ones who believed
   that wealth and power could magnify your worth!

64 Now crushed to earth, at last you will discard
   your pride, a grubby caterpillar shell
   splitting to loose angelic butterfly,

67 soaring to God upon His Judgement Day."
   I quite forgot I might be one of them.
   Brackets supporting ceilings on high walls

70 are sometimes carved like men, knees squeezed to chest.
   Those here were just like that, sorely oppressed,
   and the most patient ghosts were weeping most.

73 Their state was nearly more than they could bear.

11: The Proud

Our Father in Heaven, unlimited   1
except by your great love for all you made,
and everything you've given us on Earth,

we praise your name as angels do above.   4
Teach us to find your House of Peace on high
which by our strength alone we cannot reach

however hard and painfully we try.   7
Give everyone the nourishment we need
to rightly follow in the steps of Christ

and not slide backwards into sinful ways.   10
Forgive our sins as we also forgive
those who have hurt us. Dear Lord, most of all

do not let enemies become so strong   13
they drive the virtuous to doing wrong.
Lord God, you know that prayer is not for us,

but souls alive whose state is not redeemed.   16
Thus those ghosts prayed for us while toiling on
beneath such weight as we have never dreamed.

Let we with any goodness pray that they   19
are quicker lightened, raised above the moon
to their appointed place in Paradise.

22 Reading my mind I heard kind Virgil say,
    "May all who stoop here be unburdened soon
    and wing their upward flight. I lead a man

25 still clad in Adam's flesh, so we need stairs
    to climb this cliff. Can any of you say
    if nearest way is to our left or right?"

28 We could not see who spoke, but heard a voice.
    "Go with us to the right, where there's a place
    a man may climb. Were I not bent so low

31 I might see a face, recognise a friend
    who pitied me. I was Italian,
    my dad the great Bill Aldobrandesco –

34 Surely you know his name? Pride in my birth
    and famous ancestors made me forget
    all of us share one common mother, Earth.

37 Arrogance killed me, dragged to infamy
    my name and kin. In Campagnatico
    children know this and in Sienna too.

40 I am Umberto, whose excessive pride
    will crush me until God is satisfied."
    To hear him I'd bent low and so saw one

43 who did not speak but twisted round his neck
    to see me, knew me, kept his eyes on me
    as he crept onward very painfully.

46 Bent almost double at his side I cried,
    "You, Oderisi! Pride of Gubbio
    for illustrating books, or (as they say

in Paris) for illuminating them."   49
"Brother," said he, "Franco of Bologna
does that much better now. His claim to fame

is partly due to what he learned from me.   52
When living I denied how good he was.
Here I am purging all that pettiness.

The emptiness of glory in a name   55
is obvious. Florence once gloried in
the radiance of Cimabue's art.

Giotto's fame has cast a shade on it.   58
Guido Guinizelli's verse was once
the splendour of our tongue. Cavalcanti's

is now more highly sung. Who's next? Are you?   61
Who cares? A thousand years, two thousand, ten,
are eye-blinks to the slowly turning spheres

of Paradise. Fame is a brief noise.   64
He crawling before me once had a name
shouted through Tuscany, and adored

in Sienna, where it's now ignored, though   67
he helped it smash a mad Florentine horde."
"Your true words humble me, but tell me more,"

I said, "about that lord who crawls before."   70
"He, Provenzan Salvani, tried to be
Sienna's tyrant prince and so creeps thus

like all of us who raised ourselves far too   73
presumptuously high." Said I, "But why,
is he not below with other princes

76 not yet fit for your purifying pain?"
Oderisi said, "He earned this higher place
because once, when a despot but not rich,

79 he begged for money in the public square
to ransom a dear friend, though his proud soul
found this humiliation agony.

82 You too will know the pain of beggary."

12: Going from Pride

Like two slow oxen harnessed in one yoke   1
I, bending almost double at his side,
crept onward till my gentle master spoke:

"Leave him; we must go faster now." I did,   4
though inwardly depressed, but very soon
followed my leader eagerly. We seemed

lighter of foot. Said he, "Start looking down.   7
There's splendid entertainment where we tread."
As flat stones in a graveyard often show

carvings provoking memories and tears,   10
each vivid surface of the mountain street
was paved with wonders of mosaic art,

all showing penalties of too much pride.   13
I saw the noblest creature God first made
falling like lightning. On the other side

I saw the fifty-headed, hundred-armed   16
Briareus dismembered by Jove's dart;
I saw Jove's armoured children as they viewed

the scattered limbs – Apollo, Pallas, Mars;   19
I saw King Nimrod, Babel's architect
bewildered, staring at his futile heap;

22   and poor Niobe, statue who bled tears
      with seven sons and seven daughters dead;
      and Saul, the conquered King of Israel,

25   on Gilboa self-slaughtered by his sword;
      and mad Arachne, half a spider now,
      still clinging to the woeful web she wove;

28   and Rehoboam, boastful coward king,
      fleeing by chariot, though none pursued.
      That pavement also showed me how and why

31   Alcmaeon slew his mother, who betrayed
      his father for a jewelled ornament;
      Assyria's great king Sennacherib,

34   stabbed in a temple by his ruthless sons,
      afloat in a big cup of his own blood;
      Cyrus's head, popped by Queen Tomyris

37   who said, "You liked bloodshed? So drink up this."
      It showed Assyrians in panic flight
      when General Holofernes lost *his* head;

40   and lastly saw the broken walls and ash
      of mighty Troy, brought pitifully low.
      No human artist could contrive to show

43   these histories in carving or in paint
      so wonderfully well. The dead looked dead,
      the living seemed to breathe. I came to see

46   the fate of pride spelled on that road for me,
      but go your haughty ways, great sons of Eve!
      Do not believe what's written on the ground.

I had not seen how far we and the sun   49
had circled round the hill when Virgil said,
"The time for brooding's past. Look upward – see,

the hour is noon. An angel's coming fast   52
who will direct us to the upward way,
so give him all the reverence he's due.

Today, you know, will never dawn again."   55
Knowing my master hated waste of time
I followed him in haste. We came to halt

before a lovely creature clad in white   58
whose face gleamed on us like the morning star.
Spreading his arms to us and then his wings,

he, pointing to a deep cleft in the cliff,   61
told us, "Climb here! It is an easy way.
Why do so few arrive to share it now?

Mankind was made to soar. What little flaws   64
detain the multitudes so far below?
But up you go." His wings then brushed my brow.

The cloven rock contained a noble stair   67
like that arising from the Arno bridge
(built when my city had just government)

rising to where all Florence can be viewed,   70
before the church of Miniato's door.
Then as we climbed I heard a sweeter voice

than words can tell, sing *Blessèd are the meek*,   73
unlike the lamentable screams I heard
between one level and the next in Hell.

76   I found that climbing up that holy stair
     was easier than walking on flat ground.
     "Master," I asked, "what weight has been removed?"

79   "The weight of that first P and what it means,
     rubbed from your brow by the angelic wings,"
     said he. "The rest are there more faintly now.

82   All will be cancelled, one by one, until
     your body is so lightened by good will,
     you'll not be capable of weariness."

85   Then I behaved like all those unaware
     of how they look before the stares of folk
     begin to worry them: they use their hands

88   to feel what they can't see and don't yet know.
     With five spread fingertips I felt my head
     and found six Ps where seven were before.

91   My guide smiled as he saw me doing so.

13: The Envious

We reached the summit of the stair and stood   1
upon the second terrace of the hill
that heals its climbers. Here another road

was winding by a steeper curve, a road   4
empty of people, shadow, ornament,
and colour: just dull stone. The poet said,

"Waiting to ask the way will cause delay,"   7
and turning right to face the sun he cried,
"Sweet light of day I choose you as our guide,

until it's obvious we've gone astray."   10
We strode so briskly to the right that soon
a mile was passed, and then toward us came

clear sentences, spoken by none we saw   13
who sounded kind. "They have no wine" came first,
flew by us, went repeating on behind,

fading, but not quite lost in distance when   16
"I am Orestes" followed it, and then
while I said, "Father, what do these words mean?"

a third voice came: "Love those who injure you."   19
My kind guide said, "Envy is cut back here
by whips of love, which are its opposite.

22 More sounds like these will strike your ear, I think,
before you leave this street, but look ahead.
See, at the cliff-foot many people sit."

25 I, staring forward harder, could detect
in robes coloured like stone on which they leaned
a mournful row, and nearer heard them groan:

28 "Pray for us, Mary", "Peter", "All the saints",
I do not think there walks on Earth today
any so hard that pity would not pierce

31 at sight of those I saw in so much pain.
Each, wearing coarse grey hair-cloth, lay with head
propped on a neighbour's shoulder like the blind

34 paupers who beg beside confessionals.
Tight iron wires stitched their eyelids shut.
Ashamed to see and not be seen I turned

37 toward my counsellor and he advised,
"Yes, question these, but use the fewest words."
He stood beside the road's perilous edge

40 which had no parapet, facing the shades,
whose cheeks were wet with tears squeezed sorely through
their eyelids' horrid seam. I turned to them

43 and said, "You who are sure to see one day
when consciousness and memory run clean,
are there among you some Italian souls?

46 It may be good for such a one or two
if I speak for you on the Earth below."
"O brother, all of us are citizens

of one great city. All Italians   49
are pilgrims to it, and not only they."
These words came from a little further on.

I moved to where a small expectant face   52
was tilted up. "Spirit, if it was you,"
I said, "who spoke, make yourself known by place

or else by name." "Sienna was my town,"   55
said she, "and here I mourn my sinful life
weeping to Him who gave Himself for us.

Named Sapia, although not sapient,   58
failure in others more delighted me
than my good luck. I was an old woman

when Sienna's Tories fought Florentine Whigs.   61
Seeing the faction that I hate retreat
with mad delight I loudly swore to God,

Now I don't fear you! as the blackbird sings   64
at sight of briefest sunlight in the spring.
This blasphemy will be forgiven since

Peter (a saint who lived by selling combs)   67
in charity both grieved and prayed for me.
But who are you who ask about my state?

You have I think, wide eyes and talk with breath."   70
I said, "My eyes will not be here for long.
Envy has never been my greatest sin.

My fear is of the punishment for pride –   73
I dread that crushing misery below,
but let me know what I can do for you

76 when I return to Earth." "How strange," said she.
"God loves you, letting you go up and down.
Please pray for me sometimes, and tell my kin

79 if you pass through Sienna, I am here.
They invest in schemes to renew old streams
and at Talamone build a new port

82 by trading oversea. Alas, the cost
will be private and public bankruptcy.
My family's great fortune will be lost,

85 and hopeful admirals will lose the most."

14: Of Envious Rulers

"Who now ascends our penitential hill   1
before death makes him rise, and who at will
opens and shuts his eyes?" "I do not know

but he is nearest you. Speak well to him,   4
to gain a fair reply." We saw two souls
conversing thus in that blind row. One said,

"O living man bound Heavenward, please tell   7
in charity your birthplace and your name.
A special grace protects you, so your words

can do us good." "I was born near," said I,   10
"a stream that flows more than a hundred miles
from Falterona to the sea. My name

you do not need. It's not yet known to fame."   13
"Mount Falterona is the source," said he
"of Tiber and of Arno, therefore you

are from Romagna or from Tuscany,   16
and probably the last. Why not say so?
Is Arno a bad word?" "It is indeed!"

the other speaker cried, "All living by   19
that evil flood should die and be forgot.
They flee from virtue, dread it like a snake.

22 The place corrupts them, or bad custom spreads
corruption through them like a deadly plague.
Close to the Arno's source the folk are brutes

25 like those whom Circe once turned into swine,
fit to eat acorns, not to dine like men.
Leaving these hogs the stream enters a land

28 of snarling mongrel dogs, more full of spite
than bravery or any strength to bite.
Lower the stream swells wider, and as

31 it swells, the dogs become rapacious wolves.
Leaving them by a winding glen it flows
through land of cheating foxes none can trap,

34 so great is the support for their deceit.
But now the future has grown clear to me!
I'll say what I foresee, and do not care

37 what ears may hear. Your grandson will become
hunter of wolves beside that horrid flood,
selling young flesh, butchering it when old.

40 He will be infamous for slaughtering,
will leave so few that centuries will pass
before the state of Florence is restored."

43 This coming woe showed on the troubled face
of he announcing it and he who heard.
Said I, "If you want word of that conveyed

46 to Earth below, I'd better know your names."
Chief spokesman of the two replied, "You ask
what you denied to me. I can't refuse,

for you are in God's grace. Know that in life   49
I, Guido del Duca, felt so much spite
at sight of folk enjoying life, my face

swelled and turned scarlet in my jealous rage.   52
I sowed bad seed, now chew the bitter crop.
No wonder I am blind, for envy's whip

drove me away from human fellowship,   55
engrossing good things for myself and heirs.
O humankind, our mad wish NOT to share

repels the sympathy and love we need,   58
brings endless war. You Tuscans know that well.
Rinier of the house of Calboli

is my companion, last true nobleman   61
of an old family. None after he
have been or will be good, and this is true

of every great family between   64
mountains and Po from Reno to the sea.
Once they were generous and chivalrous.

Art, sport, good manners flourished under them.   67
Now fields of their estates grow fouler weeds
than decades of good farming can repair.

Where now exist Arrigo Mainardi,   70
Guido di Carpigna, good Lizio,
also the good Pierre Traversaro?

In the Romagna a vile bastard race   73
replaces every one; and when again
will a Fabbro be found in Bologna?

76 A Fosco in Faenza? – noble sprout
from a most humble herb. Do not wonder,
Tuscan, if now I weep recalling how

79 Guido da Prata, Ugulino d'Azzo
lived and ruled, Tignoso and company,
the Traversaro and Anastagi,

82 both now without an heir. O Tuscan, think!
I knew these knights, these ladies moved by love
and courtesy, where now is villainy.

85 O Bertinoro, why do you remain?
Your lords abandoned your corrupt old den –
follow them! Bagnacavallo does well

88 in failing to breed men. Castrocaro
does ill, Conio worse by breeding lords
deserving Heaven's curse. The Pagani

91 still keep old honesty, or will when free
of that sly fiend Malnardo, even so
their name cannot regain its ancient fame.

94 O Hugo Fantolini, your good name
is safe since no one now possesses it.
Tuscan, depart. I'd rather weep than speak,

97 our conversation has so wrung my heart."
We knew that these dear spirits heard us go.
Their silence made us sure our way was right.

100 A mighty cry suddenly cleft the air:
"All seeing who I am desire my death!"
Before our ears recovered from that shout

another deafening outcry burst out,   103
too loud to be an echo of the first:
"I am Aglauros who was turned to stone."

Silence returned. Instead of following   106
I stepped beside my guide. Without surprise
he saw the question in my eyes and said

"You have heard Cain, his brother's murderer,   109
and sister-killing Aglauros. These two
are reins to hold back human jealousy,

if we will bite God's bit on Earth below,   112
but most prefer His enemy's sweet bait,
whose hook then pulls them downward into Hell,

while those who wish to see can raise their eyes   115
to starry wheels of Heaven high above,
created beautiful, given in love,

inviting all to soar into the skies."   118

15: Ascent to the Wrathful

1 Each starry and each planetary sphere
circles the Earth, running like child at play
over and under us from day to day.

4 Although it was midnight in Italy
the time was now late afternoon when we,
rounding the hill, walked west toward the sun

7 and level with it, so it warmed my face
pleasantly, till new dazzlement ahead
caused me to raise my hands and shield my sight,

10 and cry aloud, "What radiance is this?"
"All Heaven's housekeepers bring extra light,"
said he. "This one beckons to the next stair.

13 The sight of such will soon not dazzle you
but give as much delight as you can bear."
We neared that angel and I saw he stood

16 where in the cliff a flight of steps began
broader, less steep than any we had known.
A glad angelic voice said, "Enter there,"

19 while his angelic finger pointed up.
We bowed our heads, set feet upon the stair
and climbing heard him very sweetly sing

the fifth beatitude of Jesus Christ: 22
Blessed are the merciful, followed by
You who have overcome a sin, rejoice.

Since we were now ascending side by side   25
I thought to profit by my master's speech.
"You are the voice of reason and my guide,"

I said to him, "so please will you explain   28
what Guido of Romagna meant when he,
blinded for envy, spoke of partnership?"

Said Virgil, "He now knows the social cost   31
of his worst sin, and so condemns it most.
When goods are kept instead of being shared

goods become selfish gain, so fear of loss   34
drives owners to care nothing for the pain
and poverty they cause by seizing more –

more than they need out of the public store   37
of goodness God has given everyone
our common Earth. The more that folk say *ours*

instead of *mine*, the more their charity."   40
I said, "Forgive me, but I cannot see
why riches some enjoy deprive the rest."

Said he, "Your worldly greed has blinded you,   43
for property makes darkness of God's light.
True charity enlarges all we share.

Like sunshine, love enriches all it shows.   46
If these words do not satisfy your need
to know how Heaven's justice works, then wait

49   'til you meet Beatrice, who will wholly
     supply that craving more than I can do.
     Two wounds upon your brow are now erased.

52   Strive to erase five more, though healing them
     will cause some pain." I was about to say
     "Your words have satisfied", when suddenly

55   we reached the topmost stair where I was
     silenced by my eyes. They were surprised
     by a vision of a congregation,

58   in a great temple. A woman there wore
     a sweet maternal look and meekly asked,
     "Son, why treat us so? Father and I feared

61   you were lost before we found you here."
     She said no more, vanished, was replaced by
     a woman with a fretful tear-wet face

64   crying aloud resentfully, "Husband!
     Pisistratus! Athens' almighty lord!
     Are you content that a youth publicly

67   kisses our daughter without punishment?"
     I thought I saw smiling Pisistratus
     and heard his calm reply: "If I punish

70   those who love me and mine, how will I treat
     others who offer hate?" Then I beheld
     a frantic mob all yelling, "Kill! Kill! Kill!"

73   while stoning a youth sinking to the ground
     praying in his death agonies that God
     pardon his enemies. Realities

claimed my mind again. I found my master   76
held my arm as he remarked, "As if drunk,
with shut eyes you have walked for half a league."

Said I, "But I saw visions! Let me explain . . ."   79
"No need, for if you wore a hundred masks
I would still know your thoughts," said he.

"Those visions should have taught you to accept   82
waters of peace from God's eternal source.
I spoke of how you walked upon this road

only to wake you up, put conscious force   85
into what had been blindly stumbling feet.
A dreaming pilgrim sometimes needs a prod."

We walked on through the evening, gazing ahead,   88
when there sped to us from the setting sun
an airborne shred of what seemed smoke or fog

followed by larger darker shreds, and then   91
dense black cloud overtook them and us too.
There was no escape. Spreading everywhere

it robbed us both of sight and the pure air.   94

16: The Wrathful

1   The gloom of night and Hell hid Heaven's light
more wholly than the thickest curtain could
and stung my eyes. Again I shut them tight.

4   My trusty guide offered his shoulder now,
told me to take good hold and not let go,
so in a blind man's state I went ahead

7   led through foul air while he kept telling me
to have great care we did not separate.
Then voices came, singing sweet harmony

10   in prayers for peace and mercy, and each one
beginning with these words, *O Lamb of God.*
"Master," I asked "are these souls penitent?"

13   "Quite right," said he. "By vocal unity
they untie knots of wrath still binding them,
preventing progress on their upward path."

16   A new voice spoke: "Who are you walking through
our smoke, talking as though months and years still
measured time for you?" My master told me,

19   "Answer, and ask how to get out of here."
I said, "O soul cleansing yourself of sin
till fit to face Him who created you,

if you keep company with us I'll tell   22
what brings us here. It is astonishing."
He said, "I will – as far as Heaven allows.

Hearing will join us, though we cannot see.   25
So now, astonish me." "I am not dead,"
said I, "though I have travelled here through Hell.

God's grace demands I see His Heavenly court,   28
a strange idea to modern ears, but true.
Who were you when alive? And if you know

where the next stair is, please escort us there."   31
"I was a Lombard. Marco was my name.
I knew the world yet loved the good at which

people no longer aim or greatly love.   34
To climb up higher go straight on," said he,
adding, "Please pray for me when you're elsewhere."

"I promise that," I said, "but dreadful doubt   37
of human virtue, doubled by your words,
is swelling me. If I don't speak it out

I will explode. Your view of things confirms   40
what Guido of Romagna said below –
the world is overwhelmed by wickedness.

Folk break God's laws. Help me to see the cause   43
that I can make it known. Astrologers
blame stars for our sins." He cried out "Brother,

alas! Be not as blind as those!" Sighing   46
he said, "We would have no *choice* if ruled by
blind necessity. Each would be a part

49 of process without consciousness! Justice!
    Joy in doing well! Misery for sin!
    Our sense of choice is fact, like sense of light,

52 sound, heat, weight, pleasure, pain. Denying one
    rejects all common sense reality.
    Appetites are from Heaven and therefore good,

55 but lead to greed if wrongly understood.
    Our senses let us work out what is right
    and so oppose mistaken appetite.

58 Strengthened by exercise this virtuous fight
    conquers all things, making a free new mind
    just limited by what is nearer God.

61 If the world goes astray, then search within!
    Find in yourself the root and source of sin.
    As you want guidance let me be your guide.

64 Listen. When a tiny soul comes from the hand
    of Him who loved it while creating it,
    the soul knows nothing. The joyful maker

67 lets it move eagerly to take delight
    in many small things, some of which are bad.
    Thus it needs parents who will curb it well,

70 direct it to the best things it should love.
    Thus we need laws and kings enforcing them,
    priesthoods who point to New Jerusalem,

73 the happy state God wills us to create.
    That is why he makes laws. Who do they curb?
    None. None. Our shepherds do not lead their flocks

by peaceful waters and through pastures green   76
where they may safely graze. They fleece their sheep
and sell the wool for gain. When people see

their leaders worship wealth they too adore,   79
greed multiplies itself. All fight for more.
Bad government makes Earth a wicked place –

nature is not corrupt. There was a time   82
when Rome strove hard to make the whole world good.
Two grand authorities like double suns

showed men the laws of Earth and laws of God.   85
These quell each other now. When King and Pope
equally try to wield the sword and crook,

neither corrects or fears the other one.   88
Observe the modern state of Italy!
Courage and courtesy were here before

King Frederick attacked the papacy,   91
which fought back just like he. Now you may go
by Arno, Tiber, Adige and Po

nor fear to meet with honest company.   94
Just three old men do well in ancient ways
and won't be there for long: good Gherardo,

Conrad di Palazzo, also Guido   97
da Castel, all famed for their honesty.
Tell people that the Church of Rome's attempt

to seize both Heavenly and Earthly power   100
corrupts itself, corrupting others too."
"I see you're right," I said, "and also see

103 why Hebrew law forbad that Levi's sons
   (the Jewish priests) inherit property.
   But who is this Gherardo that you say

106 still shows old virtues to this rotten age?"
   "You puzzle me," said he. "Your speech is Tuscan.
   Surely all Tuscans know good Gherardo?

109 I won't say more of him except to give
   his daughter Gaia's name. God bless you both.
   Here now, alas, we have to part since I

112 see light through smoke ahead, and so goodbye."

17: On and Up

Those who have been in mountain mists too thick   1
for eyes to pierce, then seen them thinning down
to let the sun show as a small, pale disc,

know how the setting sun appeared to me   4
as the thick fog dispersed. Shorn of bright rays
it hung above the sea, while far below

dim shadows hid the shores. As we walked on   7
imaginary visions mastered me,
visions of ancient anger and past wrong,

so great that I believe no trumpet blast,   10
or stormy thunderclap, however strong
could have recalled my eyes to where I was.

Procne appeared, changed to a swallow's form   13
for punishing unfaithful Tereus
by feeding him their son, baked in a pie.

Then I beheld another fantasy   16
of Haman, fierce and scornful, hanging high,
thus rightly punished by an angry king

for outrage against Jewish Mordecai.   19
Lastly I saw a daughter's wild despair
at sight of mother who had hanged herself

22 because the man her daughter was to wed,
Prince Turnus, had been slaughtered in a fight.
As sleep is broken when a sudden light

25 strikes through a dream, a brightness wakened me
whiter, more dazzling than the sun at noon.
On looking round to see just where I stood

28 a gentle voice said, "Here is your ascent."
This drove away all other thought, but though
longing to look upon the speaker's face

31 its brightness baffled me. My leader said,
"This angel showing us the upward way
without us asking, hides in his own light.

34 Accept his courtesy. Climb upstairs now.
We cannot move at all when it is night."
My foot was on the uphill path's first step

37 when a wing brushed my face, a soft voice said,
"Blest are peacemakers, free of sinful wrath."
As we went up, the setting sun's last rays

40 were slanting steep. On each side stars appeared.
"O strength!" I inward groaned, "Why disappear?",
for as we reached the highest step my weight

43 felt heavier than stone. We both sank down
like boats left high and dry upon a beach.
I listened and heard nothing, asked at last,

46 "Dear Master, say what sin is purging here?
Our legs can't move. Don't let that stop your tongue."
He answered thus: "Sloth prevents energy

achieving what it should, so here you'll see   49
how healthy active love must be restored.
Listen and pluck good fruit from our delay.

Since love is God's creative force, all things   52
(time, space, star, sun, earth, insect, human child)
keep going by God's love. Love has two kinds:

the natural, and of the mind. Mistakes   55
are never natural. Only minds can err,
loving wrong things, or good ones with too much

or with too little force. Thus love brings both   58
good deeds and deeds requiring punishment.
When we attend to God, the Source of All,

our desires are kept in proper measure.   61
We are not then seduced by sinful pleasure,
until we look away and therefore stray.

As none can harm the source of what they are   64
(trying to wound the sun would be as mad)
the only law of God that we can break

is that which says, *Love neighbour as yourself,*   67
the rule for Jews that Moses carved in stone
and God when born as Man gave to us all.

And so the only evil folk can love   70
is harming other folk in three main ways
you know by having seen them punished below:

first, trying to excel by doing down   73
those by our side – perversions born of pride.
Second, by fear of losing wealth or fame

76 when those nearby do well – envy's the name.
    Lastly, when insult, real or by mistake
    inflames blind anger hungry for revenge.

79 You know these states of lamentable love.
    Think now of those you'll see lamenting here
    who loved true good with insufficient zeal,

82 and higher still you'll find three kinds of grief
    endured for not loving the best stuff well.
    I leave you to work these out for yourself.

85 My son, believe me, I have said enough."

18: Love and Sloth

Silent once more, my teacher closely watched 1
my face for understanding of his words.
Though thirsting to hear more I held my tongue

lest further questioning would pester him. 4
That good instructor guessed what I suppressed.
With smile and nod he told me to ask more.

"Master," said I, "you clarify my brain, 7
so say again how love induces both
virtuous actions and their opposite."

"Give me your full attention now," said he, 10
"and concentrate your analytic mind
on truth that Plato gave humanity

before Epictetus made scholars blind. 13
All souls are born with appetite for love,
so bound to look at what most seems to please

whenever pleasure beckons them, and thus 16
attractive visions from outside ourselves
enter our souls. Love is what draws them in,

makes soul and vision a new entity. 19
Thus nature's objects take a hold of soul,
and as the flames leap upward to the sun

22   (the source of every fire) no soul can rest
     before she blends with objects that she loves.
     But they are wrong who say all love is good.

25   Substantial minds possess material shapes
     and yet are different, though only seen
     in what they do and show, like grass when green.

28   None know how virtue starts. It moves our hearts
     as bees are moved to building honeycomb.
     No praise for such instinctive skill is due,

31   because such instincts should not be obeyed
     till brought in tune with other wills as right
     and communal, as are the busy bees.

34   We have to choose between bad love and good
     by freely reasoning, as all folk can
     when love submits to reason as it should.

37   Indeed, necessity creates our love,
     but free-will only gives it right control.
     Reason and free-willed souls are gifts from God

40   to everyone: Greek, Roman, Pagan, Jew
     and those like you born since that hero died
     who conquered death. My words sound cut and dried.

43   They point to Heaven's Grace but they stop short
     at gate of Paradise, where that pure soul
     Beatrice will become your only guide."

46   Now it was midnight and the rising moon
     upon the wane had reached its height, and hung
     among the stars like tilted golden bowl.

The poet who had brought his birthplace fame   49
now dropped the burden of instructing me.
As we reclined I pondered drowsily

on all the noble thought he had made mine,   52
till noises at my back awakened me,
for round the mountain track there came a mob

who seemed at first a wildly charging herd   55
of peasants drunk on half-fermented wine,
but as they neared I saw most were well dressed.

Not revelry but pain was driving them,   58
a frantic pain allowing them no rest.
I and my guide, our energy renewed,

sprang to our feet and sprinted at the side   61
of two in front who alternately cried,
"Hail Mary, pregnant with our Saviour,

rushing uphill to greet her cousin Beth!"   64
and, "Caesar, in haste to conquer Lerida,
routed Marseilles and then swooped into Spain."

Meanwhile the horde behind were shouting out,   67
"Go faster! Faster still! Slowness in love
prevents the Grace that blesses from above!"

My master cried, "Your mighty urgency,   70
O souls, will one day purge the laziness
delaying your salvation when alive,

but this man lives. Heaven has ordered him   73
to climb above you when the sun appears.
Please teach us how to reach the nearest stair."

76 Someone among these racers answered him,
    "Follow us. You will see a staircase soon.
    Forgive me if I have to run away

79 and seem discourteous. I lived in great
    Emperor Barbarossa's day, he who
    plundered Milan. I was then abbot of

82 San Zeno in Verona, and can say
    who rules it now has one foot in the grave,
    and soon in Hell will curse what he has done.

85 He has made certain that his bastard son,
    crippled in legs and mind, will take his place,
    keeping a good priest from that benefice . . ."

88 He raced so far ahead I heard no more,
    but I was glad to recollect his words
    before my master said, "Now look behind.

91 Here come the two who goad the slothful on
    by telling them some things to keep in mind."
    At once I heard a strong voice loudly say,

94 "Of those to whom the Red Sea opened wide,
    three only lived to see The Promised Land
    because of slothfulness upon the way."

97 Another cried, "When Aeneas led forth
    his Trojan band to the grand enterprise
    of founding Rome, many abandoned him

100 in Sicily, and died there without fame."
    I paused then till that multitude had passed
    quite out of sight. My head was in a whirl.

Each thought that came inspired another one   103
or two, or three that contradicted it
with hectic fancies, frivolous or deep,

until I sank beside the road, asleep.   106

19: To the Avaricious

1   In a cold hour before the vast dark cone
    of shadow we call night is split by dawn,
    I dreamed I was approached by a foul crone,

4   hunch-backed, club-footed, hands like vulture claws,
    bald-headed, stammering from drooling lips.
    Her wrinkled skin was corpse-like yellow-grey.

7   I stared and saw her change like frosty field
    with bright sun warming it. Her skin grew smooth,
    blushing a lovely rose. She stood up slim,

10   erect. Her young face kindly smiled on me,
     framed by rich locks of chestnut-coloured hair.
     Her soft throat crooned so blithe an air, my ears

13   drank each note eagerly. Here's what she sang.
     "I am Sirena. Sailors love my voice,
     leaving the sea for joy on land with me.

16   My singing stopped Ulysses wandering,
     and none I satisfy try to depart."
     Before that sweet sound died a stern voice cried

19   "O Virgil Virgil Virgil, what is *that*?"
     I found a stately lady at my side
     glaring on Sirena indignantly.

Virgil appeared, saw my companion   22
and then abruptly stripped Sirena bare.
The belly he exposed gave off such stink

it wakened me. I sat up. There he stood   25
saying, "I've called you thrice. Let's find the stair."
I rose and saw the day was well begun,

light flooding all the circles of the hill.   28
We marched right on the road where the bright sun
now cast my shade ahead. I stared at it

with downcast, brooding face, my body bent   31
like half a bridge's arch until I heard,
"Here now you may ascend", in tones more sweet

than spoken by the tongue of any friend.   34
An angel pointed to an opening
between two walls of flinty stone. He said,

"Blessèd are mourners: they shall be consoled,"   37
and as we passed, fanned us with swanlike wings.
When we had passed above the angel's head,

my master asked, "What's wrong with you?" I said,   40
"A recent dream has filled me full of fear."
He answered, "That old hag you saw was she

who makes all those above us weep. You saw   43
how to reject her – be content with that.
Strike heels into the earth and climb! Look up!

Beyond that blue, God's starry wheels revolve."   46
The hooded falcon stares down at its feet,
but when released, soars up into the sky.

49 Now like that bird was I. Sped by desire
   I ran right up that stair to the fifth ledge,
   then stopped astonished. Where the road swept round

52 folk laid out flat covered each foot of ground,
   face down in dirt. They sobbed words hard to hear
   but I made out, "We sold our souls for dust."

55 My master cried, "O you whom God permits
   repentance by such pains, I truly know
   Justice and Hope have saved you from despair.

58 We pass among you to a greater height.
   Will someone please tell us a shortcut there?"
   From just ahead of us a voice replied,

61 "Since you are free from having to lie prone,
   walk with right hand toward the outer rim."
   My master saw my eyes imploring him,

64 knew what I asked and nodded his consent.
   Stooping beside that unpurged sufferer
   I said, "Please tell me of the man you were.

67 I know the more repentant tears you shed,
   will bring you sooner into Paradise,
   but for a little time tell me instead

70 why you must lie with backside to the sky.
   Say too if I may serve you in some way,
   when I at last return to Italy."

73 "I'll tell you why Heaven turns me upside down,"
   said he, "but speak first of the man I was
   before elected to the papacy.

Into the Gulf of Genoa there flows 76
a limpid river down a pleasant glen
called Lavagna, which also is a name

my people used and I inherited 79
from count and cardinal no better than
the other priests whose greed disgrace the Church.

But when Saint Peter's shoes were on my feet 82
a purer spirit suddenly was mine,
too late! Too late I struggled with the weight

of the Pope's mantle. For one short month 85
and a few days I tried to shake it free
of parasites who clung as I had done.

That struggle killed me. It will save my soul 88
when I have cleaned the foul thing I've become:
a creature given up to selfish greed.

Here is my punishment. There is no worse 91
pain on this Holy Mountain. We refused
to see the shining multitude of stars.

Enchanted by our wilful avarice 94
we fixed our eyes downward on Earthly things,
so Justice now must clamp us here face down

quite motionless in dirt, as in a vice. 97
This distress was our own choice! Tears alone
can wash away the dirt I partly am,

freeing what God created me to be." 100
I knelt and he, sensing my reverence
demanded, "Why do you lower yourself?"

103 "I have to bow. I cannot stand," said I,
"before your dignity in suffering."
He commanded, "Brother, straighten your legs!

106 I am like you and all of us, servant
of only One. There is no slavery
or mastery for equals under God,

109 who calls His Pope *servant of my servants*,
which several forget. And now please go.
You asked if you could serve me down on Earth.

112 My niece Alagia is thriving there.
Let her know what and why I suffer here.
Her inborn goodness can relieve my soul.

115 Uncle in Purgatory tells her so."

20: Hoarders and Wasters

While thirsting for more words with that good Pope   1
I found his silence stronger than my will,
so had to leave before I'd drunk my fill.

Between the prostrate mourners and cliff base   4
a narrow space left something like a path.
I paced along this, close behind my guide,

appalled by lamentations on our right   7
from those who now felt greed's iniquity.
To Hell, you wolf of Greed! Your poisoned fangs

have damned more souls than any other beasts!   10
Your gluttony enforces poverty.
You spread starvation by your wasteful feasts.

Having to place our footsteps carefully   13
we slowly moved along this narrow way,
then from in front we heard a clear voice cry,

"Sweet Mary!" Like a woman giving birth   16
in agony that yet suggested joy,
adding, "What could exceed the poverty

of labour pains within a trough of hay,   19
between the muzzles of an ox and ass?"
A pause, then the voice said, "Fabricius

22 chose virtue and poverty, not riches
by military conquest. So should we."
Wanting to see the soul who said these things

25 I pressed ahead, hearing him talk about
Saint Nicholas, whose generosity
brought marriage to the poorest of young maids.

28 I said, "O soul in pain announcing good,
please tell me who you were. Your words will be
recorded down on Earth when I return."

31 Said he, "I will reply, though not because
your good report will do the Earth much good.
You have a radiance that pleases me.

34 From me sprang up that monarchy of France
which overshadows Christendom and stops
much good fruit growing there. If Douai, Lille,

37 Ghent, Bruges had strength, they'd cast it off,
for which I pray to He who judges All.
In Paris Dad was butcher. I became

40 head of the royal household when the last
of Charlemagne's great line, a monk, expired.
I had such wealth and friends that very soon

43 my son was wedded to the widowed queen.
From me, Hugh Capet, grew that lengthy line
of Philips, Louises, commanding France,

46 their bones entombed in consecrated earth.
As long as they inherited Provence,
they did no good and very little harm

but riches strengthened their rapacity.   49
To further it, by force and fraud they took
Ponthieu and Normandy and Gascony,

then went beyond, killing in Italy   52
Conradin, and better still, poisoning
Saint Thomas Aquinas. Soon you will see

another prince to bring my France more fame.   55
Using hypocrisy (that Judas lance)
he will burst in the guts of Florence,

gaining no land by it but gold and shame.   58
The less he thinks of this, the worse for him.
His brother sells his daughter to an old

and evil count, also for gold. O Greed,   61
what fouler misdeeds can you bring my race?
To make these crimes seem less, I can foresee

the fleur-de-lis flag enter Anagni,   64
see Christ's appointed Vicar, captured, mocked,
fed with vinegar and slain between

two live thieves by a new Pontius Pilate   67
so unscrupulous, he goes on to loot
the treasury that good Knights Templar use,

escorting pilgrims to Jerusalem.   70
O Lord my God, when shall I gladly see
your vengeance smiting down these evil men?

You heard me calling on the Holy Ghost's   73
one Virgin Bride. By day we think of Her
and others without greed; at night we brood

76 on those whose sin resembled ours, such as
Pygmalion, traitor, thief, parricide
through lust for gold; Midas, whose silly greed

79 made him ridiculous – a king with ass's ears.
We think of foolish Achan stoned to death
for keeping gold Joshua meant for God;

82 Ananias and Saphira his wife,
stealing coin from the first Christian kirks,
and dropping dead, rebuked. We praise the kicks

85 the angel's horse gave Heliodorus
when by force he tried to steal the treasure
from Jerusalem's temple. We lastly

88 shout in chorus, "Crassus, how does gold taste?"
remembering Rome's grasping millionaire
whose mouth and throat a Parthian monarch filled

91 with molten gold. Sometimes we yell aloud
or softly sing the stories that we share,
or ponder them. You heard me praising Mary.

94 Others were also thinking of her then."
We parted from him, trying to walk fast,
but suddenly the whole great mountain shook

97 as if it fell. I felt a deathly chill.
Delos, floating island, quaked not more
when sunk and fixed by Jupiter, to be

100 a birthplace for the gods of sun and moon.
Mourners on every side shouted aloud.
My master drew me close, said, "Do not fear,

for I am guiding you." Then I made out   103
from the folk nearest us the words they cried
were *Gloria in Excelsis Deo*.

Like shepherds who first heard this news proclaimed   106
we stood stock-still and stupefied until
they shut their mouths. The mountain ceased to shake.

Again we walked upon the narrow path   108
beside those spirits weeping as before.
Never did ignorance make me so keen

to understand, or so afraid to ask.   111

21: Statius

1   The thirst for truth not to be satisfied
until Christ quench it was tormenting me.
I picked my steps upon that awkward way

4   while grieving for the mourners' long delay
when all at once I noticed we were three.
Luke writes of how two followers of Christ

7   after his crucifixion, found themselves
joined on a road by One they did not know
at first, or recognise as He. We two

10 were overtaken from behind, nor knew
until we heard, "Brothers, God send you peace."
Said Virgil, "May you find it with the bless'd

13 in that high court of God which exiles me."
"But why?" the stranger asked as we walked on,
"If you are still excluded from God's Grace,

16 how did you climb so high on Heaven's stair?"
At this my poet said, "See this man's face!
It still has marks the angel at the gate

19 wrote on his brow. He'll reach a greater place
though still his thread of life is being spun.
Death has not slit it yet. His soul – sister

of yours and mine – could not climb here alone,   22
having no eyes like ours. I was released
from Limbo as his guide and do my best.

But can you tell what shook this sacred hill?   25
What made it ring with shouts of jubilee?"
These questions chimed so well with my desires

I listened for the answers eagerly.   28
The shade replied, "Nothing disorderly
like rain, dew, hail, frost, snow can rise above

the three steps where Saint Peter's curate sits.   31
To wind and lightning also we're immune
and subterranean shocks. What moves us

is a soul released by love from sin,   34
free at last to rise where it wants to be.
I lay in pain over five hundred years,

and my release is a most glad surprise.   37
You felt the tremor, heard the shout of praise
from the devout. God send them soon above!"

The drink is more enjoyed the worse the thirst.   40
How this intelligence delighted me!
My wise guide said, "I now perceive the cords

of conscience that hold these mourners down,   43
have been untied for you, hence jubilee.
Please tell us who you were, and why you were

thus pinioned down for many centuries."   46
"I lived when Titus was our Emperor,
he who made deadly warfare on the Jews.

49 My gift of song was such that from Toulouse,
Rome drew me to itself, and placed the crown
of myrtle on my brow for poetry.

52 My name's still spoken there – it's Statius.
I sang the wars of Thebes: and tried to make
Achilles hero of an epic song,

55 but that was rather more than I could do.
The spark that kindled my poetic aim
leapt from the flame of Virgil's *Aeneid*,

58 where many other poets have caught fire.
He taught me how heroic history,
the strife of gods and men in daily life

61 is the pure substance of morality.
Without his *Aeneid* none would believe
my verses worth a penny. Could I live

64 when Virgil lived I gladly would endure,
what? . . . an extra Purgatorial year."
These words turned Virgil to me with a look

67 that silently said, "Silence!" Willpower
cannot do all. Laughter and tears are so
near passions causing them, sometimes they show

70 whether we will or no. I only smiled,
at which the spirit looked into my eyes,
where most expression is, and said, "Forgive,

73 but I must ask what caused that gleam of mirth?"
Between command for silence and these words
begging for speech, what could I do? I sighed.

My master understood for he too sighed   76
and said, "Reply. Answer his eagerness."
"You wondered, ancient spirit, at my smiling,"

I began. "Hear now a greater wonder.   79
He leading me is he who taught you how
to sing of gods and men – Virgil, I mean.

I only smiled because you spoke of him."   82
Statius, stooped to cuddle Virgil's feet,
was told by him, "Brother, that can't be done.

We both of us are shades, so bodiless,   85
and neither nobler than the other one."
Statius, rising, said, "It proves my love

that I forgot we lack solidity."   88

22: To the Gluttonous

1   We three then passed the angel of the stair
    taking us up to the next mountain ledge,
    but not before his wing brushed from my brow

4   the scar of the fifth P, as he announced,
    "Blessèd are they that thirst for righteousness."
    Lighter of foot than I had ever felt,

7   I followed easily these two swift souls
    conversing as they climbed; heard Virgil say,
    "All good and selfless love inspires a love

10 reflecting it. I heard from Juvenal
    (who came to Limbo and had been your friend)
    how highly you regarded me, also

13 he praised your work so much I thought of you
    far more than others I have never met.
    I hope you will consider me a friend

16 if I ask something many might think rude.
    How came (with all the wisdom you possessed)
    the sin of avarice to foul your breast?

19 You need not answer. That is understood."
    Statius smiled a little at these words
    then answered, "All you say declares your love,

although appearances have led astray.   22
Because I lay face downward in the grit
among the hoarders, I appeared like one.

My sin, however, was the opposite.   25
I was a wastrel, spending money fast
to glut my appetites: a jolly sin

I thought, but squandering is just as bad   28
as hoarding money tightly in a bank.
That I'm not where wasters jostle hoarders

endlessly in Hell, I have you to thank,   31
for in your *Aeneid*'s third book I read
To what crimes have not many been misled

by that infernal appetite for gold?   34
This made me stop and think because I saw
that if I did not rectify my flaw

I'd sink to be more beastly than I was."   37
"I'm puzzled by another mystery,"
my master said. "Your Theban epic deals

with history, but gives no hint of Faith,   40
lacking which no good effort sets us free.
Faith releases you from prison here

to find (as I will not) a higher home.   43
Some guide in Rome directed you into
Saint Peter's holy ark, which has no place

within your poems. Why?" Statius said,   46
"Cowardice stopped me emulating you,
in your third Eclogue heralding the birth

49 of one whose reign would bring us peace on Earth
    and happily restore true Golden Age,
    creating thus a better human race.

52 You died before our Saviour was born,
    I lived after the Resurrection.
    Your poetry first made of me a poet,

55 then taught me how to be a Christian
    in days when there were preachers of Christ's faith,
    and these I visited. Their upright ways

58 soon taught me to despise all other sects
    so I was baptised when Domitian
    was persecuting theirs. I meanly chose

61 to seem a Pagan still. Four centuries
    I raced around the slothful circle till
    my lukewarmness for that was purged away.

64 Now say (if there is still time as we go)
    where that old Latin author Terence is,
    and Plautus, Cecilius, Varius.

67 Are these damned? And in what place?" My guide said,
    "In Limbo, where I meet them face to face
    with that great blind Greek Homer, he

70 whose genius gave new life to all the arts,
    with thinkers, playwrights and historians,
    and the heroic folk of whom they wrote."

73 The poets, having reached the topmost stair,
    were not quite sure which way to turn until
    my teacher said, "Let us go to the right."

They did. I followed very close behind,   76
learning much from their talk of poetry
how I should write my own. And then we saw

a tall tree in the middle of the road   79
with many fruits whose scent was sweet and good.
As a fir tapers from great width to height

this tapered downward, so could not be climbed.   82
From the high cliff upon the left a stream
of pure clear water fell among the boughs

which, glistening, absorbed it while a voice   85
among them cried, "You may not eat this food!"
It added, "Mary, at the marriage feast,

cared more for nourishment of other guests   88
than for her mouth, and anciently in Rome
women preferred pure water for their drink.

By hungering the prophet Daniel   91
grew wiser still. In the first Golden Age
hunger made acorns seem the sweetest food.

The Baptist thought honey and locusts good."   94

23: The Gluttons

1   I gazed aloft through the green foliage
     like hawker who wastes hours pursuing birds
     until my more-than-father said, "Come, son!

4   Make better use of time." Turning my face
     and running after him I heard a hymn
     sung by a chorus mingling joy and pain:

7   "Lord, open up our lips." I asked my guide,
     "Father, please tell me what this signifies."
     Said he, "Souls paying God what is His due."

10   Like travellers absorbed in thought who rush
     by others with one quick enquiring look,
     so, coming from behind and speeding on,

13   a crowd, silent and devout, overtook
     and passed us with astonished stares. Their eyes
     were deeply sunk, their white skins clung tight

16   to bones beneath. Erysichthon who gnawed
     his limbs when wild with hunger was as gaunt,
     and those starved in Jerusalem's great siege

19   where Miriam ate her child. Skull sockets
     seemed gemless rings. The nose-bone M was plain
     to any who read OMO in a face.

I knew not why the sight and scent of fruit   22
had famished them, but greatly wondered at
their harsh emaciation, scabbiness,

and agony. One turned his eyes on me   25
and cried, "Rejoice! What goodness brings you here?"
Not by his looks I knew him, but his voice —

he was my friend, Forese Donati.   28
"Ignore," he begged, "my withered skin and flesh.
Please tell me about you. Who are the two

you travel with? You must explain all this."   31
"I wept to see your face when dead," I said,
"and weep to see it now. In God's name say

what starves you? Upset by your present state,   34
I don't see how to answer questions yet."
"The spring of water nourishing that tree,"

said he, "makes me as lean as all of us   37
who sing as we pass under branches of
that fragrant fruit and spray. It renews our

hunger and thirst. We glutted appetite   40
to such excess in life these painful pangs
are needed to restore our holiness.

It feels like pain but is a comfort too,   43
bringing us closer to the tree where One
who died to make us free was crucified —

our Lord Himself." I said, "But Forese,   46
you only died five years ago. I know
you were not very bad, but men as good

49 are waiting centuries outside the gate
before admitted to ascend the stairs.
What lets you come so fast and far?" He said,

52 "My widow Nelly's tears and constant prayers,
heard in the court where love is highest law.
She's that rare thing among our womenfolk,

55 a widow who still loves the man she wed
and does not seek romps in another bed.
Her prayers have raised me up and through the gate

58 and stairs above to here. She's one of few.
The savage women of Sardinia
are chaste beside most female Florentines.

61 Brother, I prophesy an evil time
when priests from holy pulpits will denounce
our noble dames for how they flaunt their tits.

64 I hear that Muslim wives dress modestly,
and wives from equally barbaric shores
need none to tell them not to dress like whores.

67 I wish they saw ahead what tragedies
will come before their baby boys grow beards.
Dear brother, it is time to tell your tale

70 not just to me: also my company.
Your shadow on the road amazes them."
At that I said, "Farese, I will not

73 give tongue to all we did when we were young.
I left such wildness just four days ago
when my best teacher led me bodily

through Hell then up to here, circling this hill   76
that straightens folk made crooked by bad will.
He'll be my guide till I meet Beatrice.

He is Virgil, the other Statius   79
for whom all Purgatory shook like mad
releasing him, as you will one day be.

How great that both of us can now be glad."   82

24: Toward Temperance

1   This conversation did not slow us down.
     We went on like a yacht before fair winds.
     The former gluttons who appeared twice dead

4   found us astonishing. Continuing,
     I said, "Please speak of how Piccarda is,
     and of these gazing, may I know their names?"

7   "My lovely sister is in Paradise,"
     said he, "as for the rest of us, although
     almost featureless from fasting, none seek

10 anonymity. There is" (he pointed)
     "Bonagiunta, poet and toper
     of Lucca. He with the most wizened face

13 is Martin, Pope, Defender of our Faith,
     who died because he over-ate the eels
     of Bolsena, stewed in sweet Vernage wine . . ."

16 He mentioned more who did not seem ashamed
     but pleased by my attention: Ubaldin
     de la Pila who made new recipes

19 and now from hunger bites the air; Archbishop
     Boniface who kept a mighty table;
     Lord Marquess of Fornay whose thirst got worse

the more he drank; but Bonagiuta   22
of Lucca seemed most keen to speak with me.
I turned to him again. From his dry throat

the word "Gentucca" came. "I do not know,"   25
said I, "what that means. Can you speak more plain?"
"A woman born but not yet wed," said he,

"will make the town of Lucca kind to you.   28
If you don't understand that, never mind.
Thus it shall be. Let us now speak of verse.

Surely you wrote the poem which begins,   31
Ladies who have intelligence of love.
That was a splendid novelty. Your lines

have sweetness, strength, passionate nakedness   34
that almost made me blush." I shrugged, replied,
"I write as love commands." He cried aloud,

"Yes, that is why you beat a poor old bard: 37
like me, and he they call the Notary
of Sicily, and Tuscan Guittone.

Compared with yours our style is cold and hard.   40
Our grandest efforts were just good enough
to point you on the way to better stuff,

but love is what has made your lines excel."   43
Then he fell silent with a sigh and smile.
Cranes wintering upon the Nile take wing

to fly much faster in a single line.   46
So too the former gluttons rearranged
to travel forward at a swifter pace.

49 As some let others race ahead while they
    regain their breath, Forese paused to ask,
    "How long before we meet again?" I said,

52 "I do not know how long I have to live
    but think my healthy years ahead are few.
    Our Florence mocks at virtue, praises sin,

55 and hurries down the road to ruin's brink."
    Said he, "And one who'll help to push her in
    is my own brother, Corso Donati,

58 and he will meet his end by being tossed
    and dragged behind his horse along the ground.
    Dear friend, farewell. I must exert myself

61 to make up for the precious time I've lost."
    With lengthened stride he disappeared ahead.
    Beside these captains of the human mind

64 I followed at a slower pace behind
    until the curving road brought into sight
    another tree fruit-laden like the first.

67 A mob with arms stretched upward underneath
    were begging, though I could not hear their speech.
    The tree, like adult teasing greedy child,

70 wagged fruit above their grabbing fingers' reach
    until the starving grabbers ran away.
    As Virgil, Statius and I drew near

73 a voice out of the leaves commanded us,
    "Go forward! On the summit of this hill
    you'll see the tree whose fruit made Eve so ill.

This is a shoot from it. Recall fights lost   76
by those who gave way to their appetites:
drunken centaurs Theseus had to slay;

the Jews whom Gideon chose not to use   79
because they quenched their thirst incautiously."
At foot of inner cliff we picked our way,

hearing more punishments for gluttony.   82
We walked on far beyond that second tree
in sombre meditation without talk

until another voice astonished me: 85
"What are you three thinking of?" Timidly
I raised my head, beheld a figure glow

more red than furnace-heated glass or steel.   88
"If you would go above, turn here," it said.
"This stairway is for people seeking peace."

I could not face this figure, kept my eyes   91
on Virgil's heels, following close behind.
As the soft breeze in May before the dawn

feels with its scent of dew-wet grass and flowers   94
I felt a wing brush my brow, heard these words:
"Blessèd are those without foul appetite

whose only hunger is for what is right."   97

25: To the Lustful

1   The time had come to climb without delay
    for it was after noon. The narrow way
    made us go single file. Within my brain

4   a question formed. Just like a little stork
    wishing to fly, raises a wing, but since
    it fears to leave the nest, drops it again,

7   I was like that, hardly dared clear my throat
    when without backward glance my master spoke:
    "You are on fire to ask me something. Shoot!"

10 Assured once more I said, "Shades do not eat,
    so what makes some of them so very thin?"
    Said he, "Our figures in a looking glass

13 are bodiless, yet show us as we are,
    thinner or fatter though they do not eat.
    I know a better explanation's due.

16 Statius, may I pass that job to you?"
    Came the reply, "You know as much as I,
    but your request is one that I accept."

19 Statius told me, "Listen son, and learn.
    The human male's creative fluids go
    through vein and heart, infuse and shape each part

until in loving acts they overflow   22
the female vessel, thus fertilising
her passive fluids into a new life

with whole new soul, but not yet rational.   25
Think it a plant containing seeds. These sprout
into organs that it needs, moving like

water creature, jellyfish or tadpole   28
stirring in the womb. By natural growth
these turn into a complex animal.

How animal becomes a child with mind   31
is mystery. A wiser man than we,
Arabian Averroes, could find

no organ of self-consciousness so said   34
it naturally grew in new-born brains.
Untrue! Believe what Aquinas deduced.

As soon as nature forms the foetal brain   37
the First Creator welcomes it as His.
Rejoicing, he breathes into it His own

freedom that can reflect upon itself.   40
Think of how sunlight changes grapes to wine.
God's gift of free thought is far more divine.

When, after life, the soul is loosed from flesh   43
it keeps those faculties it gained in life –
memory, intelligence and will –

but more enhanced, much keener than before.   46
These rush it to the one or other shore
where wait the ferries that will take them to

49 fit states in Hell or here, for what they've made
    of their immortal souls now radiate
    on air their shapes and size while still alive,

52 as sunbeams build across a rain-wet sky
    a bow of colours to entrance the eye.
    That shape moves as the soul moves, for each sense

55 has organs letting it walk, speak, smile, weep
    as you experienced. Passions change
    souls, shapes, as appeared in glutton's ring,

58 prompting you to ask for explanation."
    We set foot on the last road round that height,
    turned right and I was terrified to see

61 huge flames that blasted from the inner cliff
    to almost reach the ring-road's outer edge.
    A strong up-draft of wind from down below

64 drove back that fiery hedge a little way,
    leaving space along the precipice's edge
    where we could walk in single file, me last

67 between cremation and a deadly fall.
    My master said (but did not need to say)
    "Be careful here and do not swerve at all."

70 Then from the endless bonfire at my side
    that mighty hymn, *O Lord have mercy* came,
    sung by a band of spirits in the flame.

73 Fear for my skin and curiosity
    made me stare to and fro between my feet
    and choir of shades who, finishing the hymn

then cried aloud the words that Mary said   76
on hearing she was carrying a child:
But I have never known a man! They then

softly began singing the hymn again.   79
After each hymn they chanted a new phrase
denouncing lust or praising chastity,

and with these penances they pass their days.   82

26: The Lustful

1   While my good master still called out to me,
    "Take care! Beware!" we walked in single file
    along the precipice's outer rim.

4   The sinking sun made bright the Western sky
    and being at our altitude it cast
    my shadow on the flames we travelled past,

7   so yellow flames appeared to burn more red.
    As all the shades were journeying our way
    the nearest ones attended to that sight.

10 A pair on whom I eavesdropped near me said,
    "That man lives in the flesh." "Yes, I agree,"
    whereupon both came close to me although

13 carefully keeping in the fire because
    escaping it was not their main desire.
    One questioned me, "O you who walk behind

16 the other two, tell me (burning with thirst
    in dreadful heat) what others want to know.
    How come you here without having to die?"

19 A strange sight silenced me before I spoke.
    From far ahead I saw a running crowd
    come down that blazing road, and rushing past

they kissed the crowd advancing on my side   22
so fast that no delay was caused, like ants
exchanging nose-rubs to convey good will.

Not stopping all tried to out-shout the rest.   25
"Sodom! Gomorrah!" those departing yelled.
Those going my way bawled, "The Cretan queen

in wooden cow got fucked by bull!"   28
As cranes divide, one flight departing north
to Arctic snows, one south to Egypt's sands,

both sides went different ways, singing hymns,   31
chanting scripture, with tears confessing sins,
and thus in pain obtaining holiness.

Those who had first approached me came again,   34
and I, respecting their desire began,
"O souls whose thirst for righteousness will be

as Jesus said, fulfilled at last one day,   37
in Paradise a saint has ordercd me
to look at what God made for humankind

from the world's centre to the outmost stars.   40
But say (for I will write it in a book)
who were those folk going the other way?

And also, who are you?" The couple gaped   43
like Highlanders bemused by city streets
but soon resumed civility again.

The first shade said, "Your soul is truly blest.   46
It will learn how to die better than most.
Those you saw run the other way have sinned

49   as Caesar did, whose soldiers called him 'queen'.
     They shout 'Sodom' in self-reproach. We too
     enjoyed unlawful feasts of lust. My crowd

52   shout the disgraceful name of Pasiphaë
     who in lust turned into beast. I do not know
     all who are here. Guido Guinicelli

55   is my name. I so sorrowed for my sins
     death sent me quickly here. I'll soon be free."
     In King Lycurgus' time two orphan boys

58   found that their mother lived. I partly felt
     their joy on hearing Guido's name for he
     wrote best the earliest Italian verse,

61   in sweet and graceful songs of love. I gazed
     speechlessly 'til, after my sight was fed,
     I offered my respect in humble words

64   he could not doubt, and said, "Thank you but why
     with words and looks you value me so high,
     I cannot think." Said I, "Your noble verse

67   in common speech of shop and street enrich
     our talk and thought. Thus, sacred is the ink
     you wrote them in." "Brother," said he, "look there!"

70   He pointed to a shade ahead. "In verse
     and prose romance he had more craftsmanship.
     Fools deny this, misguided by the cry

73   of other fools who set mere fashion high
     above good rules of reason and of art.
     Let me be selfish, if you will be kind.

When you ascend to Paradise and find   76
that monastery where the abbot is
our Lord Christ Jesus, there please pray for me.

He sank back into flames like fish in sea.   79

27: Chastity

1   Midnight in Spain; high noon in Asia;
sun nearing dawn at Calvary where Christ
was crucified; here, ready to depart.

4   Upon the cliff edge, close beside the flames,
God's happy angel welcomed us and sang
in voice more clear than any I had heard,

7   "Blest are the pure in heart! Come, holy souls,
pass through this fire and climb to Paradise!"
His last words struck me with a deathly chill.

10   I have seen people burned alive. Raising
clasped hands I glared into the flame. Virgil
turned to me, said, "Son, here is agony

13   but certainly not death. Recall, recall
our ride on Geryon. I brought us through!
I'll do the same now we are nearer God.

16   If you were in this flame a thousand years
it would not burn a hair upon your head.
Go closer if you fear I'm fooling you.

19   Test it with your garment hem. Put away,
put away fear! Enter with confidence!"
But still I stood, in spite of conscience.

My fearful stubbornness now troubled him.   22
"Remember that this fiery wall," he said,
"divides from Beatrice." Hearing that name

I softened, stared at him. "So now we go?"   25
he murmered, with a smile as at a child
beguiled with promise of a sweet. He then

told Statius to come behind me and   28
strode first into the fire. On entering
I felt a bath in molten glass would be

a cooling change, so terrible the pain,   31
but my sweet father spoke of Beatrice
to lead me on: "I seem to see her eyes,

rejoice!" he said. A new voice led me too,   34
singing, "Come you whom God the Father blest!"
Once again I came out into a light

too bright for me to see. Now the voice said,   37
"Evening has come. Don't stop. Start up the stair
before the west grows dark." Straight through the rock

the narrow staircase went, with sun so low   40
my shadow filled it up ahead. Night fell.
That hill lets none go forward after dark.

Each sank to make his bed upon a step   43
as goats in morning light that leap at play
in noonday heat rest, chewing cud in shade,

watched by the goatherd leaning on his staff –   46
as shepherds also watch their flocks by night,
ensuring no wild beast attempts a raid,

49 I, like a goat between two herdsmen, lay
in that high-walled ravine where I could see
only a few stars overhead, but these

52 were bigger, brighter than I'd ever seen,
and as I gazed sleep seized me, sleep that brings
sometimes good news of things to come. Venus,

55 our morning star, had risen from the sea
I think, and cast a ray upon the hill
when I dreamed that a lady came to me,

58 beautiful and young, through level meadows
gathering spring flowers. She also sang,
"Know, if you want my name, that I am Leah,

61 and weave these garlands to adorn myself,
unlike my sister Rachel who all day
sits before her mirror, loving her eyes,

64 while I adore the garments that I weave."
And now the dawn in splendour touched the sky.
Shadows fled everywhere and so did sleep.

67 The poets had arisen. So did I.
"The fruit that mortals seek on many trees,
you will pluck today," I heard Virgil say.

70 No promise ever pleased as much. Each step
made me feel wings were sprouting on my heels.
Reaching the top he looked at me and said,

73 "You've seen the Hellish, also purging fires.
I've led you by intelligence and skill
up to this level where I have no power.

From here, let happiness decide your way.　　76
see how the sunlight glows on you and on
smooth grassy lawn, fine trees, fruits and flowers

clothing this gracious soil. The splendid eyes　　79
that chose me as your guide must soon appear.
Rest now or roam as wide as you're inclined.

While Statius and I will follow you.　　82
I am not needed now. Your will is whole,
free, strong. Not to obey it would be wrong.

I crown you king and bishop of your soul."　　85

28: The Earthly Paradise

1   The pleasure of exploring such a wood
by easy strolling over fragrant turf
did my heart good. The green boughs overhead

4   filtered the sunlight into golden gleams.
The sweet air fanned my brows and shook the leaves
around wee tuneful birds whose vocal art

7   cheered me by blending with an undertone
of branches softly murmuring like pines
beside Ravenna when sirocco blows.

10 We strayed so far among these ancient glades
that where we entered them was lost to sight.
Then, just ahead, a stream three paces wide

13 ran past from left to right, grass on each side
wet by small waves. I never saw water
darker and yet so clear. Earth's purest wells

16 are cloudier, though density of shade
prevented sunshine entering, and made
the richly coloured petals of the blooms

19 on the far bank much more astonishing.
A lady plucking them was singing there.
"Lady," I called, "if kindliness belongs

to so majestically fair a face,   22
come nearer please, to let me hear your songs.
You gather blossoms like Persephone,

dear daughter of the goddess, Mother Earth,   25
before the King of Hell abducted her,
thus robbing us of spring for half the year."

She turned and danced toward me and her feet   28
did not depress the crimson and yellow
petals she trod. Erect, at the stream's edge,

still holding this high garden's flowering sprays,   31
she raised her modest head and smiled at me
with lovely eyes bright as two morning stars.

The strait dividing Asia from Greece   34
bound both the scope of human pride and love,
from Persia's great king who lost his fleet,

to amorous Leander, whom it drowned.   37
They loathed the Hellespont. I hated more
that little stream which would not part for me.

"This place, though new to you," the lady said,   40
"should not feel strange, for it was made by God
exactly to delight the human race.

Adam and Eve first thought it Paradise.   43
Yet wonder (which I notice on your face)
is natural, for God's creation is

almost too wonderful to understand.   46
Ask what you wish to know. I will reply."
"Below us on this hill of stairs," said I,

49 "someone said running streams and moving airs
    don't happen here." "They cannot, lower down,"
    said she. "This summit is exceptional.

52 God who delights in generosity
    made Adam good, giving him Eve for wife,
    this lovely, perfect garden for their home

55 raised far above the stormy seas and lands
    of Earth and Hell where Satan is interred.
    Here they enjoyed both peaceful ease and mirth,

58 where all good kinds of tree, herb, fruit and bloom
    flourish abundantly. By sin they lost
    this best, first human nest, exchanging it

61 for grief, pain, toil in nations you know well.
    From these their children graduate to Hell
    or rise to Paradise by climbing here.

64 Though clouds are lifted upward by the sun,
    the triple steps of penitence exist
    so high that nothing misty reaches them,

67 so no one being purified by pain
    is hurt by harsher natures than their own.
    Air stirring tree tops gently at this height

70 circles the globe, as the First Mover wills
    who turns the bodies of celestial light –
    the moon, sun, planets and constellations.

73 Thus, seeds from here are carried by the air
    world-wide to all the nations, taking root
    in soil that suits them best. No rain falls here

so far above the clouds. A fountain fed   76
by God's will flows out in two steady streams.
This we call Lethe, the other Eunoë.

Who drink this lose all memory of sin;   79
the next renews all memory of good.
Drunk later, it has sweetest taste of all.

Soon these will quench your thirst, but first of all   82
you may welcome news I'd like to add.
Ancient poets spoke of a Golden Age

when all was good and nothing went amiss.   85
Here is the former homeland of their dreams.
Nectar they sang about was in these streams."

My fellow poets smiled, nodded at this.   88

29: Revelation

1   She sang like one in love, "blessèd are they
    whose sins are purified". Like woodland nymph
    seeking or shunning shade among the trees

4   she walked upstream, and on the other side
    I also walked, fitting my steps to hers.
    Less than a hundred paces further on

7   the banks curved equally in such a way
    we both faced east again. She called to me,
    "Look, brother – listen!" for upon us dawned

10   far greater brightness through each branch and leaf,
    and with it such sweet melody rang out
    I blamed Eve for her eating of that fruit

13   which stopped me knowing such delights before.
    So on I went, experiencing joys
    that grew as brightness grew, while melody

16   became a hymnal and triumphant choir.
    O holy virgins who inspire all art,
    if sleepless toil and pain and poverty

19   have been my part in seeking for your aid,
    I beg from all of you again, but most
    Urania, muse of celestial things,

to fix in verse thoughts difficult to think.   22
On the far brink ahead I seemed to see
the golden trunks of seven stately trees,

but as I neared their place, saw them to be   25
majestic candlesticks, linked at the base.
As voices sang hosannas each one flamed

bright as midsummer moons. Awestruck, I gazed   28
at Virgil who looked back, just as amazed.
Staring again on these high things, I saw

their stems approach slow as a new-made bride   31
down a cathedral aisle. The lady said,
"Why love big lights more than their followers?"

I saw behind men clad in purer white   34
than seen on Earth. I paused and saw the stream
reflect my left side mirror-like. Above

I saw each flame staining the air behind   37
with the bright colours sunshine paints through rain,
which left a rainbow flag or canopy

ten paces wide, whose end I could not see.   40
Twenty-four elders walked in pairs beneath.
With wreaths of lilies on their heads they sang,

"Hail, loveliest of Adam's daughters who   43
in paradise is now divinely blessed."
They passed, and flowers filled the further bank

while brightness grew as four great beasts arrived,   46
crowned with green leaves and having six wings each,
wings spotted with gold eyes like peacocks' tails,

49 but these were watchful eyes. Ezekiel
in the Old Testament tells how these came
from freezing cold through cloud, storm, flame, with more

52 of how they look than I have time, reader,
to tell in rhyme. He says they have four wings.
Saint John's *Apocalypse* agrees with me.

55 Between the beasts a chariot, two-wheeled,
moved on behind a griffin with two wings
raised high beyond my sight. They neatly clasped

58 the central green band of the canopy,
nor cut the three bright colours on each side.
The griffin's eagle-half was all of gold,

61 the lion-half pure white with mingled red.
Rome never gladdened hero-emperors
with such a car, more vivid than the sun

64 when Phaeton plunged its horses down the sky.
Three nymphs danced in a ring by the right wheel.
One glowed so vivid red that in a fire

67 she'd be invisible. The second seemed
all emerald, the third like fallen snow.
Red and white led the dance alternately,

70 but red sang, and according to her voice
she and the other two moved fast or slow.
At the left wheel four nymphs in purple dress

73 also rejoiced in dancing, and were led
by she who had three eyes within her head.
Behind these groups appeared two ancient men

in gravity and dignity alike   76
but differently clad. One wore the garb
of he whose kindly art can heal the sick –

Hippocrates. One seemed the opposite,   79
holding a sword so sharp, bright, threatening
I shuddered, though between him and me

flowed the deep stream. Four elders followed these   82
with humble looks, and last of all came one
whose face was keen, though walking in his sleep.

The garments of these seven final men   85
were white, like the first twelve. Their brows were crowned,
not with white lilies, but with rosy wreaths

so red their heads all seemed to be aflame.   88
The car came opposite me and stopped
with thunderclap that halted all the rest.

The rainbow flag above them ceased to flap.   91

30: Beatrice

1   Just as at night the seven stars we call
    The Plough and Charlie's Wain and The Great Bear
    guide all good steersmen on the salt sea plain,

4   so three great Christian virtues: Faith, Hope, Love,
    with Courage, Wisdom, Justice, Temperance
    (four virtues Pagans recognise) create

7   to eyes not blinded by the fog of sin,
    the candelabrum holding seven flames
    which light for us the way to God above.

10 The Heavenly Grace I know as Beatrice
    is carried by His chariot, the Kirk
    whose baring pole is the true cross of Christ.

13 After it halted, all the twenty-four
    pure white-robed, leaf-crowned patriarchs between
    candles and griffin turned toward the car

16 with smiling faces, blissfully serene,
    and one inspired by Heaven, sang three times,
    O come to me from Lebanon, my bride.

19 The others joined their melody to his
    like blessèd souls on Resurrection Day,
    raised by the clang of the last trump to sing

hosannas with rejuvenated tongue.   22
At the great sound I saw above the car
a hundred angel ministers appear

who sang, *Blessèd is she who comes*, and then,   25
O give her lilies with full hands. They flung
up and around flowers of every kind.

I once saw in the dawning of a day   28
a rosy eastern sky, clear blue above,
while low white mist so gently veiled the sun,

my eyes could linger on its perfect sphere.   31
Thus in the cloud of blooms from angel hands
that whirled and fell inside the car and out,

a lady came, with olive garland crowned   34
and white veil, misting a green dress through which
her loveliness shone like a living flame.

I had not felt the awe now filling me   37
for many years. I had first felt it when
a child of nine, I met another child

I loved unselfishly, and so knew then   40
what press of adult care made me forget –
that love can be and ought to be divine.

The goddess now reminded me of this.   43
I turned to Virgil in my sore distress
as a child turns to mother in a fright

meaning to say, "I tremble with despair –   46
how can I make my treachery come right?"
He was not there. Virgil, my dearest friend,

49 the good guide who had led me safe through Hell,
    and washed my cheeks with dew to make me fit
    to climb so close to my salvation

52 had vanished. Gone. I wept, then heard a voice.
    "Don't weep now, Dante. You must shed more tears
    for worse than loss of Virgil's company."

55 Hearing my name I turned and saw her stand
    within the car, speaking across the stream
    as admirals commanding fleets address

58 a sailor, from a flagship's highest deck.
    The veil descending from her head, held there
    by olive-wreath-sprays from Minerva's tree

61 did not allow a clear view of her face,
    and yet the regal way she spoke conveyed
    her harshness was restrained by tenderness.

64 "Look well at me. I am your Beatrice.
    How dare you weep up here? Did you not know
    this paradise is made for happiness?"

67 Ashamed, I stared down into the pure stream;
    saw my glum face reflected; turned away.
    Stern pity has for me a bitter taste.

70 She spoke no further as the angels sang
    the psalm that starts, *My hope is in the Lord*,
    ending with, *You give freedom to my feet*.

73 They seemed to say, *Lady, why blame him so?*
    Such Heavenly compassion warmed and thawed
    ice that had bound my heart. This flowed away

like candlewax in flame, or frozen snow   76
packed hard by northern blasts between the firs
upon the Apennines (Italy's spine)

melting in breezes out of Africa.   79
I who had never so profoundly grieved,
poured from my eyes and mouth, water and sighs.

They proved my agony was honesty.   82
Still upright in her car my lady said,
"You spirits living in eternal day

know well why he's to blame. I only asked   85
to let him hear me make his falseness plain.
Repentance needs his grief to equal guilt,

sorrow to balance his dead weight of sin.   88
The starry wheels that turn the universe
let folk bring gifts from God to splendid ends,

but only through their will. He had great gifts.   91
With care they would have yielded splendid fruit,
yet in good soil foul weeds may also sprout.

Our childhood love preserved his innocence.   94
His adolescence brought new friends, but sight
of my young eyes at times still kept him right.

When twenty-five I died and was reborn   97
in purity, while his acquaintances
misled his will, because he now pursued

visions of good that could not be made real.   100
In dreams and memories I called him back.
He did not heed, sank low till Heaven feared

103 for his salvation. Only showing him
the wholly lost in Hell could save his soul;
and so I went to Limbo, found the man

106 who led him here where I will be his guide,
for I must lead him to a greater height
that poetry may show to folk on Earth

109 the architecture of eternity.
But Heaven would undo its high decrees
were he not first washed clean in Lethe's stream.

112 The saltest tears must pay his entrance fees."

31: The Cleansing

"You on the far side of this sacred stream –"   1
(she thrust this sharp point of her speech at me)
"have heard my accusation. Is it true?"

Such weakness and confusion mastered me   4
I struggled for a word but none would come.
She let me stand there dumb a while, then said,

"Reply. Say what you think. Bad memories   7
have not yet been destroyed by Lethe's drink."
Fear piercing my confusion forced a "Yes"

so faint only her eyes could know I spoke.   10
I stood like a poor archer whose bow broke
letting the arrow go, so it fell short.

Under such fierce assault more tears and sobs   13
were now my sole resort. Again she spoke.
"When love of me led you to love good things

beyond which nothing better can be found,   16
what road blocks, spike-topped fences or deep moats
stopped you from going onward as you should?

What tempted you to leave the path of good?"   19
My lips had trouble shaping a reply
but after a deep sigh I stammered this.

22   "When I lost hope of seeing you again
     domestic life and local politics
     seemed adequate distractions from my pain,

25   with some erotic dissipation too."
     Said she, "If you had tried to justify
     facts you have just declared and this court knows,

28   and done that shamelessly with a dry face,
     my condemnation would increase your woes.
     Not so. To bear the shame of your offence

31   will help resist all future siren calls.
     Stop weeping now. Hear what you should have learned
     from my dead body. Yes, nature and art

34   had never shown such beauty as was mine
     which crumbled into dust. Since death stole that,
     why dally with more bodies that must die?

37   I went to Heaven. You should have prepared
     to join me here where death does not exist,
     and let no other women hold you back

40   where all death-strokes must fall." With downcast head
     I stood, my guilt confessed, reproved. She said,
     "Since hearing gives you grief, look up for more.

43   Come, elevate your beard." No wind tore up
     tough oak tree by its roots slower than I
     lifted my rough chin at her mocking words.

46   Angels had stopped casting their cloud of blooms.
     Beatrice stood gazing with enraptured face
     upon the creature harnessed to her car –

the griffin with two natures in one soul.   49
Beyond the Lethe stream, beneath her veil
she was more beautiful than when on Earth

her face had been the loveliest of all.   52
The nettle of remorse so stung me that
hatred of all I ever liked but she,

with such self-loathing, cut into my heart   55
I lost idea of self and time and place.
When heart at last restored some gleam of sense

the lady first encountered in the wood   58
was saying, "Hold on! Don't let go my hand."
I lay throat deep in Lethe's cleansing stream,

but floating and upheld by one so light,   61
she walked upon the stream, her arm so strong
her hand was firmly pulling me along.

Near the far bank in words I can't recall   64
she sang about forgiveness, held my head,
plunged it beneath the stream, and so I drank,

then free of guilt at last could step ashore.   67
The four nymphs by the nearest chariot wheel
raised arms and linked their hands above my head.

"In Heaven we appear as stars," they said,   70
"and before Beatrice arrived on Earth
were chosen as her serving maidens here.

Now we will lead you round to see her eyes,   73
but fully to enjoy the light in them
hear the three dancers by the other wheel

76 who see more deeply into them than we."
   Led there, I stood before the griffin's breast,
   staring at Beatrice in the car behind.

79 Her serving maids then sang in unison,
   "Now you will see the eyes of emerald
   which pierced you with love's dart. Don't fear to gaze."

82 Since the veil did not hide her eyes I stared
   and saw within their depth the two-fold beast
   like sun's reflection in a looking glass.

85 Reader, this wonderful and lovely sight –
   this figure changing in my lover's eyes,
   now with a Heavenly aspect, now the Earth's,

88 was nourishing, like a delicious meal
   that never would reduce true appetite.
   Then the three virtues from the other wheel,

91 Faith, Hope and Love, danced around me and sang,
   "O Beatrice, unveil your lovely face,
   to gratify this faithful traveller

94 who's journeyed more than any man alive,
   down through the world and up to this great height
   to look upon the glory of your Grace!"

97 Though drunk with language's magnificence
   what poet, pale from studying his art
   won't find himself unable to impart

100 the greatest thing made present to his sense?

32: Of the Kirk

Her lovely smile was all I wished to see.   1
For ten years I had thirsted for the sight.
I fixed my eyes on her and in delight

forgot all else but she. Again the net   4
of her enchantment was surrounding me
until I heard the Virtues call, "Too fixed!"

when this recalled me from my dazzled state.   7
I found the sacred pageant had swung round.
Candles and prophets now marched to the sun,

passing the car just as the griffin turned   10
into the new course with an easy force
that stirred no feather of its wings. I walked

with she who'd ferried me and Statius.   13
Beside the car we crossed the woodland glades
lost to mankind because the serpent's tongue

had misled Eve. Three arrow flights beyond   16
our turning point the car stopped at a tree
far loftier than any I had seen.

Leafless and blossomless, the branches spread   19
wider while rising to astounding height.
Murmuring, "Adam's tree", our company

22 encircled it as Beatrice left the car.
The rest sang, "Hail, Griffin who ate no fruit
from this forbidden tree, thus saving seed

25 of righteousness from those who find it sweet
until its poison makes their bellies squirm."
The griffin drew the car to the tree trunk,

28 laid the pole on a branch, and as in spring
the plants renew themselves, so did the tree.
Its colour flushed through rose to violet.

31 It put forth buds, unfolded leaves and bloom
as a glad hymn was sung, but not by me
who fell asleep. Artists perhaps may paint

34 how I looked then. I can't, so pass to when
light entered eyes and someone said, "Arise",
the word Christ used to wake dead Lazarus.

37 My good guide through the stream was at my side.
I asked, "Where's Beatrice?" and she replied,
"Sitting beside the car on the tree root,

40 shaded by leaves. Around her like a cloister
the Virtues stand, candle in hand, each one
guarding a flame. The griffin is again

43 with prophets, saints, angels in paradise."
She may have said much more but Beatrice
was all I noticed now, on the bare ground,

46 her seven hand-maids near. She spoke to me.
"Now for a while become a woodlander
and citizen of Rome as Rome should be

when Christ is Roman too. Here and elsewhere   49
remember all you see. When back on Earth
write of it truthfully. Do the world good."

I saw Jove's eagle swoop down through the tree,   52
beak tearing leaves, the blossoms and smooth bark.
It struck the car, rocking it side to side,

to and fro like a boat in stormy tide.   55
Then there leapt in a filthy starving fox!
Rebuked by Beatrice the vile thing fled.

The eagle now nested within the car,   58
feathering it with golden plumes until
from on high I heard a lamenting cry,

"My wee car, O how you are weighted down!"   61
Then I saw ground between wheels opening
letting a dragon out that drove its tail

through the car floor. Like wasp removing sting   64
it pulled tail out and wandering away
left the poor broken car encased in plumes,

thick as knot-grasses clogging fertile soil.   67
No doubt the donors of the plumes meant well,
but the transforming chariot grew heads.

Along the shaft were three with oxen horns.   70
At the car corners grew another four,
each with a single horn upon its brow.

This monster never seen on Earth before   73
had riding on its back a naked whore
gazing triumphantly around as if

76 a conqueror upon a citadel,
  while at her side a shameless giant stood
  kissing, caressing her until he saw

79 her amorously try to catch my eye.
  Beating her viciously from head to toe,
  he dragged away both her and that foul steed

82 till both were hidden by the leafy wood.

33: The Final Cleansing

"O God, see heathens in your holy places!"   1
The seven Virtues chanted through their tears,
first three, then four, joining this psalm of loss.

They paused when Beatrice, with such a sigh   4
as Mary must have sighed at foot of cross
stood up and glowing like a flame, proclaimed,

"Dear sisters, we must leave here for a while   7
but will return." A gesture made them walk
ahead of her, while we three came behind

until she turned her calm clear eyes on me   10
saying, "Come nearer, brother. We must talk.
Ask what you wish." I was so far beneath

her holy state, my tongue tripped on my teeth   13
in stammering reply: "My la-la-la-
my la-la-lady knows what I should know

mu-much, much more than me." "Then start," said she,   16
"by talking sensibly, and not like one
stumbling under a load of sin. Lethe

has washed you clean. You saw the vile dragon   19
breaking my car, a giant drag it off.
Know those to blame will not escape God's wrath.

22   Know that the eagle feathering my car,
     making it monstrous, then slave to a hag,
     will not forever have heirs acting so.

25   The birthday of a hero, sent by God
     to kill the giant and his prostitute
     is registered on the star calendar.

28   Exactly when and where I do not know.
     Five hundred, ten and five are numbers where
     some find a clue. Not me. Such prophecies

31   like Sphinx's riddle, hide what should be plain,
     yet when on Earth again tell it to those
     who race to death, because it will come true.

34   Write of the tree: what you saw, what I say.
     It is the tallest tree, widest at top
     because God made it only for himself.

37   Adam learned robbing it is blasphemous,
     dwelling with Eve in Hell five thousand years
     till Jesus let him out. The latest theft

40   which you have seen is recent history.
     But now I fear your mind is like a stone
     so darkened that my words must dazzle you.

43   Remember them, though you don't understand."
     Said I, "As sealing wax receives its stamp
     I am impressed by you and all you say,

46   but why do words you utter fly so high
     over my head? The more I try (alas!)
     the less I know." "Which teaches you," she said,

"your knowledge is as far below my own   49
as Earth is underneath a Heavenly Star."
I cried, "But I have never left your side!"

She smiled and said, "You have drunk Lethe, so   52
forget how many years you walked astray.
Now you must suffer more to understand."

The splendid sun stood at the height of noon   55
(which varies with a viewer's latitude)
when the seven maids who had gone ahead

paused on the strand of what at first I thought   58
a waterfall shaded by mountain trees.
Nearer I saw an overflowing spring

diverging in two streams as different   61
as Tigris and Euphrates are, but yet
they parted as reluctantly as friends.

"O light and glory of the human race,   64
what are these waters?" I asked Beatrice,
who said, "Matilda knows." My other guide

quickly replied like one discarding blame,   67
"I've told him both these rivers' name and use."
"His memory is numbed," said Beatrice,

"by novelties, but here flows Eunoë.   70
As you know how, refresh his weakened mind."
Gentle souls gladly serve another's will.

Matilda murmured, "Come." She took my hand,   73
saying to Statius, "and you come too."
Reader, if I had time to write of it,

76 I'd speak about the sweetness of the stream
    I tasted then. I thirst to drink it still
    but now must fill more pages with the tale

79 of my long poem's third, last, greatest part.
    Commanded by the art I can't deny.
    I leave the stream of Eunoë renewed,

82 a clean soul entering the starry sky.

PARADISE

PART 3

1: The First Ascent

1   God's glory moves and shows the universe
    shining in some parts more, in others less.
    I entered Heaven with joy too great for speech

4   to glorify his light. I can recall
    only dim shadows of it now
    within this song. All you nine muses

7   led by Virgil helped me evoke the steep
    descent to Hell and climb to reach this height.
    Sun-king Apollo too inspired their aid!

10 I beg you, please give me such strength again,
    turn me into a perfect voice to sing
    of Heaven's grandest things and crown myself

13 with laurels, the one headgear fit for use
    by a true poet or great conqueror.
    Their fewness demonstrates in human kind

16 a shameful lack of will. If I succeed,
    like spark from which flames leap, some after me
    may be inspired to write with greater skill.

19 The sunrise greets us most days of the year
    from several degrees to north or south.
    When solar orbit touches other rings

(equators earthly and celestial,   22
ecliptic and the equinoctial)
four circles make three crosses and so bring

more harmony, and Summer can begin.   25
The sun this morning rose at that good point.
When Beatrice looked up at height of noon

no eagle ever fixed upon the sun   28
a gaze as clear, and since reflected rays
rebound to source like pilgrims going home,

twin beams of light now linked her sight and sun. 31
I copied her. Eden was made for ease
of humankind. There it was possible

for me to see what here would make me blind.   34
Gazing into the solar blaze I saw,
like molten silver splashed from crucible,

such fountains of tremendous light I thought   37
that He Who Can had made an extra sun.
I saw too Beatrice now looked upon

the high, eternal, starry, singing wheels   40
so lowering my eyes to rest on hers
I heard them too. Eating a magic herb

changed Glaucus to an ancient Greek sea-god.   43
The love-light in the face of Beatrice
transhumaned me in ways I cannot say.

Of new sensations knowledge cannot speak   46
unless it learns new words. Did God lift up
my eager mind to his eternal sphere?

49 No rain or river filled so vast a lake
as this whole sky now kindled into flame.
The brilliance of its harmony and light

52 provoked an appetite to know the cause,
so she who understood me perfectly
smiling replied before I questioned her,

55 "Dullard, do you not see you've left the earth?
Lightning never flashed faster from a cloud
than we ascend to your right place and mine."

58 Her smile and words erased perplexities
before I found one more. "But why," said I,
"does solid me rise above lighter things?"

61 Like mother soothing sickly child she said,
"Order is God's first law. All that He made
have places in eternal excellence, for which

64 in minerals, plants, animals they strive
instinctively, in people willingly.
When ill will leads astray our souls can't rest

67 until we reach our given place and are
at last in harmony with all that's best.
We are now soaring to our origin

70 as naturally as a waterfall
pours down a cliff. Those who forget their place
by choosing base delight, are very like

73 materials no artist can use well,
discarded in the midden heaps of Hell.
Climbing them there has purified you, so

guilt cannot weight you. That is why you rise.   76
Innocent souls who stay below defy
nature and reason, like a static flame."

Pausing, she turned her eyes toward the sky.   79

2: Moon Sphere

1 Some folk in little boats follow my ship
because they like the story in my song.
Let them turn back toward the shore they know

4 unless their craft is strong. I now go far
over a sea no poet crossed before.
Minerva fills my sails. Apollo steers.

7 The Muses indicate each guiding star.
If you are of the few like me who seek
the bread that feeds but never satisfies,

10 you too may launch your vessel on this sea
using my wake as guide. The Argonauts,
those heroes voyaging for the Golden Fleece,

13 when they saw armed men springing from the soil
after their captain ploughed down dragon teeth
were not as much amazed as you will be.

16 Our inborn thirst for God's sufficiency
kept Beatrice intent on upper skies,
me intent on her eyes, so up we went

19 as swiftly as we looked, until halted
by a wondrous sight. It stopped us short
as a struck target ends an arrow flight.

"Now praise God for His generosity!   22
This star is nearest earth," said happily
that fairest one who understood my mind.

I saw what lower down could not exist.   25
Luminous mist enclosed us now inside
a diamond-hard and perfect shining pearl,

yet we could move in it as easily   28
as light rays pass through water in a glass
without a change of character in each.

For one or more bodies to occupy   31
an equally dense body easily
defies earth's common sense. In Paradise

it was quite clear to my intelligence.   34
"Lady," said I, "my gratitude to He
who saves us from death's grip will never cease,

but why, when viewed from where most people live, 37
has this pure moon a spotted face? Some say
they can make out Cain and his thornbush there."

Amused she said, "Wits stray when seeking laws   40
for what they cannot touch, so tell me now
what you think the cause." "Varied density?"

I suggested. "Looking through dirty air?"   43
"No," said she. "God has made all the Heavens
equally good. Air here is free from dirt,

and though bodies of light within these skies   46
differ in sizes, colours, faculties,
their densities do not. On summer days

49 most things appear equally clear at noon.
  At night when you see bodies in one sphere
  what you mistake for spots are smaller lights

52 contrasted with more bright, as in the moon."

3: In the Moon

She who, sunlike, first warmed my breast with love   1
deserved both gratitude for that reply
and for correcting me. Raising my eyes,

surprise expelled my thanks. I thought she stood   4
beside a dusty glass that mirrored folk
so faintly that a pearl on a pale brow

was not more dim. They seemed to beckon me.   7
Narcissus loved reflections of himself
so gazed in front. To see these folk more clear

I looked behind myself, and none were there.   10
Turning again to my sweet smiling guide
I heard her say, "Funny, the childish way

you do not trust your eyes in Paradise!   13
These beings by my side are real although
lowest in Heaven for breaking holy vows.

Question them. Hear. Believe. They shine in truth   16
and never more will truth depart from them."
I faced the shade that seemed most keen to speak

and almost stammering with eagerness   19
declared, "O spirit made for blessedness,
who dwells in sweetness of this radiance,

22 will you be kind enough to let me know
your name and circumstance?" She eagerly
and cheerfully told me, "We can't refuse

25 kindness to those who only want what's right
because at our great height above the earth
all are like God in this. On earth I was

28 your friend Forese's sister, Piccarda,
forced to wed someone who I did not love.
Soon after I was dead. My fairer face

31 is why you do not recognise me now."
"Piccarda! Yes, I know you," I declared,
"although at first the glory in your face

34 half-blinded, dazed, distracted me. But say,
is not a higher sphere what you desire?
In higher places you'd be held more dear."

37 She smiled a bit (as did the other shades)
then answered me so gladly that she seemed
in the first fires of love. "Brother, our wills

40 are tuned by charity – by love itself.
We thirst for what we have, and nothing more.
Our wills are now identical with His

43 who keeps all things in perfect harmony –
earth, planets, stars, up to the outermost
circumference of all, which is Himself.

46 Any in Paradise who craved for more
(and once before this craving did occur)
would strike a discord through our bliss and sever

charity from necessity, and thus   49
destroy the harmony of Heaven too.
God's will is the creative sea in which

we live and move. Sharing it is our peace."   52
I now knew why the bliss of Paradise
is everywhere in Heaven – each soul

is needed by the whole domain, although   55
God is not always equally in all.
Yet in my body my imperfect will

still craved more water from her well of truth.   58
The pure cloth of the life she'd tried to weave
was slashed before the fabric was complete.

I begged Piccarda to explain. Said she,   61
"A perfect love of Christ allowed Saint Clare
to teach the vows by which a lady may

put on the bridal veil and marry Him.   64
Just such a nun was I who left the world
to join the Poor Clare sisterhood. Alas,

greedy relations came, dragged me away.   67
God knew my sufferings. Upon my right,
shining with all the splendour of the moon

is one whose plight was mine. Raped from cloister,   70
keeping bridal veil over her heart, she
is Constance, heiress to the Swabian throne,

mother of Europe's holy potentate   73
who should have been the Roman Emperor."
Piccarda, singing *Ave Maria*,

76 sank from my eyes into deeper light like
stone in pond. I looked to Beatrice who
increased so vividly upon my sight,

79 questioning her was more than I could do.

4: More Moonlight

Between two equally enticing meals   1
an idiot might starve before he chose.
A lamb between two wolves would also doubt

which way to turn, or hound between two does.   4
I hungered after what my guide might say
if asked why Heaven's justice seemed unkind,

but can a man God made doubt God is good?   7
I feared to ask that question choking me,
but Beatrice, who understood my mind

replied at once, "What ties your tongue is this: 10
how can good vows and wills deserve the less
if broken by another's wickedness?

Your other doubt is astrological.   13
Plato wrote after death all souls return
to planets ruling them. Did moons decree

these nuns' inconstancy? Both these doubts need 16
an answer. I will take the second first.
It is most poisonous, so listen hard.

No seraphim that is most one with God –   19
not Abraham, Moses or Samuel –
neither John Baptist or Evangelist –

22 not even Mary in the highest Heaven
is separated from the two you've met
although they chose to greet you in this sphere.

25 All share alike in the eternal bliss
according to their soul's capacity.
To indicate the nature of life here

28 I am compelled to talk to you as if
Heavenly Paradise has social ranks
like those on earth. This is not so, but I

31 can only make the highest things more clear
by speaking of them in the words you know,
although they may mislead. God's Scriptures say

34 He sees, acts, speaks with eyes, hands, mouth because
only thus men and women can conceive
One seeing with all light, whose deeds are days,

37 whose voices teach in all that can be heard:
thunder and waves, birdsong and whispered speech.
Plato says after death all souls return

40 to stars they left at birth, meaning perhaps
natural forces shape our characters
to some extent. If so this partial truth

43 has misled worshippers of sun and moon,
Venus and Mars, who treat these stars as gods.
Your other doubt can do no mischief here

46 or lose the smallest droplet of my love.
That in your eyes justice seems cruelty
is not a sign of heresy, but faith.

By all who know that Jesus Christ is God,   49
doubts can be logically overcome.
Doubt should make faith more sure. The facts are these.

No force can make a flame burn upside down   52
or alter any wholly pure good will,
though force may twist them sideways or depress.

To show that torture could not change his mind 55
Saint Lawrence chose to roast upon a grill
and Mucius compelled his hand to burn.

Rare are heroic virtues of that kind.   58
When stronger forces make good nuns break vows
and leave their cloisters, they are not to blame,

yet must feel shame if the strong force withdraws 61
and she does not return because the rape
has cracked her spirit, left her in the wrong.

If that is understood your doubts are solved.   64
Here is a greater doubt you can't resolve
without my aid. I told you Piccarda

is at the source of truth, so cannot lie.   67
She said that Constance, forced to be a queen
and breed an emperor, stayed nun at heart.

This means she did not linger in the wrong   70
by choosing to conform with what was forced.
Why was this so? Some sin against their will,

thinking to save themselves from something worse. 73
Alcmaeon slew his mother to escape
his father's curse. Perverse good will enforced

76 is a Hell brew, but brother, know Constance
suffered by violence, but she forced none.
Only goodness came from her suffering,

79 so absolute Good Will took no offence
but the reverse, as Piccarda told you,
and also in these other words do I."

82 Such were the ripples of that holy stream
whose source was the clear fountain of all truth.
They quenched and satisfied my thirsty soul.

85 I told her, "You who the First Lover loves,
whose speech raises my thinking nearer His
I now see intellects can never rest

88 until at last the One Truth shines on them
and further truth beyond cannot exist.
Doubt is a sturdy tree rooted in truth.

91 Nature demands we fly from branch to branch,
from height to height up to the topmost twig.
Only when that is reached can active mind

94 rest like contented bird inside its nest.
Were that not so then all desire is vain.
Lady, these facts lead to a new request.

97 Could all who fail to act as they have vowed
provide what God requires? Redeem themselves
through other acts of generosity?"

100 The eyes of Beatrice now sparkled bright
with the new interest that lifted me
so far above normality that I

103 could hardly bear the sight of so much love.

5: Free Will and Mercury

"Don't wonder that in loving warmth I shine   1
more vividly than mortal eyes can bear.
The light of truth now growing in your mind

mirrors the highest good and so is bound   4
to kindle greater love in me, though since
you loved me as a child you've been beguiled

by many gleams of truth in lesser things.   7
You ask me now if souls can be redeemed
by good works when they break a holy vow."

Having begun this chapter with the words   10
of Beatrice, here follows her reply,
her answer to the things I wished to know:

"The greatest gift God gave when He made men 13
was what is greatest glory in Himself:
free will, a function of intelligence.

Only humanity possesses that.   16
We are the only beasts who worship Him
with rights of sacrifice, with priests and nuns

who promise they will do God's will alone   19
by sacrificing all their will to Him.
A given sacrifice that's taken back

22 is ill-got gain, like any other gift
lawlessly repossessed. Can thieves use well
what they have stolen? They are robbers still.

25 Remember that chief point. Though Holy Church
sometimes releases priests and nuns from vows
which seems to contradict the truth I've told,

28 regard that as a mouthful of tough meat
to carefully chew over as I speak.
Think hard and you will come to understand

31 a sacrifice has two parts. There is first
promise of gift, and then the given thing.
A promise is not cancelled if not kept.

34 Only the keeping of one wipes it out,
but Jewish law said promises stayed good
if witnesses and parties to the deed

37 agreed upon a substituted gift
of greater value than the promised one.
Our church accepts this law of substitute,

40 but lets no single person use that law
till a just judge, weighing with equal scales,
can demonstrate no fraud or force prevails.

43 We Christians should be slow to swear an oath
and having sworn should strive to keep our word,
but not like Jephtha, Agamemnon too,

46 who slaughtered daughters rather than revoke
the hasty, cruel vows that proved them fools.
O Christians, learn to be a steadier folk.

We have both Testaments, the Old and New,   4
and further guidance, for our Holy Church
has shepherds known to every one of you.

These should be all we need to save our souls.   5
Don't leave your mothers' milk like silly lambs
who think the world is made for fretful play.

Do not be led astray by wicked greed   5
so any Jew who keeps his rabbi's laws
can point to you in scornful mockery."

I write these words as Beatrice spoke them   5
before she looked up longingly to where
the universe was sending down most light.

Her silence and her ardent face imposed   6
a quietness upon my eager will
as, like an arrow striking the bull's eye

before the string impelling it is still,   6
we sped up to the second sphere, and here
her bliss increased and Heaven brightened too.

What did this greater brightness do to me   6
who am so liable to change? New bliss
left me no words to say more than I saw.

As in a calm clear pool the fishes come   7
expecting food from one upon the rim
I saw a thousand splendours drawing near

and heard from each, "Here's one who brings more love!"   7
As these souls neared us they appeared more full,
more radiant with shining happiness.

76 Dear reader, if my story ended here,
   how eagerly you'd want to know the rest.
   I say so to make plain how much I wished

79 to hear about the state these souls possessed.
   This happened when a voice addressed me straight.
   "O you who, born for virtue, travel here

82 before the warfare of your life is done,
   since it is given you to view the thrones
   which the eternally triumphant won,

85 ask what you wish and I will answer you."
   "Ask anything you want," Beatrice cried,
   "and trust the answers as if gods replied."

88 The speaker nestled finely in a glow
   that shone from his serenely smiling eyes.
   I thanked him for his courtesy then said,

91 "Please tell me of yourself and Mercury,
   smallest of spheres between the moon and sun,
   planet least known because the rays least strong."

94 Then, like the sun seen through dissolving mist
   joy made him brighten till excess of light
   prevented seeing him. I heard his words

97 which sound in the next chapter of my song.

6: Justinian

"Three hundred years after the birth of Christ   1
Constantine led the Roman Eagle east
near ruined Troy from which Aeneas fled

and built its nest on Europe's farthest coast.   4
This new Rome was the Empire's capital
while old Rome stayed the home of Papacy.

When Goths invading Italy destroyed   7
Rome's earthly strength, they did not harm the Pope.
That was before I wore the Empire's crown

and hailed as Caesar – am Justinian.   10
God's love led me to unify Rome's laws
into one useful code, weeding out words

that might pervert the justice of a cause.   13
I was unfit for this great task at first.
My faith was still impure, for I believed

Christ was the Holy Ghost in manlike shape,   16
not flesh and blood. A letter from the Pope
corrected me, then Heaven gave me peace.

Count Belisarius, my general,   19
drove Goths from Italy, and so again
around Earth's Middle Sea one emperor

22 ruled all, and there my legal code was used,
    and thus Rome's Empire worked at giving birth
    to what Augustine said all should create:

25 God's Citadel on Earth. My peaceful rule
    made Church and State supreme yet separate.
    You know me now, but I have more to tell

28 of how the Roman Empire got renown
    and used it well centuries after me
    before the Whigs and Tories broke it down.

31 Aeneas toiled for years on lands and seas
    before his wedding to a Latin queen
    gave a new home to Trojan refugees,

34 the ancestors of Rome. For centuries
    their fighting royalty, wise senators
    conquered kingdoms and communes. Rome's Eagle

37 flew through Europe, Africa, Asia,
    forcing far-flung nations into one vaster,
    longer-lasting state than in his brief life

40 the great Alexander could create.
    The time arrived when Heaven wanted peace.
    The Roman Eagle perched on Caesar's fist,

43 none being fit to manage it but he.
    No tongue, no pen does justice to his deeds,
    quelling revolting principalities,

46 crossing the Rubicon, then putting down
    the civil war in Gaul, Spain, Egypt, Greece.
    Satan in Hell chews those who murdered him.

There Cleopatra weeps. She chose to die   49
by snakebite to escape the Eagle's beak.
Augustus Caesar was its master next.

He spread the Empire to the Red Sea shore,   52
declared the *Pax Romana* everywhere,
and needed to support it by a tax,

so ordered men back to their place of birth   55
for registration. Thus in Bethlehem
our Prince of Peace was born. Now listen hard!

Tiberius was Caesar number three.   58
Under his reign the Eagle did one thing
upon a hill outside Jerusalem

that makes all other splendid Roman deeds   61
look small and dim when viewed by Christian eyes.
Here God's wrath made the Eagle work for Him –

helped God Himself revenge Himself on God.   64
Later, when Titus reigned, Heaven ensured
vengeance on that revenge for ancient sin.

The Roman legions slew Hebrew hordes,   67
looted and burned Solomon's synagogue,
made a whole ruin of Jerusalem.

Look forward now. When Whiggish Lombard crows 70
tried to peck out Pope Leo's tongue, he found
protection in Emperor Charlemagne.

Rome's bishop and Imperial Eagle then   73
were allies though apart, as they should be.
Look at the state of politics today!

76 Now ancient symbols of the common good
   achieved by men whose fame is like my own
   are used on flag and badge to foster hate

79 by greedy statesmen with short local aims.
   The Roman Eagle and the Fleur de Lys
   are trampled by a squabbling multitude.

82 We in this little star strove to do well,
   but also strove for fame, so rose less far
   than those whose virtues lacked all selfishness.

85 This we cannot regret, happy to know
   good choirs all sound the more melodious
   where diverse voices sing both high and low.

88 In this pearl also shines the light of one
   not quite as grand as mighty emperors.
   He worked as hard for goodness as did we

91 but won no great reward. His birth was low
   and name was Romeo, and he became
   an honest steward of Count Berenger –

94 served him so well, four daughters of the Count
   got such rich dowries that they married kings.
   Envy declared he filled his pockets too,

97 which was untrue. Dismissed, he had to beg.
   Though he is famous, those who honour him
   would do it much more if they understood,

100 how sore it is to beg your livelihood."

7: Beatrice Explains

"To Heaven's greatest height now praise our God 1
who gloriously brightens with His rays
good hearth-fires everywhere on holy days!"

So sang that bright soul, dancing as he sang, 4
that ruler who had striven to connect
justice on earth and Heaven's government.

In happy play the other shining souls 7
danced with him too, until like shooting stars
they disappeared by being far away

and left me brooding in perplexity. 10
I well knew Beatrice could quell my doubts
so *Tell her! Tell her!* sounded in my head,

but reverence had overcome my tongue. 13
Parts of her name (*be*, *is*) still strike me dumb.
She did not leave me thus, for with a smile

that would have cheered a burning man she said, 16
"You do not see why justice should demand
vengeance upon revenge for ancient sin?

Listen and hear true doctrine straight from me. 19
Adam, the only man not born but made,
was given all good things men can enjoy

22 but could not bear one curb upon his will
so damned himself and we who spring from him.
Long ages passed before the Word of God

25 descending worked to free us from this ill.
By one act of amazing love God took
body with we who have rejected Him,

28 became a sinner too, deserving death
like me and you, and in Gethsemane
sadly embraced that foul necessity,

31 accepting Roman law so none can say
our Maker never felt our suffering.
If human need for death is understood

34 indeed Christ's death was good. If we respect
His righteousness, nothing was more unjust.
From that great act came opposite effects –

37 Christ's death desired by God *and* Jewish priests,
for which earth quaked and Heaven opened wide,
and Solomon's great temple was destroyed.

40 I fear your thoughts are fankled in a knot
you can't untie. Although my words are clear,
why God redeemed us thus is dark to you.

43 Brother, it is dark to everyone
with minds unripened by the sun of love.
I'll say it all again in other words.

46 God's excellence is never envious,
so all the souls He makes possess like Him
eternal life; like Him, freedom of choice.

These gifts are lost by people choosing sin.   49
Adam and Eve disobeyed God; believed
rejecting God would make them equal Him,

thus they exchanged eternity for time.   52
Justice cannot ignore so bad a crime
which all folk born of women re-enact,

so gaps between ourselves and Paradise   55
are far too big for penitence to fill
by any single act of human will

though penitence is certainly required.   58
Only a miracle could reconcile
justice with mercy, and at last it came.

God's overflowing goodness made His Word   61
human, like us; offered new birth, new life,
eternally to all who follow Christ

and grasp their cross – forgive who do them wrong –   64
love enemies and promise not to sin.
What better thing to save us could God do

than show all people how we ought to live?   67
I see you want more news of sacred things,
a thirst I'll satisfy before you ask.

What troubles you is instability.   70
God made the earth and water, fire and air
so must have made them pure as Paradise –

pure as these starry spheres, this shining space   73
through which we rise. Why on earth do all things
change, age, sicken, die and rot? Here is why.

76 Our God Himself did not directly make
all of the world below. Live plants and beasts
are generated in His elements

79 by things He made before. Sunlight is one.
Yet on the sixth day of the Genesis
He breathed His own soul into human clay.

82 All other earthly life will suffer death.
Men, women are the great exception,
created by His love to love Him back

85 eternally, after resurrection."

8: Venus

Pagans have wrongly thought the brightest star   1
at dawn and dusk provoked the wildest love.
Venus was offered hymns and sacrifice

as lover of Mars, playboy Cupid's mother,   4
provider of erotic joy beside
sorrow that drove Dido to suicide.

I only knew we'd soared up to love's sphere   7
on seeing Beatrice grew lovelier.
Bright dancing lights were in that shining globe

like sparks in a flame, like many voices   10
harmonised in one great organ tone.
The lights spun fast and slow like seraphim

according to (I think) their view of God   13
until, aware of us, a stream of them
unwound and, comet-like, sped to our side

singing a welcoming *hosanna.* How   16
I wished and always wish to hear that sound!
The first light said, "May we share happiness?

Instruct us, poet, how to please you best.   19
On earth you wrote of how our intellects
move the third star. We love you much for that.

22 Pausing, conversing now with you will be
   a very blissful interval of rest."
   I looked to my bright guide to find if she

25 accepted this, received her smiling nod,
   so asked, "Please, who are you?" – not words that said
   how glad I was, and yet he knew because

28 I saw his glow increase as he replied,
   "If dazzling joy did not disguise my form
   like smooth cocoon protecting a silk worm

31 you would see Charles Martel, a long-gone friend
   who dwelled too short a time on earth to stop
   the Whigs and Tories rending Italy.

34 O Florentine, had plague not ended me
   (king of Naples, Sicily, Hungary,
   count of Provence) you would not be exiled.

37 My father's second son is Naples' king
   and has not learned the art of ruling men,
   for brother Robert does not even know

40 taxing the poor too much must breed revolt.
   One of our blood who did not heed that fact
   incited massacre in Palermo –

43 mobs filling streets and yelling *kill kill kill!*
   Unlike our dad, Robert alas is mean,
   grabs wealth through knights who share his greed for gold.

46 He won't get rid of them, although the cost
   of keeping them wrecks all good government."
   "Sir Charles," said I, "the Heaven-sent joy you bring

is also yours who, now so near to God,   49
knows from Whom purest loving wisdom flows.
You've made me glad, so now please make me wise.

How can good seed grow into rotten fruit?   52
Why is bad son bred from a decent dad?"
"If you can grasp the truth of my reply,"

said he, "you will understand many things   55
upon which you have so far turned your back:
what moves and satisfies this Paradise

you now ascend, gives planets influence   58
over those born below. Each embryo
receives a starry ray, like shaft from bow,

that shapes its character.   61
No soul is quite alike, yet can combine
in godly ways with other souls on earth,

just as the planets circulate above.   64
Were this not so the universe would be
a chaos too confused to form a star

or any form of life, but all we see   67
amounts to one tremendous work of art.
Even its smallest part has unity

through balanced interchange of energy.   70
Is that quite clear?" I said, "Yes, I agree.
Nature has made the world just what we see."

"Can men live well without societies?"   73
asked he. I said, "One perhaps sometimes may,
but not for long. None could begin to live

76 without a family." He answered, "Right.
    A family is a society,
    but think as citizen. Cities require

79 all kinds of skill: nurses for babies and
    farmers for food, builders, tradesmen, doctors
    for the ill, engineers like Daedalus

82 law-givers like Solon, artists like Phidias,
    priests like Melchizedek and commanders
    like Xerxes. Cities can exist because

85 star influence insists that lads are *not*
    exact copies of their dads. That is why
    pagans believed gods fathered their heroes.

88 Bastard Romulus was called son of Mars.
    Brothers (as well I know) can differ too
    even when twins, as Esau and Jacob show.

91 I love you, so will tell you something more.
    When by bad luck people are doing work
    unsuited to their nature, things go wrong

94 and a good land has chosen the wrong way
    when fighters preach in time of peace, and then
    in time of war the loud-mouthed clergymen

97 climb up to seize the general command."

9: Prophecies

Mother or wife of Charles, if you read this, 1
know that he spoke of woe ahead for you
and his posterity, but also said,

"Don't speak of it. Let the years take their course. 4
Tell them that Paradise will note their tears,
and justice crush who causes them. That's sure."

He, loving holy light, now faced the sun 7
whose goodness is the main wealth we require.
Alas, for foolish creatures who admire

only the works of human vanity. 10
Another shining soul approaching me,
revealed delight by its increasing glow.

Beatrice once more signalling assent 13
I cried out, "Bless'd spirit, please let me know
what you have come to make me understand."

The light whose face I could not see replied, 16
"In the degraded land of Italy,
between the isles of Venice and the springs

from which the Brenta and Piave flow, 19
is the Romano stronghold, whose tough lord
with fire and sword plunders the plain below.

22 He was my brother Ezzelino, who
    is boiling now with other brutal men
    in Hell's hot river of the blood they shed.

25 I am Cunizza, widely known because
    so often conquered by this brilliant star.
    Venus helped me inspire a troubadour

28 and follow where he led. Though often wed
    I always could forgive myself, although
    good citizens like you will find that strange.

31 The poet you see gleaming at my side
    has written what ensures his lasting fame.
    In our first life we all should do so well

34 that people later smile to hear our name,
    but who thinks so in Padua where mobs
    now dominate that unrepenting state?

37 Defeated once, destruction comes again
    and the day nears when Paduan blood will stain
    boggy Vicenza's mud. In Travigi one lord

40 still holding his head high will die
    by assassin's hand. Feltro will bewail
    her bishop who breaks sanctuary vows

43 giving to slaughter those he should protect.
    No fouler priest was ever clapped in jail.
    The barrels must be big if they'll contain

46 gore of Farrarese slain by courtesy
    of that vile cleric's proof he is a Whig.
    Such vileness suits his city's evil ways.

Angelic mirrors up in Heaven's height   49
(you call them thrones) reflect God's judgement down
to we who have the right to say such things."

Here she returned to dancing in her sphere,   52
leaving the other spirit at my side.
Like a rare jewel caught in ray of light

he now was sparkling with a ruby glow,   55
for in that place a greater brightness comes
with gladness, just as laughter happens here,

and darkness deepens grievous gloom in Hell.   58
Said I, "The seraphim robed in six wings
well know what God perceives, and so do you.

Were I in you as you exist in me,   61
I'd not delay in saying what you will."
Said he, "The vastest valley in the world

flooded by ocean, is the Middle Sea.   64
My birthplace on its shore was Genoa
where the third planet's ray moulded my clay.

Called Folco, I was bishop of Marseilles   67
after my hair turned grey, but earlier
I doubt if Hercules, Phyllis, Dido,

were more amorous. I do not rejoice   70
in having sinned. Forgiveness blesses us
so happily, we know and share the love

moving our Heaven above the earth below.   73
Please listen more before ascending more.
This brightness like a sunbeam at my side

76 gleaming in clearest water, was the whore
   Rahab, one of Christ's ancestors
   freed from death by His Resurrection

79 with Adam, Eve, Abraham and the rest.
   Jesus made Rahab foremost in this sphere
   (last planet touched by shadow of the earth)

82 for she helped Joshua to victory
   when taking Palestine, that holy land
   God gave his chosen folk, land conquered since

85 by Saracens, whom modern popes ignore.
   O Florentine, a founder of your state
   worshipped the first sworn enemy of God!

88 There grow the golden florins, currency
   of worldwide trade and worldwide jealousy.
   That gold has led astray both sheep and lambs

91 by turning shepherds into hungry beasts.
   The Words of God and theologians
   are studied less by popes and cardinals

94 than books of canon law telling how fines,
   penalties and wills can accumulate
   property for priests. They think less about

97 Nazareth where Gabriel spread his wings
   announcing Christ will come, than about Rome
   where Peter and many who followed him

100 came to be crucified; think more about
    the Vatican's bank vaults than saving souls.
    Why will Church and Nation not win free of

103 wealth's despicable adulteration?

10: The Sun

The Father, Son and Holy Ghost unite   1
to nourish worlds below in time and space
with flow of endless love and endless light.

Raise your eyes with me, reader, to the skies!   4
Who recognise the glory there, taste God,
giver of warmth even the blind can feel

combining bodies in the universe.   7
Each part of it shows the Creator's art
keeping the movement neat. A fool may think

the cosmos squint. No planet goes agley.   10
If planets strayed a fraction more or less
out of their orbits, crashes would ensue.

Reader, stay with this book. Because you glimpse   13
the daring of its scope before the end
you may feel weariness, yet find delight.

Now comes the food I cannot make you eat.   16
Here I describe experience beyond
reach of both common sense and common speech.

Beatrice raised me to each higher state   19
so softly, instantly, it took no time.
I did not notice how I came to be

22 within the sun, that ministry of light
revealing breadth of space and time of day.
The people in the sun were all so bright

25 I saw them clearly through its radiance
which is our source of light. How this could be
I cannot say. Believe me, it was true.

28 Said Beatrice, "Praises and thanks are due
the Son of God who lifted you into
this sun of Paradise." No mortal heart,

31 I think, loved Jesus more than I did then,
in adoration quite forgetting she
who laughed aloud with joy to see me thus.

34 And then I saw a ring of shining souls
surrounding us like halo round the moon.
Only the sweetness of their tongues excelled

37 the glory of their smiling eyes, a sound
more wonderful than words can tell. Take wings –
fly to the solar sphere to hear that song.

40 The splendours circled us like stars around
the Arctic pole three times, and then they paused
like dancers waiting for another tune.

43 Before it came I heard a near one say,
"Your thirst for knowledge glows within your face.
I cannot keep it from you any more

46 than clouds can keep their showers from the sea.
You wish to know the flowers in this wreath
garlanding lovingly the fair one who

strengthens you here. Know that I was a lamb   49
of that well-ordered flock Dominic led,
where is good fattening, unless we stray.

That great instructor Albert of Cologne   52
is on my right. He taught me how to see
Greek science strengthens Christ's theology.

I am Thomas Aquinas. Let my words   55
lead your eyes round this circle of the bless'd
and introduce the rest. Gratian is next

who reconciled the laws of Church and State;   58
then modest scholar Peter Abelard,
wise commentator on prophetic lore.

See the fifth light, most beautiful of all!   61
Solomon he, whose wisdom was so great
none ever rose as high; then Dionysius,

teacher of angelic hierarchies.   64
Orosius, the small light after him,
taught Christian history to Augustine.

My praises now have led you through seven lights. 67
The next is excellent Boethius
whose writing shows the world's deceits, and how

we all can gain peace here through martyrdom.   70
See flaming after him four lights of God:
encyclopaedic Isadore; and Bede

the venerable English monk; Richard   73
the mystic Scot; and then before your eyes
return to me, see one from whose grave thoughts

76 came truths some did not want to know – Siger!"
That twelfth name sounded like a striking clock
telling the time when a whole Church must rise

79 to sing the praise of Jesus Christ our King.
Now half the solar voices drew or drove
the rest to chime in harmony so sweet

82 my spirits soared to join the melody
as the glad golden sun-sphere carried round
that choir, adding such glory to word

85 only in endless joy can they be heard.

11: Of Francis

O daft deliriums of earthbound men! 1
With force or fraud you fight to gather wealth
by trade or law, priest-craft or shedding blood,

then glut your appetites on luxuries, 4
corrupting sense by wasteful indolence,
driving your mental wings into foul mud.

Freed from such emptiness by Beatrice 7
I stood a guest among the bless'd who danced
around us like a splendid galaxy.

Then pausing as before, that radiance 10
who first had spoken spoke to me again,
smiling and glowing brighter as he did.

"Because all here share in the mind of God 13
I see some words of mine engendered doubt:
there is good fattening unless we stray;

as also these: *none ever rose so high*. 16
To clarify I'll speak at greater length.
The Providence that rules the world of men

cannot be absolutely understood 19
by human minds. To wed His human Church
Christ married Her with cry of dreadful pain

22 and loss of life. To keep Her true to him,
    Providence sent the Church two princely men.
    One was for wisdom like the cherubim

25 and one whose ardour matched the seraphim
    who I will speak of first, since praise of him
    applies to both. They toiled for the same end.

28 The Porta Sole of Perugia
    faces the Apennine, whence winds blow down
    both hot and cold. Small rivers too descend,

31 surround a town where Mount Subasio
    slopes to the plain. Assisi is its name.
    A better name for it is Orient

34 for here dawned Francis, Italy's new sun.
    While still a lad he revelled in the sins
    most folk forgive the child of a rich man,

37 or even praise. He fought in petty war,
    caroused and whored, was very popular,
    then illness made him face the fact of death,

40 forced him to see he was not fit for it.
    He read what Jesus said to the rich youth
    who wanted Heaven, and knew these words were true,

43 then tried to give away the wealth he had,
    resulting in a quarrel with his dad
    because he chose a bride all wished to shun.

46 Her first spouse had been taken from her side
    over eleven hundred years before.
    Though known to famous men much earlier

(Diogenes was one who scorned a great   49
world conqueror), the proud rejected her.
None took example from her constancy.

Even Christ's mother stayed below when she   52
climbed up the Cross to share Christ's agony.
In case you cannot guess of whom I speak

the bride who Francis wed was Poverty,   55
in church renouncing his inheritance
on earth to live on just what Heaven's Dad

gives everyone who does not seek for gain.   58
With such a wife he came to love her more
and poor himself, worked hard to help the poor.

Though old companions flung mud at him,   61
his happiness and harmony moved some
of contemplative mind to emulate.

His wealthy neighbour Bernard was the first   64
to kick off shoes and follow him barefoot.
Egidius, Sylvester followed suit.

Eight others too, delighting in his bride,   67
wore rough wool robe tied with a simple cord
and did not fear the sneers of vulgar wealth.

The scorn they all found very hard to bear   70
came from those thinking them competitors
in holiness: the confirmed clergymen.

Francis and his eleven followers   73
walked forth to Rome and showed Pope Innocent
the nature of Franciscan brotherhood.

76 Thus it was tolerated by the Church,
   and when the flocks of Francis grew much more
   through missions to France, Spain and Germany

79 Pope Honorius made its status sure.
   Francis then sailed to Egypt and when there
   preached Christ until the sultan promised him

82 far better treatment of the Christian slaves,
   and in Jerusalem Christ's tomb would be
   placed firmly in Franciscan brothers' care,

85 after which he returned to Italy.
   Twixt Arno and the Tiber is a crag
   where stands the cell where Francis found good proof

88 that Jesus loved him well: on hands, feet, side
   the bloody wounds of crucifixion came.
   For two more years he bore those stigmata

91 till Christ who destined him to so much good
   disclosed that his last day was drawing near.
   He then bequeathed the poverty he'd wed

94 to all his brothers, begging them always
   to love her faithfully. Then from the ground
   (he had rejected any other bier)

97 his ardent soul rose up to Paradise.
   Consider now which colleague is most fit
   to help God keep Saint Peter's boat afloat

100 on troubled seas under our stormy skies.
    Surely my own patriarch Dominic!
    His followers carry good merchandise

although too many wander far away   103
to fields remote from where he guided them,
thus yielding to their fold much less sweet milk.

Some dutifully keep their shepherd's path,   106
so few their cowls require but little cloth.
Now know my meaning when you heard me say

there is good fattening unless we stray."   109

12: Of Dominic

1 And when that holy flame said his last word
the shining chorus circled once again,
and I beheld that now surrounding it

4 a ring of other shining souls revolved.
The outer ring echoed the middle one
in colours of the purest harmony.

7 As sunbursts pierce the clouds after a storm
in double rainbows they enhaloed us,
also in dancing movements and sweet song.

10 And then this festival of light and sound
suddenly paused. From one new vivid heart
came speech. Like compass needle to the pole

13 I turned to that bright soul and heard it say:
"A love of justice forces me to speak
of Dominic. You heard Aquinas say

16 for wisdom he was near the cherubim.
Because Aquinas, a Dominican,
praised Francis to the height where he belongs

19 it is but right that I, a Franciscan,
equally celebrate Saint Dominic.
Christ made our Church to be God's force on earth.

It ended European paganism.   22
Since then its foes have been hypocrisy
(which Francis fought) and heresy.

Heads of some well-fed priests had grown so thick 25
they did not clearly understand Christ's laws
or know exactly what heresy was.

Dominic came to teach these things, and did.   28
This mighty athlete for the Christian cause,
this hero keen to counteract God's foes,

came from a tiny village in Castile   31
near the Atlantic shore. His mother dreamed
when he was in her womb she bore a dog

with flaming torch in mouth to kindle faith,   34
then his godmother dreamed before baptism
a guiding star was glowing on his brow.

She chose a Christian name whose greatest part   37
is Latin word for master: *dominus*,
so he became a master gardener

tending the vines of Christ. When infant, he   40
stared at the ground, as often pondering
Christ's early words, *seek for God's kingdom first*.

His father's name, Felici, meant delight;   43
his mother Giovanna's grace of God.
Suitable names! Their son became a priest

renowned for honesty and industry   46
not rich by mastery of canon laws
but earning Heaven's bread: enough to feed

49 his strength by working for the poor and weak,
   in wasted fields where vines were withering
   because they'd been in need of proper care.

52 Then he approached the highest priest of all,
   one much less friendly to the upright poor
   than better popes who filled that seat before.

55 He did not want wealth left for pious use,
   or for a chance to rob from charities
   or for a more exalted job. He begged

58 for leave to preach against the erring world
   and use both learning and his holy zeal
   to combat false beliefs where these prevailed.

61 Permission thus requested was received.
   Like torrent pouring down a mountainside
   he and his preachers flung themselves upon

64 thickets and undergrowths of heresy,
   using most force in scouring up the roots
   where they had clung most deep. He is the source

67 of many pure streams watering young shoots
   and keeping faith's Catholic garden green.
   Men like Saint Dominic compose the rings

70 shining like double garlands in this sun,
   or like two wheels on which our chariot,
   the Church, should run when strife is overcome.

73 Both deserve praise that Thomas Aquinas
   politely gave Francis before I spoke.
   I am the soul of Bonaventura,

once head of Francis' order who well knew   76
honour and wealth are traps we can avoid.
I fear that sorrow reaches me in Heaven.

My order now is troubled by a schism   79
for some now bind themselves to poverty
too painfully for many to endure;

some find the right track hard so go too slow   82
retarding men who walk behind their back.
These shirk our rule; the former narrow it.

Read our book carefully and I admit   85
you will find pages truly written with
I keep those rules of Francis I have vowed,

yet foul weeds sprout within our field of corn.   88
When it is time to bring the harvest in,
how loudly they will shout as they complain

of reapers who won't garner them as grain!   91
I'll introduce you to my circle now.
Illuminato and Augustine were

first barefoot brethren to become God's friends.   94
See Hugh of Paris, theologian;
two Peters next of Troyes and of Spain.

The first expounded Bible history,   97
the Spaniard made the use of logic plain
in twelve small books before elected pope.

Now two who preached on sins of royalty –   100
Nathan rebuked David of Israel,
Empress Eudoxia winced from the tongue

103 of Chrysostom or Golden Mouth who was
Byzantine patriarch. Anselm came next,
England's Archbishop representing Rome,

106 who argued with its kings; then Donatus,
grammarian and teacher of that art
on which speech, writing, law depend, then next

109 Rabanus the German Latinist and
commentator. Lastly, here at my side
shines Abbot Joachim, who drew divine

112 prophecies from Saint John's Apocalypse.
And now I must acknowledge yet again
the splendid courtesy of Aquinas

115 to saintly Francis, my own paladin,
which moved me here to say the good I know
about the equally great Dominic,

118 who also showed how to live free of sin."

13: Sun Wisdom

To comprehend, though faintly, what came next,   1
keep as you read this firm in your mind's eye
each image as if chiselled upon rock.

Remember all the biggest, brightest stars   4
that, piercing misty vapour in the air,
illuminate the deepest midnight sky.

Think of that constellation, the Great Bear   7
swinging in so much space round the Pole Star
no part is hidden by the highest hills.

The axle of the turning universe   10
ends in that Pole. Between it and the Bear
a smaller constellation swings. Think now,

both galaxies made of the brightest stars   13
and in concentric spheres, not simple rings,
and oppositely moving round we two.

My words can only show this state of things   16
as a full noonday sun reveals itself
reflected in a muddy shallow pool.

They tell you nothing of that golden sound,   19
that holy anthem all those wise stars sang,
grander than paeans to Apollo were.

22 That anthem glorified the Three-in-One,
    divine and natural and singular
    united in our Jesus Christ, God's son.

25 Their singing, circling halted yet once more.
    The lights were pleased to stop and tutor me
    as he who'd told me of God's poorest man

28 (Saint Francis of Assisi) spoke again.
    "One of your doubts about this company
    has been resolved. Sweet charity requires

31 I solve the next you formed too hastily
    in thinking I called Solomon wiser
    than greater men we both revere. Attend!

34 All things that cannot die and all that can
    are ideas that our loving God pours out
    in torrents of creative light, whose rays

37 first form angelic potencies and then
    Nature reflects them in her elements
    so they appear as bodies among men.

40 While making visible divine ideas
    Nature's hand often shakes, so what she makes
    is not quite right. The living upon earth

43 must propagate themselves by birth or seed,
    and doing so, incline to accidents
    obstructing slightly Heaven-sent design.

46 Thus, better and worse fruit may grow on trees
    of the same kind, while similar folk show
    astonishing varieties of mind,

but Highest Love created by Itself 49
two prototypes, because a living man
was first perfected from earth's dust, and then

a second made within a virgin's womb. 52
You heard how Adam's side bestowed a rib
taken to make his bride, the lovely Eve

whose appetite for fruit led to disgrace. 55
When a spear-point stabbed our Redeemer's side
the dear cost of that sin at last was paid.

Adam and Christ were perfect men and so 58
none others were as good, I quite agree,
but think of Solomon and what he said

when God enquired, "What should I give to thee?" 61
Solomon prayed for knowledge to rule well.
I only meant that in wise government

no men or kings could rise higher than he 64
and most are far below. Remember this!
Be slow in making judgements, like those men

imagining great harvests when ripe corn 67
stands in their fields before storms lay it low.
A winter briar bush showing bare spikes

may in the spring months bloom into a rose. 70
I saw a ship sail swiftly across seas
then suffer wreck on entering a port.

When in church we see one rob the poor-box, 73
one contribute alms, do not judge at all.
One may be Hell-bound, one for Paradise.

The first one may repent, the second fall." 76

14: From Sun to Mars

1 Water contained by bowl flows out to rim
if pebble is dropped in. When rim is struck
the water ripples back. The flow of words

4 from shining Thomas reached our ears then stopped.
As if struck by a thought, Beatrice spoke.
"Dear Sir, more words are needed by this man

7 who does not know what he should ask. I do.
All Paradise is made of light, souls too.
On the last day who must unite again

10 with their old fleshly bodies raised from dust,
even their eyes? How will they see without
(at least at first) intolerable pain?"

13 This question, eager and devout, aroused
in the wise stars a storm of tuneful mirth.
With swifter melody they danced in form

16 of blossoms, falling snow, butterfly wings,
for with these words I try and fail to tell
the lovely, wondrous things this dance conveyed

19 until Saint Thomas said, "The miracle
of Resurrection painlessly restores
all the First Will intended us to be,

with bodies free as minds too seldom are,   22
except for those of the angelic kinds,
and of Our Father, only One In Three,

Eternal, Natural and Singular   25
replenishing, refreshing such as we."
Then the full chorus of the solar choirs

sang what the sainted Thomas said three times,   28
sang it so beautifully that the sound
will satisfy the ferventest desires

of all who come to merit Paradise.   31
From out the central globe spoke Solomon,
his voice as archangelically soft

as if announcing Mary's pregnancy.   34
"When bodies finally complete our souls
we will surpass in brightness what you see,

as flaming coals surpass black stones from mines. 37
And yet we shall not be consumed because
God's virtue wills we share in His delight."

So quick were both the choirs to sing *Amen*   40
I knew they longed to have their bodies back
not for themselves alone. They wished to see

mothers, fathers, more they had dearly loved   43
in times before they were immortal flames.
And then I saw beyond the outer sphere

a new horizon form of equal stars   46
like galaxies seen here when day is done,
but these were shining round our undimmed sun!

49 The brilliance was more than I could bear,
    banishing both my sight and memory.
    Only the fair and smiling Beatrice

52 survives from later visions of the sun.
    We reached a higher zone of Paradise
    when I at last recovered use of sight.

55 The planet with the glow of ruddy light
    which to the heathen indicated war,
    kindled in me a need for sacrifice.

58 In words of heartfelt silent inner prayer
    (the only speech all share) I pled with Christ
    to take this thing I am, and fought to give

61 with every living particle of will,
    then found my offering acceptable.
    The Crucifix appeared within that star,

64 its beams from side to side, from foot to top
    wide as a crossroads made of the same stuff
    as, bridging the night sky, that thoroughfare

67 from pole to pole – the gleaming Milky Way.
    This cross so flamed forth Christ, my memory
    defeats my skill to speak of it, but all

70 who lift the cross of Christ and follow Him
    will forgive me for what I cannot say
    about His vision flashing in the dawn.

73 From arm to arm, summit to base and back
    lights travelled, sparkling as they met and passed,
    some swift or slow, some dazzling, and some dim

because they sparkled less but happiness   76
was equally in all. Harp and viola
combine so well we cannot tell apart

what each gives melody. The moving lights   79
gave out a hymn whose words I did not catch
and yet the whole conveyed *arise and win*

so sweetly none had ever bound my soul   82
in such enchanting chains of lovely sound,
which sight of Beatrice did not prevent,

whose beauty grew more pure with each ascent.   85

15: Martial Hero

1   Bad manners grow from greedy selfishness,
    as courtesy reflects Christ's charity
    which, as we know, is kindness to the weak.

4   I needed silence if required to speak
    and so it came. The choirs of Paradise
    silenced their song when, like a shooting star

7   down gloaming sky, from right arm of the cross
    yet linked to it by arc of finer fire
    a light swept down to join me at the foot.

10 It greeted me with the same welcoming
    that Virgil tells us in *The Aeneid*
    the soul of dead Anchises gave his son

13 who, living, met him in Elysium.
    "O my own blood! O wondrous grace of God
    that Paradise will open to you twice!"

16 The light said that. Amazed, I turned my eyes
    to Beatrice again, whose smile was such
    I fully knew how blessèd I'd become.

19 And then, although the sound was ecstasy,
    the light said things I could not comprehend.
    Their meaning was too great till heat of love

cooled down enough, letting it condescend   22
to sentences of much more common sense.
"Divine foreknowledge we in Heaven share

has kept me long expecting this delight.   25
Holy the guide who dressed you in such wings
as raise you to this height! You rightly think

I know your thoughts, so do not ask my name,   28
or why my joy appears much greater than
the others in this sphere. You are about

to satisfy my thirst to share the bliss   31
of perfect truthfulness. Ask what you wish."
Encouragement from smiling Beatrice

gave me the confidence to boldly say,   34
"Just as the sun's ray pours out equally
both warmth and light, you equally possess

love and intelligence, which mortals lack.   37
I am still mortal. My ability
cannot support my will. Not tongue but heart

declares my depth of gratitude for this   40
paternal welcoming. I beg you now,
O jewel in the Cross and Crown of Christ

say who you are." "O branch I greet with joy,   43
I am your root, your ancestor," said he.
"My son became your great-great-great-granddad

who has been trudging for a century   46
round Purgatory's ring where pride is purged.
Pray to reduce his toil when back on earth.

49 We knew a Florence that, seen from afar,
did not appear to outshine Rome as much
as one day it will look a great deal worse.

52 Back then our town was peaceful, sober, chaste,
filled smaller ground. No wife or daughter wore
jewellery, embroidered gown, rich stuff seen

55 before the wearers. No dad lived in dread
of baby girls growing too old to wed
before he got enough gold for dowry.

58 People were buried in their native soil –
no exiled owner left an empty house.
No families had rooms they did not use

61 or houses like the palaces of kings.
Nobility dressed plain. Our honoured knight
good Bellincion wore a leather suit

64 and had a wife with clean unpainted face.
Wives were lucky. Husbands did not desert
the marriage bed to trade abroad for years.

67 Mothers rocked cradles, soothing infant fears
by crooning songs that pleased themselves and dads,
then later, spinning thread, told older bairns

70 brave tales of Trojans; how they fought and spread
to Italy, Fiesole and Rome;
then told of Cincinnatus and Lucrece,

73 who both chose death rather than break an oath.
Kids would have marvelled more to hear about
those who now dominate Florence's state:

corrupted lawyers! Blatant prostitutes!   76
To life in Florence as the town was then,
with lovely streets, good neighbours, honest men,

my mother no doubt bore me crying out   79
Mary, as women do when giving birth.
Then in our ancient baptistry the priest

christened and called me Cacciaguida.   82
My wife came from the valley of the Po
bringing your surname, Alighieri.

I followed Conrad, Emperor who led   85
the next Crusade to free Jerusalem:
was knighted by him for my part in fight

to free Christ's sepulchre from pagan hands.   88
We lost, as Christendom is not – *should be* –
united by the popes. Death shifted me

into this perfect bliss called Martyrdom."   91

16: Old Families

1 How daft you are, great pride in noble birth!
On earth I knew proud men deformed by you
and here in Paradise you ruled my mood.

4 Since evil could not influence my soul
I freely gloried in my noble birth.
That Cacciaguida died on a Crusade

7 as many others did is widely known.
How wonderful to find my ancestor
had once been knighted by the Emperor!

10 Pride is a splendid robe. Alas, it shrinks
as time goes round us with its snipping shears
cutting off hems, while pride makes us sew on

13 new widths of extra cloth. I spoke again
addressing him as *Sire*, once common speech
but now a title fallen out of date.

16 My lady stood apart, but near, and smiled
reminding me of something I had read.
When Lancelot was courting Guinevere

19 a waiting woman who was standing near,
hearing what hinted at adultery,
gave a wee warning cough. My lady's smile

suggested that *ahem*, but still I spoke.   22
"Dear Sire, you are my great progenitor!
Sire, you embolden me to speak my mind,

for Sire, you lift me up so high I feel   25
much more than me! So many happy streams
flow down into my mind, I do not know

how I can entertain them and not drown!   28
So please, dear Sire and source of all my blood,
when were *you* born? Who were *your* ancestors?

What people flourished in your days of youth?   31
I know that pagan Florence worshipped Mars,
then took the Baptist John as Patron Saint

and shepherd too. How many were his flock?   34
Which families were worthy of respect?"
As puff of breath makes red-hot coal flare up,

so did my grandsire brighten at my prayer.   37
His voice grew gentler, sweeter as he said,
"From when the Virgin heard she was with child

to when my sainted mother gave me birth   40
Mars, moving round the starry zodiac,
had told eleven-hundred-eighty years.

I and my forefathers were born between   43
the Ponte Vecchio and Baptistry.
Where they came from before I do not know.

When Florence was a fifth its present size   46
they carried weapons to defend the town
in time of war. I know their blood was pure

49 like all in Florence then, labourers too.
      None had been tainted by their intercourse
      with Campi, Certaldo and Fighine.

52 If kept beyond our walls these hives of boors
      would not have their offspring's offsprings knocking
      hard at your doors, if not at home inside.

55 No stinking clowns out of Aguglione
      and Signa could be swindling or preside
      over Florentine citizens today.

58 The priesthood who, of all the men on earth
      should most uphold the laws that Caesar made
      that Europe might be unified in peace,

61 undid the ties of right authority.
      They let some people become Florentine
      who live by lending, borrowing and pawns.

64 You have a banker who, were justice done,
      would be returned to Semifonte where
      his grandsire was a beggar in the streets.

67 Good counts would still own Montemurlo;
      the Cerchi, Acone; the Buondelmonte,
      Valdegrieve. Admitting strangers begins

70 municipal decline, as too much food
      destroys a body's health. Blind bulls fall
      heavier than sightless lambs. A swordsman,

73 neat and trim, can cut down five obese
      oponents. Think of Urbisaglia,
      of Luni too, cities that disappeared,

and how Chiusi and Senigallia   76
are following. People and cities die.
It is not strange great families fade too.

Don't think it marvellous if now I name   79
great Florentines whose fame is dimmed by time.
I saw the Ughi, Greci, Ormanni,

the Filippi and Alberichi too: 82
illustrious, though near extinction then.
Others I saw, ancient but also great:

del Arca, Sannella, Soldanieri,   85
Ardinghi and Bostichi, also the
Ravignani, famed now for perfidy

soon to eclipse that line. Among them was   88
Count Guido, descended from the splendid
Bellincion. Della Pressa by then

knew how to rule. Galigaio wore   91
a knight's sword. So did Galli, Sacchetti
and a few more who bore the Pigli arms.

So did the cheat who falsified the weights   94
for salt he sold. The Calfucci forebears
had become great. I saw pride bring them low.

When three gold balls flourished over Florence   97
Sizii, Arrigucci were officers.
So were grandsires of those who, noticing

vacancies in the Church, fill them, grow rich   100
– mean men of base blood, dragons to the weak,
lambs to those showing teeth, or a full purse!

103 That crew was rising. The Caponsacco
from Fiesole was in our market-place.
Giuda and Infangato had become

106 respected citizens, Argenti too,
though Ubertino Donato was peeved
when his father-in-law made *him* their kin

109 by wedding his wife's sister onto one.
I'll tell you something strange. Those inner walls
the ancient Romans built were entered once

112 by a gate named after della Pera;
people forgotten now. Then everyone
who bore the arms of Tuscan marquis Hugh

115 were Tory through and through, although today
one, Guiano della Bella, is a Whig
cheered by the mob. The Gualterotti and

118 Importuni still had not sunk so low
as to become the tradesmen that you know.
The Borgo district would have stayed at peace

121 had the Buondelmonte not arrived,
that family from which your tears have sprung
from just resentment of the death it brought,

124 ending your chances of a happy life.
O Buondelmonte, you were wrong to jilt
she you had sworn to wed, and take instead

127 a daughter of the Donati. Many
now sorrowful would have led happy lives
if you had drowned before you reached our town.

The family whose daughter you jilted   130
slaughtered you fittingly on Arno's bridge
beside that wasted stone, statue of Mars,

thus starting endless Whig and Tory wars.   133
My tranquil days were passed before our strife
became continual, but then our flag

(never taken in battle by a foe)   136
became two: Tory lilies on white ground;
Whig lilies upon red. This fatal split

led to more bloodshed, many thousands dead."   139

17: Dante's Future

1 That shining soul my very great grandsire
could read my mind. My wish was now to hear
what Florence held for me when I returned,

4 but he was silent. I began to fear
this was a thing he wished me not to know.
I looked to Beatrice who gently said,

7 "He wants to satisfy your thirst but first,
to prove you understand what you desire,
say what it is in words that make it clear."

10 I cried, "Dear root of me, your intellect
has soared to such a height, you share with God
His view of time past, present and to come.

13 If I should live to be three score and ten
I have run halfway through my time on earth.
When deep with Virgil in the cone of Hell

16 and up Mount Purgatory, I heard tell
dark prophecies about my future years.
They told me these would bring much suffering.

19 Let fuller knowledge please reduce their sting,
for that is what I pray you give me now.
Forewarned is forearmed, we in Florence say."

Unlike those riddling oracles struck dumb 22
by Christ's triumphant Crucifixion
what he now spoke had no obscurity.

"Do not believe your future agony 25
is willed by God because it is foreseen.
He no more plans the world's contingencies

than an observing eye moves ships at sea. 28
You know how slander drove Hippolytus
from his Athenian home. For Whigs like you

the very same is being planned in Rome. 31
Of course the injured parties will be blamed,
though vengeance one day will reveal the truth.

The first pains that you feel will be the worst: 34
the agony of leaving all you love,
eating the tasteless bread of charity,

learning how steep are stairs you do not own. 37
Heavier too will be the company
of those also expelled, a senseless crew

vilely denouncing you. Their vicious fuss 40
will grow as brutal as notorious.
None will believe them; fame will make you be

a political party of just one, 43
and favourite guest of della Scala,
Lombard Count of Verona. His regard

will give what you most need before you ask. 46
You will know his brother, born below Mars
and now a child. After the Papacy

49 moves to Avignon, and French Pope Clement
   fools the Emperor Henry, you will see
   that boy heroic, fearing neither wealth

52 nor toil, his generosity so great
   his foes will praise it while he makes beggars
   change place with millionaires. You will see this

55 and not say how you knew it would be so."
   He said more, which only those who see
   them happen can possibly believe, adding,

58 "My dear son, this explains the worst rumours
   of the foul snares awaiting you in years
   that are to come. Don't envy Florentines

61 able to stay at home. You'll live to see
   them suffering for their foul perfidy."
   That shining soul fell silent, having shown

64 the woven pattern of my tapestry.
   I needed better news from He who sees
   all that exists, and rightly wills and loves.

67 "Father," said I unhappily, "since now
   loss of my dearest home is known to me,
   advise me how to keep the place I've won

70 in people's minds by my poetic song.
   In Hell, and on that Hill my lady's eyes
   have raised me from, I learned many things that,

73 immortalised in art, are bound to hurt.
   I am a timid friend of truth, so fear
   danger from folk who want their crimes forgot."

The light from which my grandsire smiled now blazed   70
like golden mirror in the brightest sun.
He said, "Consciences dark with their own sin

or shame at another's guilt will indeed   79
feel pain, but do not nurse hypocrisy!
Make the truth plain! Let them scratch where they itch.

Your verses may taste bad at first; digested   82
they will be nourishing. Write like the wind,
hitting high mountains hardest. What more

can poet do? That is why you have been shown   85
only the famous down below in Hell
and up Mount Purgatory. Folk ignore

examples set by those they don't know well."   88

18: From Mars to Jupiter

1   My ancestor, reflecting Paradise,
    seemed in a pleasant dwam. I, blending thoughts
    bitter and sweet, grew gradually calm.

4   My guide leading me Godward said, "Time now
    to change your mind. Think, I am leading you to
    He who heals the pains of every wrong."

7   I turned toward her lovely voice and saw
    more love within her eyes than I can tell,
    not just because I distrust words I use,

10 but all I felt in Heaven has grown dim.
    I only knew, gazing on Beatrice,
    this was the only thing I wished to do,

13 when smiling she said, "Hear your good grandsire!
    Learn that my eyes don't hold all Paradise."
    As strong emotion will transform a face

16 new brilliance in my grandsire's vivid light
    told me that there was more he wished to say.
    "In this fifth sphere the tree with living top

19 is always fruitful, never sheds its leaves,
    which are heroic spirits from the earth.
    Your verses must be brightened by their fame.

Watch the crossbeam on which our Saviour hung.   22
Each soul I name will glow like lightning there."
When he said, "Joshua," the lightning flashed,

nor did I hear the word before the light.   25
As he said, "Maccabaeus," one light spun
fast as a top whipped into ecstasy.

My eyes pursued like falcons in their flight   28
Charlemagne, Roland, Robert Guiscard,
Renuard the Saracen Crusader,

Duke Godfrey King of Jerusalem and   31
William of Orange. Other fighting saints
also drew my attention through the cross,

and then my grandsire swooped back up to join   34
these mighty glories in their harmonies.
Looking back to Beatrice for a sign

of what came next, I saw her eyes so clear,   37
so joyful, she surpassed in loveliness
even herself before. I felt as free

as man in whom virtue and wisdom grew,   40
or a good woman freed from wrongful shame.
We swung in wider arcs among white lights

of the vaster, higher sphere called Jupiter.   43
Language commanded in this temperate star,
since words themselves make shared love possible

for folk not brutes. Good Latin was the speech   46
of this sixth planet, used by the Roman
Empire, Catholic Church, Law, Sciences.

49 I saw lights soaring like great flocks of birds
and forming shapes that, flowing through themselves,
became the letters of the alphabet.

52 In swathes of living light they shaped a **D**,
then **I**, then **L**. Singing and soaring they
suddenly ceased flight and silence ensued.

55 O sacred Pegasus! You Christian steed
that raises humble souls to genius,
you true imagination that creates

58 vigour and unity in men and states!
Let me spell out the letters, one by one,
as they appeared, and so pronounce their sense.

61 I read **DILIGITE JUSTITIAM**
QUI JUDICATIS TERRAM, words which mean
Love justice, you who judge the earth! Lights then

64 congregated within that final **M**,
making all Jupiter a galaxy
of gold and silver jewels. After, between

67 the two sharp summits of the **M** I saw
thousands of other lights descend, settle
and sing (I think) of God convening them.

70 Like sparks that leap from burning log when kicked
– sparks in which fools see auguries – these lights,
both large and small, rose up between those peaks.

73 When each had settled in its place I saw
the shape of an enormous eagle's head,
sides of the **M** its downward sweeping wings,

a shape designed by He who taught each bird
the way to build a nest. These blessèd souls
by movements made a lily's shape appear

within the eagle's breast. O splendid star!
How many and how bright the gems of light
making it plain justice is consequence

of the high Paradise You decorate.
I pray the Mind that started everything
will mend the Papacy broken in two.

From there comes the black smoke that dims Your beams
thus leading Christians astray. You must be
furious again to see Your temple

plundered and changed by thieves into a den
where Salvation is sold and bought for gold.
Popes should not make war with spear and sword,

in competitions to command more men
and tax more land, refusing Holy Bread
due to all Christened souls, in spite of God.

You Popes who write now only to condemn,
should start believing Saints Peter and Paul
are still in Heaven and still judging you.

Well may you say, "My heart belongs to John,
the saint whose head Salome once danced off.
Forget the Fisherman, forget Paul too!

Give me gold coins stamped with the Baptist John!"

19: The Eagle Speaks

1 In front of me appeared with open wings
   that great bird made of congregated souls,
   each a wee ruby with a star inside.

4 What I tell now no tongue has ever told
   and none has written down. No one before
   ever conceived of such a splendid thing.

7 I saw and heard the beak begin to speak,
   say *I* and *mine* while meaning *we* and *ours*.
   "For being just and merciful," it said,

10 "I once possessed a glory none surpassed.
   Though rulers praise my memory on earth
   none have continued my great story there."

13 I cried, "O everlasting fruit of bliss,
   you represent a Justice higher still,
   yet you reflect it pure and know my mind.

16 Please feed the hunger that has famished me.
   How keen I am to hear you end the doubt
   upsetting my digestion many years."

19 Like an unhooded falcon flapping wings
   and preening them in readiness for flight
   so did that unity of noble souls,

then it spoke out: "Turning his compasses   22
to draw the ring that holds all space and time,
the Universal Architect made no part

of the diversity within its bounds   25
greater than His creating Mind and Word.
As proof, the foremost intellect He made,

thinking itself His equal, would not wait   28
to be ripened by His gift of light. Pride –
overweening pride – led Satan to rebel,

expel himself from height of Paradise.   31
All natures less than God are far too small
to measure the Eternal Infinite.

Each thought is one ray of the Divine Mind   34
but none can comprehend all other rays
except by basking in their plenitude.

Believe that ignorance and sin obscure   37
most things you cannot understand. You think,
Indians live who never heard Christ's name,

yet guided by straight reason, do no wrong,   40
like some born before God was crucified.
What justice can condemn such souls to Hell?

That thought came when you could not see beyond   43
the hills around your town, so could not know
anything about those in Asia

more than a thousand miles away, or guess   46
how God will deal with them. His Gospel tells
everything a good soul needs to know

49 for living sinlessly. Thinking further
    can show His wonders for your admiration.
    Apparent contradictions in His schemes

52 come by speculation further knowledge
    will solve, either before or after death.
    They cannot blight an honest Christian life."

55 That glowing heraldry that spread respect
    for Roman government over the globe
    soared round above my head, as mother stork

58 will fly in circles over a young chick
    gazing lovingly up from the warm nest
    where it has just been fed. The eagle sang

61 a hymn whose words I did not know, then said,
    "Just as my song is meaningless to you,
    God's justice is beyond men's reasoning.

64 None rise up here who have not faith in Christ
    before or since they nailed Him to that tree,
    but now we hear too many cry, *Christ! Christ!*

67 who on Judgement Day will be deeper damned
    than Africans who never heard His name.
    What will Asians think when they hear read out

70 the deeds of Christian kings? How Prague was made
    a wilderness by Emperor Albert?
    How the French King, debasing currency,

73 brought poverty to both banks of the Seine?
    There shall be seen arrogance maddening
    English and Scots who battle constantly

across the border nature built for them.   76
They will discover Naples' crippled king,
his single virtue and his thousand sins;

know too why crimes of the Sicilian king   79
must be described in shorthand, to save space,
and how they have dishonoured good King

William, their noble relative. Kings of   82
Norway and Portugal seem just as bad
as he of Serbia whose forged coins spread

distrust of Venice's minted silver.   85
O Happy Hungary if Martel's son
saves you from such misrule! Happy Navarre

if mountains can protect you from the French   88
and their king's foul stench! And you can see how
miserable Cyprus is, like all states

or islands that have Frenchmen as their mates!"   91

20: The Eagle's Eye

1   The sun that fills our eyes with daily light
    curves upward through the sky and down again,
    then passes underground, and it is night

4   when multitudes of galaxies appear.
    This change from one to many brilliances
    happened when, ceasing speech, that single voice

7   became a mighty choir singing a hymn.
    At times, O love, you're only seen in smiles.
    How glorious you sounded in that song!

10 I cannot now recall that harmony
    of holy thought, but noticed when the gems
    enriching the sixth sphere altered their tune,

13 became a murmuring of waters like
    many clear streams trickling from rock to rock.
    As a lute's plucked strings resonate, I heard

16 murmurs climb the bird's hollow neck until
    articulate within the beak again
    they spoke these words my heart hungered to hear:

19 "Look closely to the part of me that sees!
    Of all the fires I use to make my form
    these sparkling in my head are surely best.

The pupil of my eye was he whose Psalms   22
truly proclaim news of the Holy Ghost.
He brought the Ark home to Jerusalem.

Five others make my eyebrow's arch. Trajan   25
is beside my beak. To the poor widow
who lost her son he was most just, and yet

damned as an infidel. Gregory's prayers   28
lifted him from Hell so he knows full well
the state of those with Jesus and without.

Hezekiah next, whose true repentance   31
after divine reproof prolonged his life.
He knows decrees eternal are unchanged

on earth when the right prayers extend our days. 34
Next, Constantine who went east, became Greek,
christened the Roman Empire, giving Rome

to the popes. Though these deeds redeemed his soul 37
too many have been ruined by the last.
See good King William on my sloping brow,

mourned by Naples and Sicily. These weep   40
under his brother Charles, son Frederick.
His shining shows that Heaven loves the just.

Who in the erring world below believes   43
that in this sphere of perfect governors
pagan Ripheus is fifth guiding light?

Virgil called him *most just of Trojan kings*.   46
His soul knew more of Divine Grace than most,
though none have sight that penetrate the whole."

49 Then suddenly the great bird seemed a lark
    soaring and singing up the face of space
    to hover silently, sweetly content,

52 a perfect image of eternal joy
    whose will allows all things that are to be.
    In my perplexity I felt like glass

55 that cannot see the colour staining it.
    Failing to wait for wisdom I cried out,
    "How *CAN* that be?" provoking a great storm,

58 a revelry of vivid flashing light.
    With even brighter eye the bird replied,
    "You see the things I show, not what they are!

61 Like those who know the names of many things,
    you cannot grasp their substances unless
    many more words are said. Strong Hope and Love

64 you met in earthly paradise with Faith.
    Faith, Hope and Love occupy Heaven, *not*
    like men invading men: Heaven invites

67 good to be part of it. You are amazed
    to see in me a Jew and pagan king,
    but death revealed their souls were Christian.

70 Their faith in Hope and Love had been so strong
    they never doubted justice could prevail
    on earth as it prevails in Paradise.

73 They prayed for that, and so for them it did.
    We, close to God, don't know all His elect –
    cannot know all He knows. This ignorance

refines us. We have always more to learn."   76
This eagle's teaching brought me to accept
my ignorance, pride's sweetest medicine,

and as he spoke each star around his eyes   79
dancingly twinkled, almost seemed to play
a fine orchestral symphony of sound

to emphasise all he was moved to say.   82

21: Saturn

1 My lady, reading worship in my eyes,
   gravely regarded me and then declared,
   "I must not smile. My beauty shines the more

4 at each new height we reach. If not restrained,
   the blaze of it will turn you into ash
   like Semelé who gazed on Jupiter,

7 or cleave you as the lightning splits a tree.
   We have ascended to the seventh sphere –
   Saturn, beneath the Lion galaxy.

10 Waken the mind behind your eyes! Reflect
   deeply the image that will now appear."
   Though very sad to look away from her

13 it was a pleasure to obey. I saw
   deep in the crystal circling our earth
   a ladder, golden, flashing in the sun

16 to such great height my eyes could see no top,
   and on it moved so many splendid forms
   all lights in Paradise appeared thereon.

19 And as at daybreak flocks of birds will fly
   higher to warm their feathers in the sun,
   and scattering while others flutter down,

I saw one settle on a nearby step,   22
seeming to grow more bright with love for me!
Or so I thought, but did not dare to speak

till Beatrice said, "Say what you desire."   25
Said I, "Although unworthy of reply,
since I am granted leave to speak, say why

silence is so profound at this great height?   28
Heavens below are jubilant with sound."
The light replied, "Your ears are as mortal

as your sight. Your deafness to our music   31
is from the same reason why you must not
here be allowed to see Beatrice smile.

I have descended, cloaked within my light   34
to welcome you, guided by charity
that rules, as you perceive, the universe."

"O holy lamp," said I, "indeed I see   37
how free love here serves the Eternal Mind.
I do not understand why you alone

are commanded to speak with me." At once   40
round at centre the light spun like a millstone
or Catherine wheel and said, "Divine light

focused on me adds to my radiance,   43
but seraphs who directly look on God
won't answer questions that created minds

can't grasp. When back on earth tell people that 46
what here is clarity seems smoke down where
too few have lifted themselves Heavenward."

49 Checked by these words, I humbly asked his name.
"Within Italian shores near your home town
are crags so high thunder sounds far below.

52 They form a ridge called Caria on which
a hermitage is built. There I served God
so constantly, in contemplative mood

55 in heat or cold my need of food was small.
That cloister raised for God good crops of souls –
now it sends none, and soon will be condemned.

58 Named Peter Damian, then called to Rome,
I became Cardinal where hats now pass
from bad to even worse, so signed my name

61 Peter Sinner, to remind me when priests
were barefoot, thin, begged bread at any inn.
Pastors are now too fat to stand without

64 one on each side and one holding his train.
Their fur cloaks hide palfreys on which they ride,
two beasts beneath one skin. How long must we

67 endure such sin?" He paused as bright wee globes
came wheeling down from step to step, shouting
words meaningless to me but so intense

70 their clamour fast annihilated sense.

22: Saint Benedict

Slowly my sense returned. Like a hurt child   1
I turned at once to she I trusted most:
my Beatrice. She calmed with kindly words

the trembling caused by that wild shout and said, 4
"Know you are in the sky of holiness –
pure Paradise. One cry unstrung your nerve.

How would you be if the full choir had sung?   7
Or had I smiled in my new ecstasy?
You did not hear the prayer within that cry,

or know the vengeance it was calling down   10
on those deserving that, which you will see
before you die. Neither too soon or slow,

sinners must feel the weight of Heaven's doom.   13
Now gaze around you at the company
of contemplative souls who learned to look

lovingly upon God's full radiance."   16
I obeyed, saw a hundred vivid globes
sharing the glory of their brilliance.

Halfway between desire and modesty   19
I stood, afraid to speak, tried not to say
questions that might have caused immense offence.

22 The biggest globe among these glowing pearl
then granted what I lacked the guts to ask,
saying, "If you knew that we like to help

25 asking would be no task. Not to delay
your journey on the upward track, I shall
answer the simple query you hold back.

28 The Abbey of Cassino on a hill
was pagan shrine until I carried up
the name of Jesus Christ, who died to teach

31 all people how to live. God's grace was with me.
Many heeded, left their false creed and I
baptised them in Christ's name, and two became

34 these great and Christian contemplative souls,
Makarios of Alexandria,
founder of monasteries in the east,

37 and Romualdus, stern reformer of
my holy order here, with more who stayed
strictly within their cloisters saying mass

40 nor strayed from duties of unselfish prayer."
Said I, "Your kindly speech so full of love
gives me a confidence that grows, unfolds

43 like petals in a rose. Perhaps too bold,
I beg a favour. May I see your face?"
He said, "Yes, at last in the highest place

46 where everything we want will be revealed
as perfect, whole, and outside time and space.
That sphere does not revolve around a pole.

This ladder reaches it, and that is why   49
the very top is far beyond your sight.
Patriarch Jacob glimpsed that summit once

laden with angels. None on earth below   52
now lift a foot to climb. The rules I wrote
for monks who followed me are wasted ink.

Monte Cassino is a den of thieves   55
whose robes now stink like sacks of rotten grain.
Even a moneylender can't offend

God like a lazy monk who spends on kin   58
and luxury and prostitute the cash
our Kirk collects to feed the destitute.

So weak is mortal flesh that, starting well,   61
good conduct hardly ever lasts for more
than oak trees need to grow new acorn crops.

No gold or silver helped Saint Peter found   64
our Roman Kirk. My order grew and spread
by fasts and prayers. Francis wed Poverty.

Now no Franciscans do, and thus you see   67
how white transforms to black. God saved the Jews
from Pharaoh's wrath by a dry path across

the Red Sea's bed, reversed the Jordan's flow.   70
Today our Kirk needs miracles like these."
So spoke Saint Benedict, moving away

to join his company who suddenly,   73
as if swept up by tempest, soared above.
She I love made a sign that overcame

76 my nature so completely that I too
    went flying up that gold stair to the stars.
    Nothing on earth was quick enough to match

79 the swiftness of our flight. When purged of sin
    that chains me to the earth, how I will love
    to soar in Paradise again! None pull

82 a finger faster from a flame than I
    sprang into that part of the zodiac,
    that constellation where knowledge and thought

85 are nourished by the starry Twins. Their rays
    mingled with sunlight shone upon my birth
    when I first tasted Tuscan air. Dear Twins,

88 I owe my genius to you! It was
    my birthday when I reached your zone. I felt
    as if coming home, and prayed you for strength

91 to undertake this great work calling me.
    Said Beatrice, "A glad host soon arrives
    in this triumphant air, to be received

94 gladly, with clear eyes. First exercise yours.
    Look back and down. See what I raised you from."
    My gaze plunged down through seven planets' rings

97 to that low thing, our queer wee comic earth
    at which I smiled, now knowing thought deserved
    much higher things. The moon, daughter of God,

100 appeared pure disc, recalling how wrongly
    I'd explained her spots. I saw her siblings –
    Mercury, Venus, Sun, Mars, Jupiter –

all tempered by old Saturn's gravity.   103
Their magnitudes and speeds and inclinations
were seen by me, and how they altered climes,

weather and tide for earth's poor folk who live   106
on coast and plain and mountainside. Meanwhile
I soared on high with the immortal Twins

then gazed into the eyes of my fair guide.   109

23: The Fixed Stars

1   As mother bird among the leaves she loves
    nests all night long upon her brood of chicks
    then wakes to watch the sky for dawn of day

4   when she will fly to seek their nourishment
    to fill each gaping beak, so Beatrice
    stood gazing at the height of firmament

7   where the sun seems to move most slow. I saw
    she looked for something new and good; what thing
    I did not know till suddenly the sky

10 was glorified by splendour flooding in.
    She cried, "O see the host of souls Christ won!
    His harvest from the virtues of the spheres!"

13 I can't find words for the serenity
    of bliss we both enjoyed at what appeared.
    As in a deep blue night the full round moon

16 outshines a myriad of stars, I saw
    a thousand thousand lights kindled by One,
    not only greater far than they combined,

19 but shining through them, lighting up all else.
    With failing sense I heard my dear love say
    "None can resist if they are overwhelmed

before the open gates of Paradise."   22
As lightning vanishes into the earth
my mind was so transported, overcome,

I do not know a thing of what came next   25
until I heard, "Open your eyes, my dear!
have they gained strength to let you see me smile?"

Like waking from a dream I can't recall   28
I faintly heard these words, then heard them clear
with gratitude I never will forget.

As to her smile, if Polyhymnia,   31
muse of sacred song, and all her sisters
of poetic art joined with me to help,

I could not say a thousandth fraction of   34
how her smile lit this part of Paradise.
My verse must leap forward upon this road.

Reader, think of my theme! One mortal man   37
carries that load. Forgive me staggering.
This journey needs a ship with daring prow

cleaving the ocean waves and captain who,   40
though weak at times, will never spare himself.
"My face should not be so enchanting that

it blinds you to the loveliest flowers   43
in garden ever lit by Christian light,"
said Beatrice. "Look at the Word of God

embodied in a rose! Virgin Mary,   46
Queen of Paradise, beside twelve lilies –
twelve apostles whose scent should draw us all

49 onto the path of truth." I turned to look.
Sometimes upon a day darkened by clouds
we see a slanting shaft of sunlight on

52 one field of lovely flowers. Now I saw
many fields of loveliness lit by rays
flashing from high above. O gracious light,

55 making them visible to one without
the strength to see their source. What courtesy!
When praying night and morn I say the name

58 of that fair virgin rose. Seeing the ray
that lit her, I then mystically knew
it had to be Archangel Gabriel.

61 And when at last I saw the magnitude
of that angelic rose, as more sublime
than all the lesser blooms beside her there

64 as she was more than those on earth below,
there came a torch descending through the sky.
Circling, it made a glory round her like

67 a halo, like a crown. Music began.
The sweetest tune that soothes us here below
would crash like thunder on the ear of those

70 who ever knew the music of that sphere,
the angels' coronation song for she,
the pure sapphire who ensapphires Heaven.

73 They sang, "O holy love surrounding joy
in womb that was the inn where came to be
One wanted by created folk who need

salvation. Now crowned the Queen of Heaven,   76
follow your Son to glory in the sphere
highest of all!" The choral music stopped.

The crowned rose vanished upward and I saw   79
all the white radiances raise their flames
like babies stretching chubby arms toward

their mother when she suckles them. They sang   82
their hymn to Heaven's Queen again. The joy
of that sweet music will be always mine.

How great are riches of delight heaped up   85
in Heaven's treasury for those on earth
who, by their exile, tears and poverty

will triumph in the total victory   88
of God, His Son and Mary, with the saints
of Old and New Testaments, and holder

of keys to the gates of so much glory.   91

24: Saint Peter

1 "O fellow diners on The Blessèd Lamb,
   both Food and Host – Host who makes sure each guest
   is satisfied, will never hunger more!

4 God's Grace permits this man to drink with us
   before his death returns him to our feast.
   He thirsts for highest truth. Please let him drink!"

7 Thus pled my loving Beatrice. These souls
   then moved like comets turning round fixed poles
   or wheels within a clock, the innermost

10 so slow they did not seem to turn at all,
   while outer ones so whirled they seemed to fly.
   I gazed amazed at wheeling meteors,

13 fast, horizontal, vertical and slow,
   a dancing revolutionary choir
   with one whose vivid flame outshone the rest.

16 Nearing, it spun three times round Beatrice
   singing a song too sweet for memory,
   nor will I try to make my pen describe

19 a vision that no artist could depict.
   The fiery soul stopped circling her and said,
   "O holy sister who can pray so well,

your loving nature draws me to your side."   22
Said she, "O guardian of Heaven's keys,
admit my lover to the height he craves,

I know that you will find him fit for it."   25
Good students do not speak till masters ask.
Gathering my wits I waited to reply.

"Good Christian, what is faith?" said he.   28
I looked to Beatrice, whose glance told me
the time had come to pour my learning out.

"May the grace letting me confess my faith   31
to the twelve apostles' chief make my words
worthy of my thought," said I. "It was you

who, helped by the pen of Paul, ordered Rome   34
along the path to Paradise. *Faith* is
reality of what we hope to see,

with *reason* for the things we've not yet seen.   37
These are faith's substance, so it seems to me."
"Yes, both are essences of faith," said he.

"Why put reason after reality?   40
Desire before convincing argument?"
Said I, "Up here great truths are clear to us,

truths that to mortal eyes appear obscure.   43
We cannot always see that God is good.
Faith in Him cannot always reason out

proof in all cases that He does things well.   46
Argument later must establish this."
He said, "If arguers below knew that,

49 no wordsmiths could confuse the faithful with
   such useless reasoning." Peter added,
   "Have you sincerely taken that to heart?

52 It is not parroted?" "These thoughts are mine,"
   I said, "new minted coins of gold, not worn,
   not clipped." He asked, "How did you come to meet

55 Beatrice, this gem who inspires your faith?"
   Said I, "The Holy Ghost, speaking in Old
   and New Testaments made me recognise

58 Beatrice at first sight." "How do you know,"
   said he, "the miracles to which these books
   testify are true?" Said I, "One miracle

61 they worked convinces me: The Kirk of Christ.
   That it is built by super-human hands
   is shown by how it still stands, propagates

64 the Word of Christ despite perverted priests.
   That miracle proves God is real and good,
   His scriptures true for they took root among

67 the persecuted poor. You were of these,
   and crucified like Jesus, yet that vine spread,
   converted Rome's Empire, a miracle

70 besides which all but one in scriptures are
   less than a hundredth part, but surely prove
   Christ's resurrection true." I said no more,

73 whereupon that whole great sphere resounded
   through its circles by singing the mighty
   anthem "Glory to God in the Highest".

After that my noble examiner   76
began again: "What you have said is right,
so now declare exactly your beliefs

and where you get them from." "Father," I said,   79
"I believe what you believed when you ran
to overtake younger feet at Christ's tomb,

and knew that he had risen from the dead.   82
I believe in one eternal God who,
unmoved, moves all by His loving desire.

My proofs are in philosophy, moral   85
and natural, and in the deeds and words
of Moses and the prophets and the psalms

and you, after the Pentecostal fire   88
gave you the gift of tongues. And I believe
in the Three Eternal Persons who are

One Being, threefold, reconciling both   91
He is and *They are*, a Divinity
stamped in me often by the Gospel text,

I believe this spark in me is growing   94
to a star that will shine in Paradise."
Increasing brightness signified his glee.

Excellent teachers will at times embrace   97
students who show they learned their lesson well.
Spun thrice round me that apostolic light

to show again that what I said was right.   100

25: Saint James and John

1   I have grown thin through working years upon
this sacred song both Heaven and earth require.
Perhaps it may persuade my enemies

4   who drove me from the town where I was born,
a lamb among ferocious wolves, to change
their minds, invite me back with sharper horn,

7   thicker fleece, stronger bleat, to be crowned as
Italy's Laureate within the Kirk
where I was christened of this faith that had

10   Saint Peter welcome me to Paradise.
Here he thrice circled around me before
from out that part of the sphere wherein shine

13   our Lord's apostles, a new glory came.
"See the noble James," my guide now murmured,
"Brother of Saint John and martyred in Spain

16   where pilgrims worship at his shrine." I saw
Peter and James converse, rotating round
each other like mating doves, then both gazed

19   so steadily at me, I had to cringe
and look away. Laughing, Beatrice said,
"O famous poet! Only living soul

chosen to see the court of Paradise   22
and show the world its generosity!
To make good hope resound about this height

you must meet Peter, James and John, the three   25
to whom their Master showed the greatest light."
"Lift up your head! take comfort!" declared James,

the second glory, adding, "At this height   28
everyone will be ripened by our rays."
So I raised my eyes to those whose greatness

previously held them down, then James said,   31
"God's grace has brought you to meet face to face
those of His inner cabinet, that you

may strengthen in yourself and others hope   34
that lets love flourish on the earth below.
So first of all let me examine you.

Say what hope is, how grows in you, and whence   37
hope came." She who had winged me here replied,
"Our Kirk has nobody more full of hope

than this our Sun has chosen for His Grace.   40
Yes, he may enter new Jerusalem
from out the land of bondage into which

he must return. You ask for two more facts,   43
not because you don't know his answers, but
to show how much you value hopeful speech.

He will answer for himself easily,   46
not boasting, for God's Grace will be his help."
Like student keen to see his master smile,

49 "Hope," said I, "is sure expectation of
   glory to come, made by God's Grace in souls
   purged fully of old sins. This light reached me

52 from many stars, but first King David's psalm
   inspired the surest hope. He sang *Let them
   hope in Me who know My name.* I who was

55 baptised knew it well. To David's stream
   of hope your own Epistle added more, so
   satisfied, I now try to satisfy

58 others with what I know." In that fire's heart
   flashes like lightning were repeated while
   I spoke, then it breathed this: "The love of hope

61 still burns in me and always will so please,
   say more what hope now promises to you."
   Said I, "Old and new scriptures tell the goal

64 God provides for his friends. They point me here.
   Isaiah says, *All reaching their own land
   are clothed, body and soul, in double robes.*

67 Your brother John proclaims the robes are white.
   The promised land is here." When I said this
   I heard above, "Hope is in all of you."

70 All choirs in Paradise repeated that,
   and a great star among them shone as bright
   as any in the zodiac. As at

73 wedding feasts a happy maiden dances,
   not just for fun, but honouring the bride,
   I saw this new splendour join the two flames'

dance to the anthem that proclaimed their love.　76
Said Beatrice, "See John, who Christ loved most
of His disciples and when crucified,

begged him to care for His mother Mary."　79
As after eclipse folk have been blinded
by suddenly the sun striking their eyes,

I realised my eyes had lost their sight.　82
"Why blind yourself to see what is not here?"
said John. "My earthly body will stay there

till our number equals the full sum God　85
requires. My brothers in this company
are only lights allowed to come so high.

Take this report back to your world." At this　88
the flaming sphere fell silent, with the sound
of the saints' sweetly mingled breath, just as

at a whistle's sound, oarsmen stop rowing　91
to avoid danger or fatigue. O, how
troubled I was not to see Beatrice,

though she was by my side in Paradise!　94

26: Saint John

1 While dreading blindness from the splendid flame
  that sealed my eyes, I heard these words breathed out:
  "You will not be sightless long. Your Lady

4 will mend your vision soon, and until then
  attend my words. Tell me all your desires."
  Said I, "Sight may return as soon or late

7 as she requires. My eyes were doors open
  to her. She entered them, starting the fires
  that burn within me still. She is the court,

10 Alpha and Omega, all the love that
   the Old and New Testaments mean to me."
   He said, "Make that point clearer. Your target,

13 say what that is. What goal attracts your bow?"
   Said I, "The logic of philosophy
   plus the Authority maintained here, prove

16 Love stamps its form on all that it creates;
   That Great Good is the essence of us all.
   Nothing exists outside it but stray rays

19 seeking their souls, as Aristotle knows,
   Plato demonstrates. Christians also know
   Eternity loves the products of time.

The Bible author told Moses this, said   22
I will make all my goodness pass before
your eyes, Exodus, Chapter 33.

You wrote that too, starting your Gospel with,   25
In the beginning was the Word! More than
any other words, these announce the Love

that made the universe is meant for all."   28
Said John, "Human reason and both Scriptures
all harmonise for you in Beatrice,

your strongest love that looks to God above.   31
Tell me, what other cords tie you to Him?
Name all the teeth with which love's biting you."

John the Evangelist, eagle of Christ,   34
thus made his purpose plain to me. I saw
where he was directing my confession.

I began again. "All that bites my heart   37
turns it Godward. His charity is seen
in the death he bore that everyone

might live and enjoy His works forever.   40
I hope for that as all believers do.
Love of lesser things, Beatrice expels.

Only Heaven's justice remains," said I.   43
As soon as I fell silent through the air
of Paradise resounded a sweet song

in which my Lady joined with all the rest: 46
"Holy, holy, holy." When piercing light
breaks through sleep, driving clouds of night away,

49 wakened, we may recoil from what at first
we see, but need some time to recognise.
Beatrice by her brightness now dispersed

52 my darkness. I saw better than before
and gazed amazed at a fourth brilliance
shining at our side. My Lady explained,

55 "This radiance now shows the love he feels
for being first man made to be like God."
As saplings bend before a gust of wind

58 then spring up straight again by their own force
so did I while she spoke, first bowing low
in wonder, then erect, burning to say:

61 "You only fruit created wholly ripe!
O ancient father of all folk who are
your grandsons or daughters! Please tell me what

64 you know I want to know. I will not now
delay your answer with another word."
Sparkles within that splendour made me sure

67 he answered gladly as he said, "I see
your mind can truly mirror anything
existing less than God. You're keen to know

70 how long we lived in earthly paradise –
and Hell before raised here – and the whole cause
of the Almighty's wrath – and the speech we used.

73 My son, know that Eve and me were expelled
not for only eating that fruit, but for
our pride in knowing more than people should.

In Limbo we longed to be here for four   76
thousand, three hundred and two years before
your Lady went there five days ago to

summon Virgil for your aid. When on earth   79
I saw the sun go round the zodiac
nine hundred and thirty times. Long before

Nimrod's folk built what they could not complete,   82
the tongue I spoke had vanished totally.
No work of human reason lasts more than

a few centuries. Your minds need Heaven   85
to renew them when some generations
start again. Nature forces speech on men

but lets them please themselves how it will go.   88
Before I went to Hell the Supreme Good
that gives me now such joy I then called *El*.

Later He was as suitably named *Jah*.   91
Mortal doings are much like leaves on trees.
One goes, another comes. On that mountain

rising highest from the sea we lived pure   94
then guilty from my first day's noontime bright
until the sixth day when the sun declined

leaving we two feeling ashamed at night."   97

27: To the Empyrean

1 *Glory to Father, Son and Holy Ghost!*
The full choir of the host of Heaven sang
that hymn so sweetly, I grew drunk on it.

4 Through ears and eyesight rapture entered me.
I seemed to see a smiling universe
of joy unspeakable. With love and peace

7 the four bright torches flamed before my eyes,
the first one growing brighter till it seemed
like Jupiter's eagle, feathered with stars

10 like those of Mars with rubies at their hearts.
The choir fell silent as the eagle spoke.
"Don't wonder at me changing. You will see

13 more changes soon. He who in Rome usurps
my place, *my* place, *my* place has emptied it
in the eyes of the Son of God! This pope

16 has made my tomb a pit of blood and shit.
Lucifer was expelled from here but now
triumphs below." Then Heaven was suffused

19 with angry colours that we see in clouds
that face the rising and the setting sun.
My Lady's colour changed like a chaste girl's

hearing news of a sister's shame. I think   22
this Heavenly eclipse the same as seen
when Jesus, crucified, gave up the Ghost.

His words continued in a voice as changed   25
as his appearance was: "The Bride of Christ –
our Holy Kirk – was not fed by my blood

nor that of many martyred saints, to gain   28
gold for the Vatican. Popes Sixtus,
Pius, Callixtus, Urban wept and bled

to reach this happy sphere. They did not use   31
my image on a battle flag in wars
with Christian foes, nor on sealed documents

telling the lie that purchasers will not   34
be damned to Hell. No wonder I've turned red!
From here I see in every Christian flock

a hungry wolf wearing a shepherd's frock!   37
O God defending us, do you still sleep?
The French popes are prepared to drink our blood!

O lovely Origin, what foulness now   40
engulfs our Kirk? But it will not end thus.
When she was prone, Scipio saved Rome

to be the glory of the world. Just so   43
swift Providence will bring salvation soon.
So you, my son, have now this mighty task.

Return to earth and tell what you have learned.   46
Say it out loud. Don't hide what I do not.
That is the reason you're permitted here."

49 In winter when the sun's in Capricorn
the flakes of frozen vapour fall to earth.
The coloured forms I saw now paled to white,

52 snowed upward out of sight. I was staring
after them when Beatrice said, "And now
look down to see how far we have revolved."

55 I did, saw it was noon, viewed the full globe
in a broad arc from Spain to Asia –
from the mad ocean route Ulysses took

58 to seas Europa swam astride a bull.
I could have seen more of earth's threshing floor
had not the sun below my feet been some

61 degrees ahead. But now I yearned to look
into the eyes of Beatrice, for she
to me was the full sum of Paradise.

64 If art or nature ever made a bait
to catch the eye and occupy the mind,
I never saw any whose charms, combined,

67 could move me from divine delight I found
in my sweet darling's face. Her glance gave strength
to soar to an even higher Heaven,

70 a swifter zone and yet so uniform
I cannot say just where we entered in.
She knew how love of knowledge masters me,

73 so said, with an ecstatic smile from which
God's meaning seemed to glow, the following:
"The stable order of the universe

turns round the earth, that one unmoving place,   76
but here is generated time and space.
Such is the mind of God whose love and light

creates all. Only the All-Containing   79
comprehends how everything derives
its motions from this sphere whose centre is

everywhere and boundaries nowhere.   82
Here none can see those roots whose branches sprout
the leaves and blooms and fruits of other spheres.

O why has such abominable greed   85
corrupted all who've grown from Adam's seed?
Innocent love is found in tiny bairns,

yet perishes before their cheeks grow hair.   88

28: The Angelic Sphere

1 As she who had imparadised my soul
   described the wretched human state below
   I gazed into her eyes. They snared me. She

4 Was everything I loved and wished to know.
   When looking in a mirror, if we see
   a sudden brightness shine behind our head

7 we turn to find out why. I now did that
   and saw a point of radiance so bright
   I had to close my eyes or lose my sight

10 till I received the strength to look. Sometimes
   the sun appearing through the mist will cast
   a halo round itself. This light had one –

13 a spinning ring of glory, rainbow-like,
   and round that ring a second ring; round that
   a third. I counted nine concentric rings.

16 The inmost, closest to Intensity
   of Light, was swiftest and their speed decreased
   with the much greater vastness of their arc,

19 and the inmost was incandescently
   brightest because (I think) nearest that Point,
   that Scintilla, that Essence of all light.

My lady saw how great my excitement,   22
and to ease it said, "From that one Point hangs
all the Heavens of Paradise and all

of nature's law. Of course the closest ring   25
is driven fastest by the burning love
that impels the rest." Said I, "Of course, and

if the universe showed the arrangement   28
of these wheels I would be satisfied, but
in the sensual world where I was born,

the spheres are more divine the further from   31
the earth, which is the jail of Lucifer.
If I am here to learn all good men can,

even in this angelic sphere of which   34
the only boundaries are light and love,
I must be taught why the earthly order

is reversed." Said she, "That your fingers   37
cannot untie this knot is no surprise,
since hardly anybody tries. Since your

searching mind demands satisfaction, test   40
it on this. The size of spheres depends on
how much of virtue occupies their parts.

More excellence creates more blessedness;   43
more blessedness makes bigger bodies when
the parts are perfect too; therefore this zone

which gives all motion to the universe   46
holds most people who both love and know.
If you assess the virtue, not the look

49 of spirits who appear to you as spheres
the correspondence of intelligence
and magnitude will become obvious."

52 As north-east gales clear our Italian skies
sweeping the clouds away and Heaven smiles
in all the beauty of its pageantry,

55 my Lady's answer did the same for me –
I saw the truth as plain as Heaven's stars.
She fell silent and each Heavenly light

58 in those nine zones, like iron filings flung
into flames, sparkled brighter and rang out
a hymn of praise to the Fixed Point that held

61 each in their place upon a spinning ring,
a hymn as glad as it will always be.
Beatrice, seeing my new confidence,

64 said, "The inmost circles to the Point hold
the cherubim, seraphim and also
the Thrones of Sacred Aspect who complete

67 the first trio. All angels take delight
to the extent that their sight penetrates
the truth in which all intellects find rest.

70 From this it can be seen that blessedness
depends on acts of vision, not of love
which follows it. Depth of vision gives measure

73 of merit got by God's Grace and right will,
and thus we graduate from step to step.
The second trio in this flowering,

this endless spring no autumn will destroy,   76
sing their hosannas in a threefold choir:
of the dominions and virtues and powers.

Last trio in this mighty festival –   79
principalities, archangels, angels
who spend eternity at play. All these

by gazing up to God prevail below,   82
in ranks that Dionysius described.
Pope Gregory disagreed with him till

opening his eyes in Heaven, he laughed   85
to see how wrong he'd been. Where that pure saint
mistook the Heavenly Host, no wonder

at first you found their discipline obscure."   88

29: Of the Angels

1 The long horizon of the gloaming sky
linked the declining sun in the far west
with the far east and the ascending moon.

4 It held them balanced till the moon climbed up,
the sun dropped down to their next hemisphere.
In that soft interval my Lady smiled

7 quietly, happily, at the fixed Point
whose rays had lately almost hurt my sight.
"I will not ask," said she, "I'll say instead

10 the words you want to hear, reading them from
this Point at which time–space, where–when unite
in the eternal, infinite *I AM*

13 Whose love made everything, archangels
first. Only God's Spirit can say how they
flashed into being, movers of the spheres

16 of which, with later potencies, they were
a very grand and necessary part.
Jerome believed long ages passed between

19 their coming and the first week of the world
forgetting that in Genesis we read
God's Spirit did not rest or sleep but *moved*

upon the waters of the deep before   22
creating light. Angels could not be left
without the ecstasy of serving Him,

so now your wish to know where, when and why   25
they were created should be satisfied.
Know also hardly twenty seconds passed

before rebels among them, mad with pride,   28
declared they would not serve, and so were flung
down to the lowest element, the earth,

convulsing, warping it into the pit,   31
jailing the foul monstrosities you saw
when Virgil led you through. The rest remain

delighting in their art, for it maintains   34
the universal harmony they love,
God's Grace expanding their intelligence

to fit the vastness of their mighty task.   37
Don't doubt the merit of receiving Grace
in strengthening a sure and steadfast will.

If you have fully understood these words,   40
ponder the spirits gathered in this place.
Too many Doctors of Divinity

preach about angels' mind and memory,   43
confusing hearers with obscurity.
To banish pointless ambiguity

I will say more. The angels live in sight   46
of God from whom nothing is hid. Between
Himself and they no interruption stood.

49 So they need no impressions of the past.
   Preachers who speak of what they do not know
   dream while awake. If they believe their words

52 yet still they are to blame. Some preachers spout
   doctrines to show how very wise they are,
   and this provokes less anger here than their

55 neglect of what Christ said and did. Just think
   of how much blood was shed by humble folk
   whose simple speech was first to spread the news

58 that Christ had risen from the dead. Today
   one preacher says that when He died the moon
   eclipsed the sun, a second foolishly

61 explains the miracle another way.
   Shepherds who feed their sheep with words like these
   are bloating them with wind. Disciples learned

64 from Christ a Gospel, kindling from their lips
   Faith, Hope and Love, which was their shield and spear.
   Sermons are now so stuffed with taunts and jokes

67 that if they raise a laugh the preacher's cowl
   inflates and all are pleased, but Satan builds
   his nests in hoods like these. If folk could see

70 the falsehood of the pardons they receive
   they'd fling them down like counterfeited coin.
   I have digressed enough, so turn my eyes

73 back to your interest in Heaven's hosts.
   The number of the angels can't be told
   in human speech. The visionary Book

of Daniel mentions thousands of them,   76
and also tens of thousands, but nothing
more definite because the Primal Light,

illuminating all, reflects each one   79
in ways as multiple as splendours poured
upon them. Because affection flows most

to what viewers conceive, Love's sweetness glows   82
differently in each, some more, some less,
making a myriad reflections of

the pure unchanging rose of whitest white."   85

30: The Empyrean

1 The sun behind the world's vast curvature
    cast its steep cone of shadow to the height
    where constellations gleamed throughout the night

4 until a faint dawn, shining in the east
    increased, tilted the shadow to the west.
    Sky paled. The stars became invisible,

7 even the Morning Star among the rest.
    The light to which I soared with Beatrice
    was infinitely brighter than the sun:

10 a radiance that held the universe,
    so dazzling that, apart from Beatrice,
    I could not see a thing. If all I've said

13 in praise of her before was harmonised
    in a great anthem of triumphant praise
    it could not hint at her new loveliness.

16 I am like one too blinded by sun's rays
    to recollect its colour and its shape.
    From the first day I saw her as a child

19 her beauty made my verses beautiful.
    Soon I must cease from making songs to her –
    all artists' inspirations have an end.

She would go on to finer fanfares than   22
my lips can blow. She still spoke as a guide
giving good words to a departing friend.

"We have arisen high above the spheres   25
of Heaven seen from earth – here all is bright
with purest love and intellect: goodness

beatified with absolute delight.   28
When your eyesight is strengthened once again
you will find in high paradise both ranks:

redeemed mankind with angels by their side."   31
Suddenly I was shrouded yet once more
by blinding glares of mist and could not see

until she said, "Love ruling Paradise   34
welcomes new souls like this, for it prepares
each candle for a better flame." At this

I felt my mind enlarged beyond itself.   37
My vision knew nothing would baffle it.
I saw a river of splendid light flow

between banks of marvellous Spring flowers.   40
From that bright stream living sparks leapt into
the blossoms, like rubies setting themselves

in gold, then as if drunk with sweet scent, went   43
plunging back into the glorious flood
from which new living jewels sparkled out.

"Your wish to understand what you see here   46
pleases me the more it grows. To satisfy
that thirst you will now drink these waters first,"

49 my Lady said. "The flashing jewellery
    exchanged between the river and the blooms
    are shadows of the truths you ought to see.

52 Your mortal sight is not yet purified
    enough to let in much reality."
    No baby waking hungry, having slept

55 more than it should, sucks at a mother's breast
    more eagerly than I flung myself down
    beside the stream that would improve my eyes.

58 Hardly were the two eyelids wet when both
    river and banks expanded to a space
    in which the waves and blossoms were dissolved

61 till they exposed a nobler festival –
    all courts of Paradise! Glory to God
    for giving me the strength of sight and soul

64 to view the triumph of your kingdom there!
    Now give me words to speak of what I saw!
    The purest light made the Creator seen

67 by all who find their final peace in Him.
    It spreads so wide, the orbit of the sun
    within it is a very tiny ring.

70 There the First Mover lights the mighty width
    from source and summit of its potency
    down to its base. As a fine grassy hill

73 might see itself reflected in a lake
    my eyes took in surrounding me over
    a thousand tiers of petals, God's white rose –

the seats of blessèd souls redeemed from earth.   76
The lowest level held such piercing light
I gaped at how it reached the topmost height.

No natural perspective law worked here   79
for distance made no detail indistinct.
She who had brought me to this inmost heart,

this glowing yellow centre of God's rose   82
said, "See the blessèd white-robed multitude
in the arena of our citadel.

See how few the thrones remain unfilled.   85
Notice above one an emperor's crown.
That is for the noble Henry's soul,

summoned to rightly govern Italy   88
when she is unfit – a bad child pushing
nurse away, with Kirk undermining Crown,

pretending to support. Henry will sit   91
there before you die. God will damn that pope
with Simon Magus in the malebolge

where he will thrust his predecessor down."   94

31: Heavenly Hosts

1 The host of blessèd souls redeemed by Christ
   formed round me like a rose. The angel host
   made first by God to fly and see and sing

4 the glory of His goodness, visited
   the many-petalled rose like bees in blooms,
   their faces living flames, their wings pure gold,

7 the rest whiter than snow. Their intercourse
   with the redeemed maintained ardour and peace,
   nor did their flight hide anyone from view.

10 Light here permitted no obscurity.
    I saw this joyful commune richly thronged
    with folk of ancient times and new whose sight

13 and love combined in one continuum.
    O Three-fold Light seen in a single Point
    and satisfying all beholding You,

16 look down upon this storm-torn earth below!
    Barbaric Goths were struck dumb when they saw
    Rome and her temples. How then did I feel

19 coming from human to divine? From time
    to eternity? From foul Florence to
    a people just and sane? Imagine my

bewilderment. Between that and gladness   22
I was content to say nothing. Silence
seemed best. Like a pilgrim who stands refreshed

in a kirk he had vowed to reach, and means   25
to tell my folk about at home, I stared,
down and around me, seeing everywhere

faces of happiness and charity   28
lit by Another's light and their own smiles,
each movement showing graceful dignity.

One thing I had to do: see Beatrice.   31
An old man suddenly confronted me.
His robe was white, his aspect fatherly.

"O where is she?" I cried. He kindly said,   34
"Beatrice sent me here. Direct your eyes
up to the highest tier. Count three rings down.

See her upon the throne she so deserves."   37
I looked, and saw that now she wore a crown
made from Eternal Light's reflected rays.

Distance between my eyes and Beatrice   40
was greater from the sky where thunder rolls
to the sea's deepest floor. I did not care.

Her image was not dimmed by things between.   43
I prayed, "O Lady who restored my hope,
walking through Hell to save my soul, all I

have learned is due your virtue and your grace.   46
Let me keep the goodness you made in me
till death sets free a soul that, with God's help,

49 still pleases you." This was my wee prayer.
Although so far away she smiled at me,
then turned to contemplate eternal light.

52 The old saint said, "Divine love brings me here
to help end your pilgrimage. Send again
your eyes around this place, for seeing more

55 will prepare them for higher radiance.
The Queen of Heaven is here helping us.
Bernard, her faithful servant, is my name."

58 As one who comes from far away to see
the veil of our Veronica, will think
O Jesus Christ my very God, was this

61 *the face you wore on earth?* I gazed upon
the Abbot of Clairvaux, saint who founded
monasteries, so rich in charities

64 that the Mother of God in a vision
appeared to him. He read my mind and said,
"You child of grace, stop gazing at your feet!

67 To know that joyful state look higher up,
see Mary on her throne!" and so I did.
Just as the dawn horizon's eastern part

70 outshines the western where the sun goes down
I felt as if my eyes climbed up from out
a valley to a mountaintop at dawn.

73 On the highest verge of the rose I saw
a brilliant zone of light, though on each side
no soul was less distinct, and in that zone

a thousand angels played with outspread wings.   76
Smiling upon their sport and songs was She
whose beauty gives delight to all the saints.

Were I as rich in words as visioning   79
I still could not try hinting at the joy
filling me at this sight. When Bernard saw

the vision warming him now shone on me,   82
we exchanged a smile before he, turning,
looked back devotedly on Her he loved.

We stood together sharing that delight.   85

32: The Rose's Plan

1   Gazing upon the source of his delight
    my co-adorer kindly lectured me
    beginning with these holy words: "The wounds

4   of nails and spear that Mary ointmented
    and closed, derived from Eve the beautiful
    who sits below her feet. You will recall

7   Eve opened them by eating of a fruit.
    In the third row below sits one you know –
    Beatrice; then Jewish mothers: Rachel,

10 Sarah, Rebecca, Judith, also Ruth
    grandmamma of David, king and singing
    sinner of the penitential psalm.

13 After the Hebrew women's seventh tier
    a separation starts. On the left side
    sit those who looked for Christ before his birth,

16 for they had faith in God's Old Testament.
    On the right side are seats for those who know
    that Christ did come, some of them empty still.

19 Now look behind. On the side opposite
    equal divisions reign. Facing our Heaven's Queen
    sits John the Baptist who prepared Christ's way,

suffered the wilderness and martyrdom,   22
then went to Hell before Christ set him free.
Below him see Augustine, Benedict,

Francis and others down to where we stand,   25
but split between, as on the women's side,
good Jews and Christian men, who shall remain

until both sides are filled up equally.   28
Also see that halfway down this flower
a tier encircling us has those beneath

whose merits did not win this place for them.   31
Look and listen well. Their faces, voices
tell they are souls of children who have died

before their innocence was tested by   34
fighting to conquer sin, resist Hell's snare.
I see a doubt in you, striking you dumb.

Let me untie the knot that binds your tongue.   37
Chance accidents in Paradise, like thirst,
hunger and suffering, cannot exist.

All that befalls souls here is fitting them   40
surely as rings fit fingers, so accept
God's foresight and His Grace will give to all

their rightful place. Do not try to know more.   43
Look on her face whose face is most like Christ's.
Only her brightness can enlarge your mind."

From the first angels soaring in these heights   46
I now saw gladness raining down on her.
All that appeared before was not so full

49 of such wonder and love. I seemed to see
    The Holy Dove descend, and hear the hymn
    "Hail Mary, full of Grace", saw the wings spread,

52 heard on each side the divine court respond
    tunefully to the divine voice. Each face
    melodiously grew more glorious.

55 "O holy father whose great courtesy
    in guiding me removes you from your throne,
    which angel gazes so enchantedly

58 upon the Virgin, he appears on fire?"
    I asked the saint. He answered, "He contains
    all gallantry an angel can, so brought

61 Mary word she would bear the son of God.
    Attend again, for I will point out more
    nobilities in this most merciful

64 empire of the just. Upon either side
    of our Queen sit the twin roots of this rose.
    On her left is Adam, the first dad who

67 tasted the bitter fruit, causing the Fall.
    All are engendered from his seed. Look right
    where sits the Kirk's father and foundation,

70 whose keys give entrance to this bonny bloom;
    beside him John, the prophet who foresaw
    the tribulations Christ's Kirk had to face.

73 Beside the other rests the great guide who
    led the ungrateful tribes through deserts where
    he nourished them with manna from the skies.

But now time flies and soon your dream must end. 76
Good tailors cut a coat according to
the cloth available, so point your eyes

toward the Primal Love. Look into His 79
radiance deep as you can. In striving
to advance you may, for lack of God's Grace,

fall back. Pray hard for Grace. Salvation 82
lies in prayer. Follow my words with love.
Let nothing come between them and your heart."

He began his holy supplication. 85

33: Prayer and Answer

1 "O Virgin Mother, daughter of your son!
Lowly, yet raised higher than anyone!
Goal of all human striving, you are she

4 ennobling humanity, because He
who made mankind chose to be made by you.
The love that was rekindled in your womb

7 had warmth enough to let this Heaven bloom
in endless peace where you are now our sun
always at height of noon. To the souls here

10 you are incarnate charity, to those on earth
a well of living hope. Lady so great
that those who seek for Grace without your aid

13 may just as well try flying without wings.
Your kindness not only aids those who ask;
sometimes it anticipates our prayer.

16 Your mercy, pity, generosity
unite in all the good that people need.
This man was sent up from the depths of Hell,

19 seeing the lives of spirits, one by one,
and now he begs your kindness for the strength
to bear salvation's last enlightenment.

I never sought that vision for myself   22
yet join my plea with his to strengthen it.
I pray you, cleanse his sight of mortal stain

making his vision fit for such delight,   25
and afterwards I pray that you will keep
his heart pure – curb his human appetite.

Many more blessèd souls unite in this   28
prayer of mine, including Beatrice."
The eyes God loved and His Son reverenced

fixed on the supplicant and plainly showed   31
she loved devoted prayer, then she looked
to the fixed point of light that only she

could penetrate with undimmed eye. By now   34
I had achieved the end of all desire,
did not want another thing, but Bernard

with a smile told me to look up. I did   37
and found my sight, now purified, could see
the lofty beam which is the one true light.

And from that time I parted company   40
with memory and speech. It seemed a dream
of passion that remains when dreamer wakes

yet can't recall visions inspiring him.   43
That has become my state. Only a few
small drops of sweetness in my heart remain,

and this is how our tears are lost in rain   46
and thaws dissolve our footsteps in the snow.
O light supreme, more than conceivable

49 by mortal mind, grant mine again some part
of what you let me see, and give my tongue
some power to leave a gleam of glory

52 for my readers yet to come. Please give back
a little to my memory, so that
my poetry conveys your victory!

55 So piercing was the splendour of that ray
I am convinced that had I looked away
even an instant, it had blinded me,

58 but I sustained it until my gaze reached
the central goodness. Bless abounding Grace!
It let me dare to face infinite light

61 so long that my whole mind was lost in it.
The scattered pages of the universe
were in that deepness, with its substances,

64 accidents, relationships unified
and bound by love into a single book.
God by His light creates complexity,

67 yet sees it as one good grand simple shape.
In writing this I feel my joy expand.
Twenty-five hundred centuries ago

70 the first ship was launched. A single moment
gazing at that light seemed more. I could not
look elsewhere. The good which is the object

73 of all will was there. What exists outside
is defective; all that exists within
is perfectly made. Now know that my words

will tell even less of what I recall   76
than if my infant tongue still sucked a breast.
The living light remained the same, but I

began to change. My strengthened sight saw more. 79
In the profoundest clear ground of the light
appeared three circles, different colours

and same size. Two reflected each other   82
as rainbows do, the third took fire from them.
Alas, such blethering *cannot* convey

the things I noticed in Eternal Light   85
fulfilling, knowing, loving its sweet self
in that reflecting, circling Trinity!

As my eyes dwelled on it I seemed to see   88
a human form. Like the geometer
battering his brain in vain to find how

circles are squared, I tried to see or feel   91
how such a human form could live in light
eternally. The wings of my fancy

could not fly so far, until in a flash   94
I saw desire and will: both are a pair
of finely balanced wheels kept turning by

love that revolves sun, sky and every star.   97

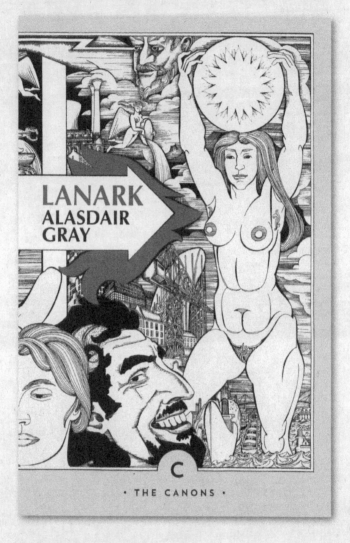

LANARK
ALASDAIR
GRAY

C
· THE CANONS ·

'Probably the greatest novel of the century'
Observer

CANON∥GATE